Phonological Analysis

Focus on American English

By Walt Wolfram and Robert Johnson

 PRENTICE HALL REGENTS, Englewood Cliffs, NJ 07632

To Our Families:

Jane

and

Marge and T⁴
[Tyler
Todd
Terry
Tanya]

© 1982 by Prentice-Hall, Inc.
A Division of Simon & Schuster
Englewood Cliffs, NJ 07632

Printed in the United States of America

10 9 8 7 6 5

ISBN 0-13-664988-2

Prentice-Hall International (UK) Limited, *London*
Prentice-Hall of Australia Pty. Limited, *Sydney*
Prentice-Hall Canada Inc., *Toronto*
Prentice-Hall Hispanoamericana, S.A., *Mexico*
Prentice-Hall of India Private Limited, *New Delhi*
Prentice-Hall of Japan, Inc., *Tokyo*
Simon & Schuster Asia Pte. Ltd., *Singapore*
Editora Prentice-Hall do Brasil, Ltda., *Rio de Janeiro*

PREFACE

Teaching introductory courses presents a great challenge for linguists. Students entering such courses often represent a wide range of backgrounds and expectations, and instructors have the constant tension of balancing a clear and straight-forward presentation of linguistic principles with an understanding of the inherent complexities of language organization. Many students are lost along the way, and many instructors approach such courses as a dutiful burden rather than as an intriguing challenge.

This text is a partial response to the challenge of teaching an introductory course in phonology on an advanced undergraduate or graduate level. It is based on years of experience in teaching students from a wide range of fields. Along with those who specialize in linguistics, students in speech pathology, foreign language and bilingual education, and language arts are among those who need a solid foundation in phonological analysis. We have attempted to write a text useful to the wide range of students we have encountered by first discussing the general principles of analysis and then showing how they are applied in particular fields.

In this text, we have incorporated some of the contributions of earlier approaches to phonology with more recent approaches. There is an obvious bias toward the "standard version" of generative phonology, but we hope that we have not been irresponsible to insights from other approaches. We have tried to show that different developments in the study of phonology are related to and derive from each other rather than present notions in terms of independent "schools of phonology." Ultimately, we are more concerned that students understand certain principles in phonological analysis that are shared by various theoretical approaches, rather than develop allegiance to particular models.

In our presentation of examples, we have focused on English, often to the neglect of the "classic" examples from other languages. We purposely made this decision because we thought it most practical in terms of the goals of the text and the backgrounds of our students. While our primary aim is to introduce the principles of phonological analysis, description, and application, we also want the student to come away with a feel for the English phonological system. Exercises are incorporated into the chapters at the point where the relevant discussion takes place, and we suggest working through the exercises before continuing reading: the subsequent discussion is sometimes dependent upon familiarity with the exercises.

Chapters 1-9 give a basic approach to analysis, description, and explanation, and the final four chapters (10-13) discuss some applications of phonological analysis. We think that the final chapters are important both for students interested in basic linguistic description and for those with more applied concerns.

We don't have a long list of people to whom we are grateful, although we probably should because we claim no particular novelty in our approach to phonology. Obviously, we are deeply indebted to those in the "who's who" of phonology, but we've also profited greatly from our students. They have forced us to sharpen our thinking on issues in phonology and to be focused and deliberate in our presentation of these issues. Sometimes we have marveled that they have been able to learn at all from us and thank them for their patience.

Allan Bell was superb as an editor, uniquely combining technical expertise on the subject matter and concern for style and presentation. Remaining improprieties of style and presentation remain the authors' responsibility, as should be obvious to those who have heard them speak or seen them behave together in public. Marge Wolfram spent many volunteer hours typing various drafts of the manuscript over the last decade, and should be as happy as the authors to see this project finished. Marcia Taylor meticulously prepared the final copy for typing, and Carolyn Piersma was exceptionally adept at deciphering several layers of scribble.

Finally, the authors would like to thank each other. We learned much from this joint endeavor and had lots of fun in the process. In all respects, it was a partnership full of respect and enjoyment. In fact, we had so much fun working on this manuscript that someday we would like to do an underground version--full of all the quips, puns, and irreverent comments which even our limited sense of propriety forced us to eliminate here.

Walt Wolfram
University of District of Columbia and
Center for Applied Linguistics

Robert E. Johnson
Gallaudet College and
Oregon State University

December, 1981

CONTENTS

CHAPTER 1
The Study of Phonology

All languages are organized in several different ways. We can recognize at least three levels of organization in a simple sentence such as *Tall people often make good basketball players*. One of these levels deals with the ways in which the meaning of a sentence emerges from the meanings of the individual words: semantic organization. A word such as *basketball*, for example, should have roughly the same meaning for most speakers of American English. On another level, there are the ways in which the words of the sentence are combined with each other: the **syntax** of the sentence. The order of the words in a sentence is not accidental. Changing the order in the sentence above would either change the meaning of the sentence or make it meaningless. A third level deals with the sounds that transmit the sentence to the listener. The **phonology** is that aspect of language organization involving the use of sounds and the relationships among them.

There are a number of different reasons for studying phonology, or for including a course in phonology in a particular program of study. Students may range from the specialized student of phonology within the discipline of linguistics, to the aspiring opera singer who has been told that a course in phonology will help singing in foreign languages. Information about the structure of sound systems can be useful for a number of different professional subject areas. And besides that, we think it is interesting.

Even before discussing the "practical" reasons for which the study of phonology is important, we should start with the role of phonology in a general study of human knowledge. Language is a unique form of knowledge, in that speakers know a language simply by virtue of the fact that they speak it. Much of this knowledge is not on a conscious level, but it is still open to systematic investigation. The sounds of language provide a potential that few disciplines can match for systematically tapping data. Looking at how we use sounds provides a natural laboratory for making generalizations drawn from carefully described sets of data. We can hypothesize about certain aspects of the system, and then check our hypotheses by looking at the data provided by speakers of a language. And we can do this without many of the technical instruments that are necessary in other disciplines. Although the formalization of particular aspects of phonology may call for some specific training, accurate generalizations and observations are not the unique domain of professional linguists; they are open to any speaker of a language. Phonology—as a part of the study of language—can contribute substantial insight into the nature of scientific inquiry.

At first glance, the notion that we use our knowledge from phonology in hypothesis formation and testing seems somewhat removed from our everyday experience, but there are certain types of ordinary occasions that demonstrate how we actually use such knowledge. Suppose we have two players nearing the conclusion of a Scrabble game. One is left with the letters *f* and *p*, and the other has the letters *s*, *l*, and *p*.[1] The only workable combination involves placing letters before the sequence *at*. The player with two letters quickly realizes that either *p* or *f* can be used, but that only one at a time can occur before *at*. This observation is based on the knowledge that no

1

sequences of English words begin with *pf* or *fp*. On the other hand, the player with three letters can use all of them to make *splat*, since there is a combination of *s*, *p*, and *l* found in English phonology. In the course of the game, the players have made a significant observation about the structure of sound sequences in English. They have noticed that combinations of the letters *p* and *f* are not permitted at the beginning of English words, but that combinations involving the sequence *s*, *p*, and *l* are permitted. This observation is based on the knowledge available to them as speakers of English. If the game had been conducted in another language, such as German, initial *pf* sequences would have been permissible, but other types of sequences would not.

Exercise 1

Examine a crossword puzzle and identify some ways in which a person's knowledge of phonological structure would be used in arriving at possible answers. What observations about phonological structure can be drawn from this?

Consider another illustration. A group of advertising agents is attempting to come up with a term for a new laundry soap. They decide that they want a completely new name for their product, one that has a "splashing" sound to it. Eventually they come to the conclusion that a short word beginning with several consonants will do the trick. They start to create new words, and, in doing so, notice that in all of the terms they come up with, the first letter is *s*, the second is *p*, *t*, or *k*, and the third is *l* or *r*. In considering alternative names for the product, such as *sprish*, *splursh*, and *skrell*, they have made a significant observation about consonant sequences at the beginning of words in English. They automatically reject new creations like *fplop* or *ptrap* because these sequences of sounds are not permissible in English. In the course of their reflections, they have tapped their knowledge about English. They have made an observation which—stripped of the veneer of technical linguistic terminology—is as valid as that of the linguist formally describing sequences of sounds in English. Both processes involve a search of available data, an observation concerning the data in terms of a hypothesis, and the rejection or acceptance of the hypothesis based on whether it accounts for the data at hand.

While the study of phonology may provide the linguistics major with basic knowledge about one level of language organization, and the non-major with an interesting laboratory for looking at one kind of scientific inquiry, the function of a course in phonology does not necessarily stop there. Knowledge of the organization of sound systems can lead to practical applications in a number of different fields.

Phonology, Writing, and Reading

One of the most important uses of phonology involves **orthography**: the use of an alphabet to represent a language in writing. In many of the world's writing systems, the printed symbols in the orthography are chosen to represent the significant sounds of the language. The earliest uses of the study of sound systems centered on this very practical goal of devising efficient writing systems. And, during the 20th century, when interest in language developed into a specific discipline of linguistics, this concern surfaced as an important byproduct of phonological analyses.

One of the earliest textbooks devoted entirely to phonology during the modern era of linguistics was subtitled *A Technique for Reducing Languages to Writing.* A primary concern of this text (Pike, 1947b) was to enable the student to arrive at a phonological analysis, which in turn would permit the development of a writing system reflecting the systematic structure of the phonology. At that time many linguists were engaged in analyzing unwritten languages. In many instances, one goal of such projects was the development of literacy programs. Many of the languages did not have orthographic systems, so that part of the work necessarily entailed developing an orthography. Rather than adopt an orthographic system which was devised to represent the sounds of another language, new orthographies were developed to represent the sound system of the particular language under analysis. During the past half century, many orthographies, based on principles of phonological analysis, have been created for previously unwritten languages.

Applications of phonological studies to such languages may seem somewhat exotic, but studying the phonology of English also offers some important insights concerning its spelling. Many people think that the English spelling system is highly irregular, representing some sounds inconsistently and others that are not pronounced at all. Although there certainly are some inconsistencies, recent work in the phonology of English has demonstrated that English spelling is much more systematic than is often recognized. When this system is examined from the perspective of phonology, certain underlying regularities are revealed. Take the case of words with the so-called silent *g*, like *sign* and *design*. If we accept that these forms are related to items like *signature* and *designation*, in which the *g* is actually pronounced, the presence of the *g* seems justified in the spelling. First impressions about the unsystematic nature of English spelling often turn out to be incorrect upon closer inspection. A spelling teacher who understands such relations in terms of phonology may have an important advantage over one who does not look for underlying regularities.

Exercise 2

If we assume that items such as *bomb* and *bombardier* are related in English, what does this imply about the existence of the "silent" *b* in *bomb*? Think of five similar word pairs in which one item has a "silent" letter (not necessarily *b*), and the related item reveals the pronunciation of the letter.

Similarly, a reading teacher who understands the relationship between sounds and symbols from the perspective of phonological analysis is at an advantage. Early readers need to know how certain spelling patterns reflect their knowledge of the language. An understanding of such processes may ease some of the frustrations beginning readers experience as they attempt to match sounds and symbols.

It appears that an efficient orthographic system will allow for different pronunciations that a native speaker uses automatically. For example, we may write the English plural with an *s* even though it is pronounced sometimes as a *z*-like sound (*beds, bags*) and other times as an *s*-sound (*bets, backs*). Speakers of English will automatically pronounce an *s* or *z* sound in the right places, despite the fact that both sounds are represented by the symbol *s*.

Phonology and Foreign Language Learning

A common tendency of students attempting to learn a second language is to use the sounds from their native language in the language they are learning. However, where the two languages are not phonologically identical, this can lead to serious "interference" problems in speaking the second language. Certain sounds will be modified to fit the phonological pattern of the native language. The resultant "foreign accent" is a common problem, well recognized by both professional and non-professional observers of language usage.

Many English speakers encountering spoken Spanish for the first time tend to interpret the Spanish *p* as *b* in some contexts. This is because there is a small but significant difference between the English *p* and the Spanish *p*. In English, *p* is often accompanied by a small puff of air following the sound. This "aspiration" is one of the major identifying characteristics of the pronunciation of *p* in English. But in Spanish, there is typically no aspiration of *p*. Without the cue of aspiration, there is a tendency for the English speaker to think that the Spanish *p* is a *b*, which in English is often identified by its lack of aspiration.

Filtering sounds in terms of the native rather than the second language is a natural tendency which must be overcome if a person is to acquire real fluency in a foreign language. Most teachers in introductory phonetics can readily testify to the problems that English speakers have in hearing and producing the unaspirated *p*, whereas a native Spanish speaker would have no difficulty at all with it. On the other hand, the native Spanish speaker learning English has difficulties with certain phonological details not found in Spanish. A Spanish speaker might not perceive the difference between the nasal consonants represented by *n* and *ng* in English, since these sounds are not distinguished in the sound system of Spanish. Or, a Spanish speaker might have difficulty with English words beginning with *st* (e.g. *steep*), because words are not permitted to begin with the *st* cluster in Spanish. In this case, the speaker might insert a vowel before the cluster, thus creating a permissible Spanish sequence (*esteep*).

Exercise 3

Consider a foreigner who typically pronounces *p* in English words which contain an *f*. Thus, both *fat* and *pat* are pronounced as *pat*. What does this information tell you about the sounds *f* and *p* in the speaker's native language?

By observing differences between phonological systems, a foreign language teacher may be able to anticipate problems and develop strategies for helping foreign language learners overcome the tendency to filter the sound system of a foreign language through the native language. Without an understanding of how sound systems may be organized, and using this as a basis for comparing systems, foreign language training seems to be at a serious disadvantage.

Understanding the basis of phonological systems is essential not only for the foreign language learner; it is also important for our understanding of first language acquisition. It shows that a child does more than simply acquire sounds in a random fashion. Sounds are acquired according to a number of principles which organize phonological systems. However, there is an important difference between first language acquisition and how an adult learns a foreign language. In the case of normal children learning their first language, simple exposure to the language of the community is enough to develop a phonological system, while adult learners of a foreign language usually need aid in overcoming the filtering tendency of the native language.

Phonology and Speech Disorders

So far we have discussed some of the applications of phonological analysis to normal language situations. Such knowledge also has implications beyond normal language, and is particularly useful in the assessment and treatment of phonological disorders. In evaluating disorders, it may be misleading–and in some cases, wrong–to identify articulation problems simply as "omissions," "substitutions," and "distortions." When an individual reveals a phonological disorder, we want to know to what extent this disorder stems from differences in the organization of their phonological system.

Several dimensions of the study of phonology are crucial to understand what are commonly called "misarticulations." For one, phonological analysis allows us to look at the **patterned nature of disorders.** Evidence indicates that the sounds of a disordered system are not simply affected in a haphazard, random way. Instead, there are patterns in the ways they contrast with the normal, adult system. A particular type of disorder may be manifested by a lack of contrast between sounds such as *p* and *b*, *t* and *d*, *s* and *z*, and so forth. In such a case, the loss of one basic distinction (the difference between voiced and voiceless sounds) is responsible for a number of problematic sounds. A speech pathologist who understands the systematic nature of the so-called articulation problem is in a good position to make a diagnosis and plan subsequent remediation strategies.

Exercise 4

An individual with a speech problem produces the following items instead of the normal adult forms:

tip for *chip*	*pine* for *vine*
ting for *sing*	*pight* for *fight*
tow for *show*	*palentine* for *Valentine*
tipper for *zipper*	*pit* for *fit*

Notice that both *t* and *p* occur for a number of other sounds. Is there a pattern to this misarticulation so that we can predict where *p* will occur and where *t* will occur? Why might *p* occur for some sounds and *t* for others?

As well as understanding the patterned nature of the misarticulation in a disorder, we also need to know how the disordered system is organized as a system in its own right. As we shall see in Chapter 11, some of the ways in which deviant systems organize themselves are rather ingenious. They may, for example, use sounds in ways that are quite different from the adult normal system. Understanding the organization of the system is crucial to determining what a speaker does and does not know about the use of sounds. It is, in fact, difficult to see how a serious speech pathologist could do without knowledge of the systematic nature of normal and non-normal sound systems.

The Phonological Component

While there is currently much discussion among linguists about the overall organization of grammar, it is generally agreed that a complete grammar of a

---

Exercise 5

Consider the following words as produced by a young child.

ring	'ring'	*bwing*	'bring'
wing	'wing'	*dwown*	'drown'
right	'right'	*kwack*	'crack'
white	'white'	*twip*	'trip'
ray	'Ray'	*pway*	'pray'
way	'way'	*gway*	'gray'

What is the pattern that controls "incorrect" production of *r* (in the right-hand column)? Does this patterning support the claim that this speaker does not know the difference between *r* and *w*? How does this demonstrate the need to know where sounds are used in words as a basis for making observations about misarticulations?

---

language must include information from at least the phonological, semantic, and syntactic levels of organization.[2] The exact relationship between phonology and the other levels, however, is still in dispute. In some traditional approaches, phonology was seen to be a separate entity, whose structure could be determined without reference to other levels of the grammar. That is, a phonological description of a language could be made without reference to the syntactic or semantic levels. In other approaches (and the one taken in this book), phonology is considered to be dependent to some extent upon elements from other levels of the grammar. That is, the phonological level is dependent on at least some syntactic information.

From our point of view, the **phonological component** of a grammar is basically a system of rules that operate on items from the syntactic level and convert them into their actual pronunciation (their **phonetic form**). There are then several prerequisites for the phonological rules of a grammar to operate effectively. First of all, there must be some sort of basic units in the vocabulary, or **lexicon**. Then, the phonological component itself contains rules that can operate on these basic lexical units, changing them to their eventual phonetic form. The ultimate output of the rules of the phonological component is the actual pronunciation of items, or the "surface phonetic form." Aspects of phonetic production cannot be ignored, but phonology is properly concerned with how sounds are organized within a system, rather than the physical details of production *per se*. In other words, our interest is in the organized **system** that leads to the eventual production of forms, not the details of physical sound production that can be described apart from an organized system.

For our purposes here, the important questions about the phonological component are:

(1) What is the nature of the rules that make up the phonological component?
(2) What is the form of the lexical units?
(3) How do the rules operate on the lexical units to arrive at the eventual phonetic form?

In the preceding sections, we have previewed what we mean when we speak of the phonology of a language, and have presented some practical applications of phonological analysis. In subsequent chapters, we will examine in detail the actual ways in which the sounds of a language are organized. We will focus on the various dimensions of organization within the phonological component of a language. While some aspects of this organization are considerably more complex than appears at first glance, it should at least give a new appreciation of the human capability to speak a language. At the same time, we will see that the study of phonology provides some exciting data for observation and analysis as a type of scientific inquiry.

We have also suggested that there are some utilitarian reasons for studying the organization of a sound system. We will return to this in our final chapters, after we have considered the actual organization and analysis of phonological systems. Hopefully, we will see that the specialized, somewhat technical, study of phonology carries considerable potential for advancing our understanding of the capabilities of the human mind, as well as a basis for applying such knowledge to human problems.

NOTES

1. The use of particular letters of the alphabet is important only in the sense that the spelling system of English, with certain exceptions, reflects the phonological system. We may refer to spelling as a reflection of English phonology, but we must keep in mind that our real concern is the way in which the actual phonological system of English is structured, not the way in which it is represented in writing. We will discuss the relationship of phonology and spelling in a later chapter.
2. A linguist's description of the organization of a language is usually referred to as a grammar of that language. There are, however, several different uses of the term *grammar* current within linguistics. One use is restricted only to the syntactic level of organization. Another (and the sense in which we are using the term here) refers to a complete model of language organization at all the various levels.

CHAPTER 2
The Phonetic Base

Phonetics is the study of the actual sounds of language. It provides the raw material that serves as the base for analyzing a phonological system. The actual pronunciation of items is the ultimate output of the phonological system rather than an integral part of its organization, but this does not diminish the importance of the study of phonetics. In a real sense, a phonological analysis cannot go beyond the accuracy of the phonetic material with which it has to work. There have, in fact, been some rather elaborate phonological analyses which have been refuted simply on the basis of phonetic accuracy. Knowledge of phonetics is essential to the serious student of phonological systems. Students of phonology cannot get very far without some knowledge of phonetics, and this knowledge must have a very practical base. Phonologists should be able to both produce the sounds they transcribe and reproduce the sounds described by others. It is more than just a practical matter to know phonetics. The sounds of a language provide the primary objects of study in phonology. That is to say, we find patterns of organization in phonology through examining the concrete products of language behavior— the speech sounds themselves.

As a field of study, phonetics has developed in three main directions:

(1) **articulatory phonetics**, which is primarily concerned with the way in which sounds are produced by the human speech mechanism;
(2) **acoustic phonetics**, which deals with the acoustic properties of sound waves in their transmission from speaker to hearer; and
(3) **auditory phonetics**, which is concerned with the physical effects of speech on the human ear and its associated mechanisms.

Each area has developed elaborate methods of investigation and experimentation. Our interest here, however, will be restricted to the less experimental aspects of articulatory phonetics. And even in this area, we shall limit ourselves to that focus of articulatory phonetics which is concerned with the impressionistic recording of speech sounds. We use the term **impressionistic phonetics** to refer to the transcription of sounds based on our perception from hearing. This approach to phonetics is the oldest in the field and still the most commonly employed.

Schane (1973) notes that there are at least three different goals of what a phonetic theory could be asked to account for:

(1) any kind of noise that the human vocal apparatus is capable of producing (including grunts, groans, and laughter);
(2) those sounds that are linguistically significant in language in general; and
(3) only those sounds that are linguistically significant in a particular language.

While goals 1 and 3 may be admissible for particular purposes of investigation, in this chapter we are concerned with a restricted version of goal 2. That is, we are concerned with sounds that are linguistically significant in a variety of languages. Ideally, we might deal with all of the sounds that occur in every known language, but our description here will be selective.

As a beginning point, it is important to counter certain myths that have sometimes found their way into folk phonetics. For one thing, there is no basis for claims that certain races or ethnic groups are physically or genetically predisposed toward the production of sounds in any particular manner. We learn to produce our sounds on the pattern of our language community, and normal individuals from any particular racial or ethnic group will learn precisely the sounds of the community in which they are raised. Evidence of this fact can be found readily by looking at the articulatory abilities of an individual born into one group but raised exclusively in the context of another group. Such a speaker will manifest the phonetic capabilities of the native speakers of the surrounding language community. Listeners who hear such individuals on tape will typically classify them as belonging to the group where they learned their language rather than to their birth group.

There is also a great deal of folk reference to speech in terms of subjective impressions such as "drawl," "flat," "guttural," or "harsh." Linguists generally dismiss terms like these as imprecise and therefore largely meaningless to the serious phonetician. This does not mean that there are no actual phonetic details which correlate with such labels, but the looseness with which they are applied severely limits their usefulness.

Phonetic Transcription

One of the goals of impressionistic articulatory phonetics is to provide a conventional notation system for representing sounds in terms of the movements of the vocal apparatus. This is accomplished by establishing a phonetic alphabet, in which the symbols correspond to particular speech sounds. Letters from existing alphabetic systems are used for particular sounds, and various diacritic marks are added to letters to modify their value in some way. An adequate notational system should be able to represent any sound uttered in any human language. The symbols are used to represent phonetic values— the sounds as they are actually pronounced. In most cases, each alphabetic symbol used in writing a particular language includes more than one actual phonetic value.

For the beginning student, the important aspect of practical phonetics is developing an ability to hear sounds as they are actually pronounced. This can be accomplished only by divorcing oneself from the alphabetic representation of the sounds of one's own language. For example, the native speaker of English does not usually think of the unit represented by *p* in English orthography as having several different phonetic forms. One of these forms is followed by a puff of air (aspiration), as in *pot* and *pin*. But when *p* follows the consonant *s*, as in *spot* or *spin*, the puff of air is absent—the *p* is unaspirated. Many instructors of beginning phonetics have had prolonged arguments with native English speakers whose initial reaction is that these two types of *p* are phonetically identical. In an effort to convince students of the different pronunciations, we can resort to a simple demonstration. The puff of air following the *p* in *pot* and *pin* blows out a burning match held several inches in front of the mouth; the pronunciation of *p* in *spot* and *spin* usually does not.

A number of such gimmicks have found their way into the teaching tradition of articulatory phonetics. The goal is to convince students of the difference between the actual phonetic production and their perceptions as native speakers of their language. It is crucial to understand that the notion of phonetic value refers to the accurate representation of sounds following a convention independent of a particular language. Alphabets are not devised to give phonetic values, so that thinking of phonetic values in terms of one's own language can often turn out to be more of a hindrance than a help in phonetics.

Conventionally, phonetic transcription is indicated by enclosing the sound or sounds in square brackets [ ], referred to as **phonetic brackets**. The aspirated type of *p* sound found in *pin* is represented as [p^h] and the unaspirated one in *spot* is represented as [p] (a chart of phonetic symbols appears in the front of the book). The unit in English which combines these different phonetic forms into one functional unit would be indicated as /p/. The slanted lines / / have been referred to traditionally as **phonemic brackets**. (We will explain their use further in Chapter 3.) There is, of course, a great range of phonetic detail that could be included in the representation of a sound, depending on the phonetician's expertise and concern for minute differences in production. Representing sounds with extensive phonetic detail is usually referred to as **narrow transcription**, whereas representing them with less phonetic detail is **broad transcription**. Intermediate stages between the two extremes of transcription are referred to as "broader" and "narrower" transcriptions.

In order to transcribe sounds independent of any particular language system, linguists have agreed on conventional phonetic values for various graphic symbols. Ideally, we would like one convention to be adopted by all phoneticians, but this has not worked out. The most widespread attempt to standardize a phonetic alphabet goes back to 1888, when the first version of the International Phonetic Alphabet (IPA) was established. Since that time, revisions and modifications have been made to iron out certain inconsistencies and accommodate more types of sounds. The principles upon which the alphabet was originally established were:

(1) There should be a separate letter for each distinctive sound; that is, for each sound which, being used instead of another, in the same language, can change the meaning of a word.

(2) When any sound is found in several languages, the same sign should be used in all. This applies also to very similar shades of sound.

(3) The alphabet should consist as much as possible of the ordinary letters of the roman alphabet, as few new letters as possible being used.

(4) In assigning values to the roman letters, international usage should decide.

(5) The new letters should be suggestive of the sounds they represent, by their resemblance to the old ones.

(6) Diacritic marks should be avoided, being trying for the eyes and troublesome to write.

International Phonetic Association
(1949; inside back cover)

The conventions of the IPA suffer from certain biases which reflect its earliest concerns with the major European languages. The values of the sounds have been defined largely in terms of these languages, so that other uses are somewhat restricted. The IPA also suffers from the fact that the units are not always defined strictly in phonetic terms. In some cases, it is obvious that the phonetic interpretation of various sounds was strongly influenced by their status in certain European languages. Furthermore, the distinction between the use of diacritics and letters seems to imply that those differences represented by distinct letters are more basic than those indicated by diacritics, but this is not always true. The decision on which sounds to indicate by letters and which by diacritic modification to these letters, also reveals a bias in favor of the European languages which the developers were familiar with.

Despite these drawbacks, the IPA remains a useful system for phoneticians and is presently used in a number of different countries. In the United

States, some differences in the convention have developed which set apart the phonetic notation used by many American linguists. Some of these simply represent the biases of English sound values, such as the use of [y] to indicate the approximate value of the English sound found initially in words like *yet* or *yes*. In the IPA [j] is used to indicate the same phonetic values, reflecting the orthographic conventions of German, Scandinavian languages, and the modern spelling of classical Latin. Some differences in the systems used by American linguists stem from attempts to adapt the phonetic alphabet to a conventional typewriter. The use of đ for IPA ð is such an instance, as is the use of š, ž, č, and ǰ, instead of the IPA symbols ʃ, ʒ, tʃ, and dʒ, respectively. One of the more common notational systems used in the United States is presented in Smalley's *Manual of Articulatory Phonetics* (1961). This treatment is extensive in the sounds represented, yet shows concern for such practical matters as the accommodation of the system to a typewriter.

In most cases, linguists will follow one system of transcription with certain idiosyncratic twists, but most instructors have attempted to be fairly consistent with established conventions. While differences in transcription systems may be somewhat distracting for the student who is concerned with mastering the rudiments of basic phonetics, a simple memorization of equivalent forms can usually solve the problem. The student who plans to become a professional linguist should be familiar with several different conventions. The student from another discipline should concentrate on the convention used most often within that field. Thus, a student in speech pathology should become most familiar with the IPA, since it is used typically by professionals in that field. A reading specialist, on the other hand, should probably become familiar with the types of pronunciation symbols used in dictionaries and their equivalents in the system most often used by American phoneticians. The beginning student, however, should not be thrown off by arbitrary differences in representing a given phonetic value.

Exercise 1

a. Consider the different pronunciations represented by the initial letter *a* in each of the following words. A number of different actual vowel sounds are represented by this single orthographic symbol. Group together the words that have the same vowel sounds.

1. America	5. Antarctica	9. approach
2. Asia	6. Alaska	10. author
3. Africa	7. anger	11. angel
4. Australia	8. acorn	12. about

b. Do the same thing for each instance of *t* in the following English words.

1. nation	5. bottle	9. little
2. party	6. got you (gotcha)	10. rotten
3. button	7. tinker	11. action
4. butter	8. caught you (caughtcha)	12. partake

The use of phonetic symbols in the remainder of this book will depart slightly from the traditional convention, in which one symbol is chosen for exclusive use when there exist alternative representations. We deliberately vary the use of symbols where it is likely that the student will encounter different representations in further reading in phonology. For example, for one sound we alternate between [tš] and [tʃ] and for another we use both [d̶] and [ð], even though both symbols indicate the same phonetic value. This will take some adjustments at the outset, but it represents the range of variation students can realistically expect to encounter in reading current phonological analyses.

Dividing the Speech Stream

So far our discussion of speech sounds has treated them as if they came to us neatly packaged and separated. In fact, speech is more like a continuous flow of sound, produced by the movement of those parts of our anatomy which, for the sake of convenience, we refer to collectively as the **speech mechanism**. In order to understand how we move from the continuous flow of speech to what we regard as isolated sounds, it is helpful to examine exactly how sounds are produced.

The production of speech sounds is accomplished through the simultaneous activity of a number of different anatomical organs, no one of which is exclusively designed for speech production. Producing a string of speech sounds involves:

(1) the **respiratory system**, composed of the lungs, the bronchial tubes, the trachea, diaphragm, and various muscles which help move air through the system;

(2) the **larynx** (or "voice box"), which can provide voice for speech sounds, but which serves the additional function of sealing off the lungs to protect them or to make the chest more rigid while using the arms; and

(3) the **articulatory system** (vocal tract), which includes the lips, teeth, tongue, and other parts of the mouth, also used for eating and breathing.

These three systems combine to produce speech sounds, and it is really their activities we are interested in when we study articulatory phonetics.

Speech sounds are carried on a stream of air, so the exact nature of the airstream itself is important. It is possible to produce different kinds of airstreams within the speech mechanism. Most speech sounds are carried on an airstream flowing from the respiratory system. In most cases, this airstream is **egressive**; that is, it flows out of the mouth and lungs, rather than into the mouth (**ingressive**). All the sounds we will describe with reference to English are made on an egressive airstream from the lungs.

Other languages make use of other kinds of airstreams. Many languages use an airstream created by a rapid movement of the closed larynx, resulting in distinctive "popping" sounds (called glottalized consonants). Others use an ingressive airstream produced in front of a closure between the tongue and velum—what are known as "clicks." Speakers of English may use an ingressive airstream of this type, but not in linguistically significant speech sounds. Examples in English are the sounds written as *tsk-tsk*, and the "kissing" sound used to call dogs. For the most part, our discussions will be concerned only with sounds carried on an egressive, pulmonic (i.e. from the lungs) airstream. Descriptions will assume that all our sounds are produced in this way unless otherwise specified.

Once the airstream is on its way from the lungs, the larynx and the articulatory system may alter it in various ways to make distinctive speech sounds. As we shall discuss in more detail below, the larynx may set the airstream into vibration, thereby producing the sound feature we call **voicing**. The articulatory system may then further shape the airstream, interrupt it, or change its course as it flows through the mouth and/or nose. It is these movements of the articulatory system as they act on the airstream that provide us with our first means of dividing a given utterance into speech sounds.

A basic unit in the division of a stream of sounds is the **syllable**. The syllable is one of those units of language that is easier to identify than to define. There are two predominant views about what constitutes a syllable, neither of which is perfectly satisfactory. From one perspective, it may be defined in terms of peaks of acoustic energy or **sonority**, the loudness of sounds relative to other sounds. From the other perspective, it has been viewed in terms of the physical activity of the chest musculature in combination with movements in the oral cavity. Our concern here is not to arrive at a conclusive definition of the syllable, but to observe that syllables seem to somehow constitute units in the perceptions of the speakers of a language.

Like other types of complex human behavior, syllables can be sorted into smaller parts. For example, while the movements involved in shooting a basketball are perceived as a unit, the "jumpshot" may actually be analyzed as a slow backwards cocking of the wrist, an upward thrust of the legs, a rapid forward thrust of the arm, and a forward bending of the wrist. In a parallel way, we may divide the syllable into the **onset**, the **peak**, and the **coda**. The syllable peak is that period during which the airstream escapes relatively freely. It usually sets the vocal bands into vibration and is associated with less obstruction of the passage of air through the mouth. Alternatively, it may be viewed as that period of time when acoustic energy is the highest. Because acoustic energy is commonly associated with degrees of obstruction in the mouth, these two viewpoints on the syllable peak are compatible. The characteristic sounds produced at the syllable peak are called **vowels**, although certain other sounds may be used as the peak. It is possible to produce just a syllable peak (i.e. a syllable with only a vowel), but it is more common to assist the beginning (onset) and ending (coda) of the syllable with a more restricted passage of air through the articulatory system. Generally speaking, sounds associated with a more restricted passage of air at the onset or coda of the syllable are called **consonants**. The word *tea* is composed only of a consonant as the onset and a vowel as the peak, while the word *teak* has a syllable-initial consonant functioning as an onset, a vowel as the peak, and another syllable-final consonant that functions as a coda.

The division of syllables into consonants and vowels provides us with the means of isolating the important sound units of a language. Notice that the substitution of slightly different movements of the speech mechanism in the syllable onset may be responsible for a change in the meaning of a word. For example, by changing the onset movement of *tea* and *teak* from an obstruction immediately behind the teeth to one at the lips, we get *pea* and *peak*. Similarly, the syllable peak may be altered slightly to provide *tie* and *tyke*. The **sound segments** identified by such substitutions are the object of the study of phonetics. These sound segments are often referred to as **phones**.

Phones differ from each other in where and how they are produced by the speech mechanism. Following our original distinction between consonants and vowels, we will begin by describing the various consonants that are produced by the vocal mechanism. Linguists have traditionally described consonants according to two major characteristics: place of articulation and manner of articulation.

CONSONANTS: Place of Articulation

Place of articulation refers to the primary region or area in the vocal tract at which the sound is produced. One scheme for classifying the parts of the vocal tract is diagrammed below. The place of articulation of a sound is determined by the contact (or near contact) of two parts of the vocal tract. Usually, this involves a **passive articulator**, typically some point on the top of the vocal tract, and an **active articulator**, typically a movable part of the lower portion of the vocal tract. The place of articulation is most often named for the passive articulator.

We can start with the front of the mouth, where the lips may function as a place of articulation in several ways. By bringing the lower lip and upper lip together, we form **bilabial** sounds. In English, the sounds *p*, *b*, and *m* are all bilabials. Sounds can also be produced by placing the lower lip against the upper teeth to produce **labiodentals**. In English, *v* and *f* are produced as labiodentals. The upper teeth may also function as a passive articulator, with the tip of the tongue as the active articulator, as in the sounds represented by *th* in English orthography. Such sounds are called **interdentals**.

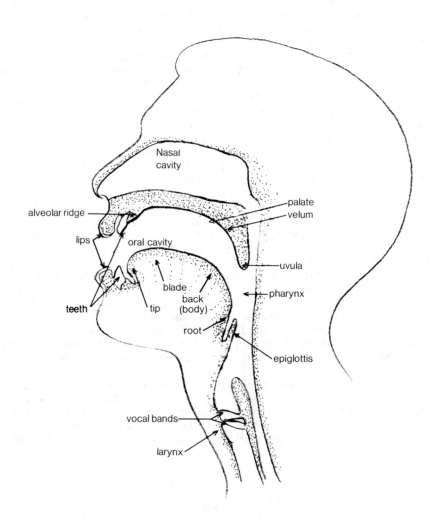

The speech mechanism

The roof of the mouth is divisible into a number of different places of articulation. Immediately behind the front teeth is the tooth ridge, the alveolar ridge. Many sounds are produced in this area, including *t*, *d*, *n*, *s*, and *z* in English. Behind the alveolar ridge is the **palate**, also called the hard palate. The front part of the palate immediately behind the alveolar ridge is sometimes referred to as the **alveopalatal** place of articulation. In English, the sound usually represented by the *sh* spelling as in *sheep* is produced as an alveopalatal. The palate itself is used as a place of articulation in many languages, including English. For example, the kind of *k* sound in words like *keep* and *kit* (but not *cot* or *kodak*) is a **palatal** sound. Behind the hard palate is the **velum**, or soft palate. Whereas the hard palate is an immovable plate of bone covered with other tissue, the velum is movable. The *k* sounds in *kodak* and *cot* are **velar** sounds, as are the *g* sounds in *God* and *good*. These are made by contact between the back of the tongue and the velum. The back of the velum can be raised against the pharyngeal wall to close off the air flow into the nasal passage, or it may remain open so that the air flow escapes through the nasal cavity. (We will discuss the movement of the velum in more detail later.) Finally, there is a small appendage hanging down at the back of the velum which is known as the **uvula**. Although there are no uvular speech sounds in English, the German and French *r* sounds often involve the vibration of the uvula against the back of the tongue. It is the uvula that vibrates during gargling.

Several sections of the tongue are important to articulation: the **tip** (or **apex**), the **blade**, the **back** or **body**, and the **root**. The tip and the blade of the tongue may articulate against the teeth, alveolar, or alveopalatal regions of the mouth, whereas the body of the tongue typically articulates against the palate, the velum, or the uvula. It is also possible for the tip of the tongue to turn back so that the bottom (rather than the top) of the tongue tip comes into contact with the place of articulation. Sounds produced with the tip of the tongue turned back are called **retroflexed** sounds. Diagrammed below are typical uses of the three main sections of the tongue in the production of certain consonants. As we shall see later, the position of the tongue is also crucial in describing vowels.

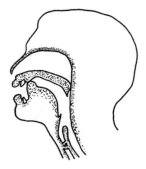 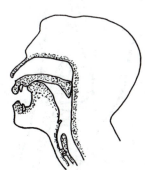 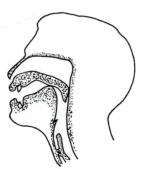

Use of tongue tip   **Use of tongue blade**   **Use of tongue back**

The root of the tongue may contact the **pharynx** to produce **pharyngeal** sounds, common in Semitic languages, but not found in English. The glottis itself is usually considered to be a place of articulation in articulatory phonetics, even though no other articulator comes into contact with it. The distinction between *mmhmm* ('yes') and *mmˀmm* ('no') is often maintained by **glottal** sound differences.

Exercise 2

Identify the places of articulation indicated by the numbered lines in the diagram below.

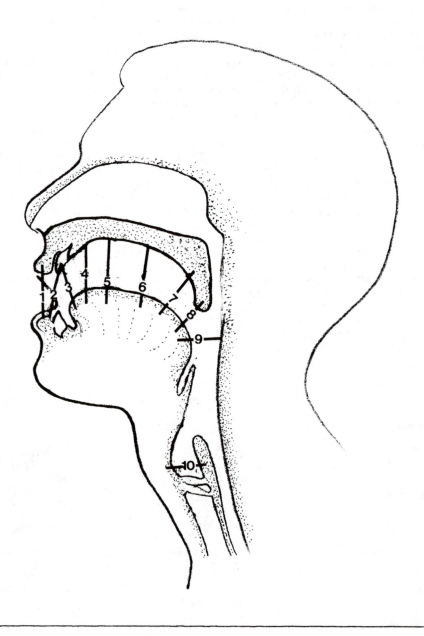

Exercise 3

Identify the place of articulation for the *first sound* in each of the following words.

1.	mother	6.	happy	11.	lathe
2.	cat	7.	kick	12.	topple
3.	cheap	8.	judge	13.	shove
4.	gross	9.	thought	14.	zero
5.	fickle	10.	villain	15.	basket

Manner of Articulation

Manner of articulation concerns the types of obstruction that can take place in the vocal tract. There are two main places where such obstruction takes place. One is the oral cavity and the other is the glottis. The two operate independently from one another and may act simultaneously.

Voicing and the Glottis. At the top of the trachea (windpipe) is a cartilaginous structure known as the **larynx**. In the production of speech, the main importance of the larynx lies in the fact that it contains the **vocal bands** (vocal cords). The vocal bands consist of two horizontal folds of elastic tissue, one on each side of the passage. In normal breathing, the vocal bands are open, but it is possible to close them partially or completely during the production of a sound. Further, the bands may be brought together so they vibrate as air passes through them. This vibration accounts for the feature of **voicing**. Sounds like [z], [v], and [d] are all produced with vibration of the vocal bands; hence they are classified as **voiced** sounds. If the vocal bands are open and not vibrating during the production of a sound, it will be a **voiceless** sound. Sounds like [s], [f], and [t] are voiceless. If you place your fingers on both sides of your "Adam's Apple" and say the word *zoom*, you will feel the vibration from the vocal bands. But you will feel no vibration producing [s] in the word *spit*. Other positions of the vocal bands produce such phenomena as whispers, murmurs, and "creaky voice."

Exercise 4

Indicate whether the *last sound* in each of the following words is voiced or voiceless. Do not be fooled by the spelling; pay attention to the actual sound.

1.	rag	8.	bathe	15.	phonograph
2.	rack	9.	bags	16.	silly
3.	realize	10.	books	17.	thorough
4.	class	11.	matched	18.	thought
5.	closed	12.	roses	19.	strength
6.	cloth	13.	mouth	20.	hang
7.	clothes	14.	laugh		

It is also possible to completely close the vocal bands and then release them in a rather abrupt manner. The resulting sound is referred to as a **glottal stop**, symbolized phonetically as [ʔ]. The most notable glottal stops in English are in pronouncing the *t* of *bottle* [báʔḷ], *little* [líʔḷ], and *button* [bʌ́ʔn̩] in some varieties. Less noticeable but more widespread is the use of a glottal stop instead of *t* in syllable-final position, as in [bɪʔ] instead of [bɪt]. In some non-mainstream varieties of English, it is also possible to use the glottal stop instead of [d], particularly in unstressed syllables, so that we get items like [stúpɪʔ] and [sǽlɪʔ] for *stupid* and *salad* respectively. Another very common context for glottal stops in English is before words beginning with a vowel when the word occurs as the first item in an utterance—for example, *apples* [ʔæplz] in *Apples are edible.*

In some languages, including many American Indian languages, glottal closure may accompany a consonant, either simultaneously or slightly delayed, giving the impression of a type of popping sound. Although these are very important aspects of the phonetic structure of such languages, our focus on English makes it unnecessary to discuss them in more detail here. The remaining manners of articulation relate to obstruction in the oral cavity.

Stops. **Stops** (or **plosives**) are produced when there is a complete closure between an active and a passive articulator during the production of the sound, followed by release of the closure. Stops may occur at any of the places of articulation mentioned above, and may be voiced or voiceless. At the bilabial place of articulation, the voiceless stop [p] and the voiced stop [b] occur. At the alveolar position, [t] and [d] occur, and [k] and [g] occur in the velar position. These are not, of course, the only positions at which stops may be produced, and many languages have stops at other positions as well. Recall here that our phonetic symbols represent the sounds themselves, and may not have a one-to-one correspondence with the same symbol in English orthography. A good example is the phonetic [k], which is represented in orthography by both *k* and *c*.

Previously we mentioned that stops may be released with or without a puff of air following the sound. This **aspiration** is indicated by a raised *h* following the sound, as in [pʰ] or [kʰ]. In English, both aspirated and unaspirated voiceless stops occur, but the difference in aspiration is not used to distinguish different words. In many languages, however, aspiration is used to make such a distinction. Both voiceless and voiced stops may be aspirated, as in Hindi, where [bʰ], [b], [pʰ], and [p] all serve to distinguish words. While both aspirated and unaspirated stops may occur in English, the presence or absence of aspiration is highly sensitive to the surrounding phonological context. Thus, we get aspirated stops at the beginning of a word, as in *pit* [pʰɪt], but unaspirated stops following an *s*, as in *spit* [spɪt].

Exercise 5

For the following items, identify those voiceless stops in English which are typically aspirated in spontaneous speech (i.e. conversational usage rather than careful, isolated citation pronunciation). At this point, do not be concerned about phonetic symbols that have not been introduced yet.

1.	[púdɪŋ]	'pudding'	7.	[kápə]	'copper'
2.	[rɪpórt]	'report'	8.	[rɪspɛ́ktəbl]	'respectable'
3.	[tǽksi]	'taxi'	9.	[kənklúd]	'conclude'
4.	[spɛ́kyəleɪt]	'speculate'	10.	[temptéɪšən]	'temptation'
5.	[prɪpǽr]	'prepare'	11.	[tíkɪt]	'ticket'
6.	[prɛpəréɪšən]	'preparation'	12.	[kántæktɪŋ]	'contacting'

Fricatives. Whereas a stop involves complete closure between a passive and an active articulator, fricatives do not completely close this gap. Rather, the air is forced through a narrow passage, creating friction. This results in a hissing or buzzing type of sound. Fricatives, like stops, can be produced at all the places of articulation mentioned above, although English does not utilize all these positions. In most varieties of English, no bilabial fricatives are used. Bilabial fricatives are produced by bringing the lips into close contact without closing them, while forcing air through them to create friction. These can either be voiceless ("phi," symbolized as [ⲣ] or [ɸ]) or voiced ("beta," symbolized as [ƀ] or [β]). In Spanish, the sound represented orthographically as *b* is produced as a bilabial fricative following vowels (e.g. [bɛ̀ƀɛ́ř] 'to drink'). Present-day English also has no velar fricatives, voiceless [χ] "chi," and voiced [ɡ] or [γ] "gamma," but there are many languages that do. German has voiceless velar fricatives in items like *doch* [dox], while Spanish speakers may pronounce orthographic *g* as a voiced velar fricative [ɡ] following vowels (e.g. [paɡár̆] 'to pay').

English does have labiodental fricatives—voiceless [f] and voiced [v]. Many varieties of English also have interdental fricatives, both voiced (represented as [đ] or [ð] 'eth') and voiceless (indicated by [θ] "theta"). English spelling represents both voiced and voiceless interdentals with one orthographic symbol *th*. The voiced interdental fricative [ð] is found in items like *the, that,* and *these,* and its voiceless counterpart [θ] in *thought, thank,* and *three.*

English also has fricatives in alveolar and alveopalatal positions, but they are produced in a slightly different manner from the interdentals. In producing the interdental fricatives, the tongue is extended in a rather flat manner. But for [s] (e.g. [sɪp] 'sip', [sɪs] 'sis') and [z] (e.g. [zɪp] 'zip', [zuz] 'zoos'), there is a trough in the middle of the tongue through which the air passes. This is also true for the alveopalatals, the voiceless [š] (or [ʃ]) of *ship* [šɪp] or *wish* [wɪš], and its voiced counterpart [ž] (or [ʒ]) in *measure* [mɛžur] or *azure* [æžur]. Because of this grooving quality of the tongue, these sounds are sometimes referred to as **sibilants.**

All these fricatives are produced entirely in the oral cavity. It is also possible for a fricative to be produced against the pharyngeal wall, or simply between relaxed vocal bands. In the latter case, the oral cavity remains unobstructed while this slight friction is formed. This is what happens with the *h* sound in items like *hat* [hæt] and *how* [haᵁ]. Although the glottal fricative [h] is normally voiceless, it may have a slight voicing quality. In English, the voiced glottal fricative [ɦ] occurs only between vowels, as in *ahead* [əɦɛ́d] or *behave* [biɦeᴵv].

Affricates. A cluster of sounds containing two segments, the first a stop and the second a fricative produced at approximately the same place of articulation, is referred to as an **affricate.** In English, the sequences spelled *ch* and *j* often represent respectively the voiceless alveopalatal affricate [tš] (or [tʃ] or [č]), and the voiced alveopalatal affricate [dž] (or [dʒ] or [ǰ]). These occur in the words *church* [tš₃ʳtš] and *judge* [džʌdž]. Affricates may be produced at various positions, so that some languages make use of affricates such as [pⲣ], [bƀ], [kx], [ɡɡ], [pf], and so forth.

Flaps and Trills. Flaps and trills are obstruents that involve a rapid closing and opening of the obstruction at some place of articulation. Flaps involve one brief tap of the articulator so that considerably less pressure is built up than in the case of a regular stop. In American English, the alveolar *t* and *d* between vowels are often produced as flaps [ɾ] or [ř], as in items like *batted* [bǽɾɪd] and *raided* [réᴵɾɪd]. Between vowels, nasals may also be produced with a flap-like quality [ñ], as in the rapid pronunciation of items like *wanted* [wʌñɪd] or *any* [ɛñi]. Laterals can occasionally become flapped [ɭ] in English, e.g. [bɛɭi] for *belly*.

Whereas flaps have only one tap of the active articulator, **trills** have two or more. The alveolar trill [r̃] is found in a number of different languages, but English does not use it, except in certain preaching styles where trills may be used in place of the common retroflex *r* (e.g. [spír̃it] 'spirit'). In Spanish, items like *pero* [pér̃o] 'but' and *perro* [pér̃o] 'dog' may be distinguished by the difference between the alveolar flap and alveolar trill. Some dialects of German use the uvular trill [ʀ] (e.g. [ʀot] 'red'), as does French (e.g. [ʀat] 'rat').

All the sounds discussed so far are characterized by articulation involving some type of radical obstruction. As a group, stops, fricatives, affricates, flaps, and trills are sometimes referred to as **obstruents**. Sounds not involving such radical obstruction are referred to as **sonorants**: nasal and lateral consonants, glides, and the vowels.

Nasals. In the production of **nasal** sounds, the velum is lowered, opening a passage from the pharynx to the nasal cavity so that air can escape through the nostrils. In nasal consonants, there is a closure at some point in the oral cavity, forcing the air to rebound through the nasal cavity. In English there are at least three nasal consonants: bilabial [m], alveolar [n], and velar [ŋ]. These correspond to the voiced stops [b], [d], and [g] at these points of articulation, except that air passage into the nasal cavity is closed off for stops and open for nasals. The difference between the production of alveolar stops [d] and [t] and the nasal [n] is illustrated in the following diagram.

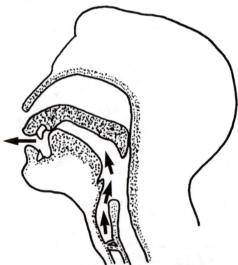
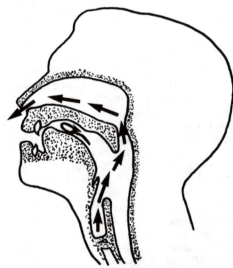

**Air passage in production
of alveolar stops**

**Air passage in production
of alveolar nasal**

Other languages use more places of articulation for nasals. Spanish has a nasal which is produced in the alveopalatal region [ñ] ([ɲ]), as found in the word [niño] 'child'. A similar type of alveopalatal is found in Gullah, an English-based creole spoken in the South Sea Islands area of South Carolina and Georgia (e.g. [bɔñ] 'tooth'). In some varieties of English, speakers produce a labiodental nasal [ɱ] before a labiodental fricative, so that *emphasis* is pronounced as [ɛɱfəsɪs] and *comfort* as [kʰʌ́ɱfət].

In English, nasals are usually voiced, but next to certain voiceless consonants and in particularly rapid pronunciations, they may become voiceless, as in some pronunciations of *Memphian* [mɛm̥fiən] (a person from Memphis). Voiceless nasals are represented here by a [̥] subscript, as in [m̥] or [n̥]. Other linguists use uppercase [M] and [N].

Liquids. Two kinds of sounds are usually considered to be liquids: the retroflex *r* when it functions as a consonant, and the laterals. The retroflex [r] which occurs in *run* [rʌn] and *rat* [ræt], is found in many varieties of English. It can be produced in several different ways. One of these involves turning the tip of the tongue upward (usually without actually touching the palate) while the sides of the tongue rest against the sides of the back upper teeth. Another type of production involves bunching the tongue together toward the back part of the palate while the tip of the tongue remains low.

Whether these liquid segments are classes as vowels or consonants depends largely on the phonological system. Thus, at the beginning of a word and followed by a vowel, the retroflex [r] typically functions as a consonant while at the peak of a syllable it appears to function as a vowel. We will return to this later.

In producing **laterals**, the tip or blade of the tongue comes into contact with the roof of the mouth and air is allowed to pass over one or both sides of the tongue. This differs from many oral consonants, in which the air escapes over the central portion of the tongue. In other languages, there are a number of different lateral sounds. English has the *l* sounds, with a difference between a "light" or "clear" *l* and a "dark" *l*. The light *l* (an alveolar lateral) is produced with the tongue tip or blade on the alveolar ridge, with the air escaping over the sides of the tongue. The front of the tongue is relatively high and the back somewhat lowered. In many varieties of English, a light *l* is produced in words such as *leap* [lip] and *lap* [læp]. Dark *l* is a velarized alveolar lateral, often symbolized as [ɫ] or [ł]. It is produced with a concave slope in the middle of the tongue. The tip and back of the tongue are relatively high while the center is lowered. In many varieties of English, *l* following a vowel, as in items like *pull* [pʰuɫ] or *golf* [gaɫf], is produced as a dark *l*. The cross-sectional difference between light and dark *l* is shown in the following diagrams. Dark *l* is described with

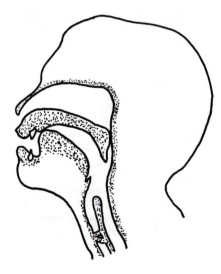

Position of light l̠ [l]

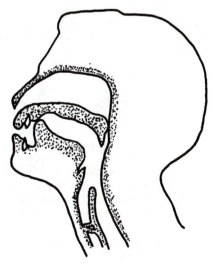

Position of dark l̠ [ɫ]

reference to its "velarized" characteristic (i.e. alveovelar or velarized lateral), stressing the degree in which the tongue is raised toward the velum. The degree of velarization depends on how much the back of the tongue is raised, and different varieties of English vary considerably in this characteristic.

Glides. The terms **glide** and **semivowel** refer to vowel-like sounds that occur in a place in the word usually reserved for consonants. Thus, these terms are often used more with reference to the overall functioning of the sound system than to the actual phonetic character of the sound. Vowel-like sounds that are prominent in the syllable (i.e. those that occupy the syllable peak) are usually identified as vowels, whereas vowel-like sounds that do not serve this function are most often classified as semivowels or glides. However, there usually is a real phonetic difference between glides and their corresponding vowels. These phonetic differences usually result from factors such as more rapid movement, or more rigid positioning of the tongue for glides.

The rounded velar (or labiovelar) glide [w] is formed by protruding the lips slightly while raising the back of the tongue to the position typically occupied in the true vowels [u] or [ʊ]. The voiced variant of this semivowel occurs initially in items like *will* [wɪɫ] or *wish* [wɪš]. In some varieties of American English, there is also a voiceless variant of this glide (often with preceding aspiration), which is usually symbolized as [hw], [w̥], or [ʍ]. This sound is found in dialects that distinguish *which* [hwɪtš] from *witch* [wɪtš] or *while* [hwaɪɫ] from *wile* [waɪɫ].

The palatal glide, symbolized as [y] or [j], is produced by raising the front of the tongue toward the hard palate and bringing the sides of the tongue into contact with the upper back teeth (bicuspid and molar). The place of articulation is much like that found in the high front tense vowel [i] (to be described later). Like *w*, this also has a voiceless variant in some varieties of English, symbolized as [hy], [hj], or [y̥]. These dialects often distinguish between items like *you* [yu] and *Hugh* [hyu] and between *human* [hyúmɪn] and *Yuman* [yúmɪn] (a person from Yuma, Arizona).

Exercise 6

In the following English items, pick out those in which the consonants have been transcribed *inaccurately*. For the time being, ignore the transcription of vowels. Correct the transcription in an appropriate way, based on your pronunciation of the item.

1.	[rɪp]	'rip'	11.	[ənʌθə]	'another'
2.	[cuɫ]	'cool'	12.	[pænts]	'pants'
3.	[tʰɛ́ɫəgræph]	'telegraph'	13.	[rɪzáɪn]	'resign'
4.	[pʰíktʊr]	'picture'	14.	[rə́bɪŋ]	'rubbing'
5.	[rɪpórt]	'report'	15.	[əɫɛktríkɪɾi]	'electricity'
6.	[néɪtən]	'nation'	16.	[tʰrænskrípšən]	'transcription'
7.	[kʰæch]	'catch'	17.	[fənáɫəgi]	'phonology'
8.	[trænskráɪb]	'transcribe'	18.	[ínlɪš]	'English'
9.	[fənɛ́ɾɪk]	'phonetic'	19.	[tʰrænskráɪbd]	'transcribed'
10.	[bə́ttə]	'butter'	20.	[rɛkd]	'wrecked'

The Description of Consonants

Although we have used various alphabetic symbols to represent the phonetic value of sounds, we have typically referred to sounds in terms of distinguishing characteristics, such as the place of articulation, the manner of articulation, and whether they are voiced or voiceless. So we call the sound represented by [b] a voiced bilabial stop rather than *bee*, and [pʰ] a voiceless bilabial aspirated stop rather than *pee*. Such **descriptors** are used to avoid any commitment to the phonetic value that a "letter" might have within the spelling of a given language system. Descriptions of consonants usually follow a convention in which factors of voicing, place of articulation, and manner of articulation are given, in that order. Consider the following sample descriptors:

Symbolization	Voicing	Place of Articulation	Manner of Articulation
[b]	voiced	bilabial	stop
[pʰ]	voiceless	bilabial	aspirated stop
[p]	voiceless	bilabial	unaspirated stop
[θ]	voiceless	interdental	fricative
[ž]	voiced	alveopalatal	sibilant
[h]	voiceless	glottal	fricative
[hw]	voiceless	rounded velar (labio-velar)	glide
[ʔ]	(voiceless)	glottal	stop
[n]	(voiced)	alveolar	nasal
[ɫ]	(voiced)	velarized alveolar ("dark")	lateral

The traditional format used for description is not entirely regular, and reflects a bias toward the English phonetic system. Thus, aspiration and non-aspiration are often specified only for voiceless stops, even though a number of languages use aspirated and unaspirated voiced stops. For English, lack of aspiration is assumed unless specified to the contrary. So [bʰ] is described as a voiced bilabial aspirated stop, but [b] is described as a voiced bilabial stop, and we assume it is unaspirated. Similarly, voicing is assumed for nasals unless they are specifically described as voiceless, so that [n] is described simply as an alveolar nasal. It is also assumed that sounds are produced with an egressive, pulmonic airstream, unless specified otherwise. In the case of a glottal stop [ʔ], it is unnecessary to specify voicing since it is impossible to produce a voiced glottal stop. Although there are certain irregularities in the descriptive format which simply have to be memorized, the basic descriptors should cause little difficulty.

Exercise 7

Identify the phonetic symbols represented by the following descriptors.

1. voiced alveolar stop
2. voiced velar fricative
3. voiceless bilabial fricative
4. alveopalatal nasal
5. voiced alveopalatal affricate
6. voiceless velar unaspirated stop
7. voiced glottal fricative
8. labiodental nasal
9. voiceless alveopalatal glide
10. alveolar lateral
11. voiceless labiodental fricative
12. voiceless velar fricative

Exercise 8

Give descriptors for the following phonetic symbols.

1. [v]
2. [ɑ̶]
3. [š]
4. [ɾ]

5. [ᵽ]
6. [ʀ]
7. [r̃]
8. [ɸ]

9. [ñ]
10. [hy]
11. [w]
12. [ʃ]

Detailed Consonant Descriptions

The inventory of consonantal segments we have presented is fairly selective. We have omitted many consonants that occur in languages other than English. But even if we had presented a more complete phonetic inventory of consonants, we would still find a need to specify some sounds in more detail than that provided by our basic inventory. These additional details are usually viewed as modifications of basic consonantal forms, such as aspiration of stops. Others must be added as our expanding knowledge of phonetics leads us to the transcription of finer detail. In most instances, this further detail is added through the use of diacritics. In English, for example, stops in utterance-final position may be momentarily unreleased, or "held." This is indicated by adding [ˈ] to the basic symbol, as in [rɪpˈ] 'rip' (*Let's rip!*).

Similarly, an examination of the production of *t* preceding an interdental [θ] in English reveals that it is actually produced on the teeth (a "dental" *t*) rather than the alveolar ridge. When a sound is articulated at a point further forward than that indicated by the conventional symbol, we say it is fronted. This is shown by [‿], (e.g. [eɪt̪θ] 'eighth'). On the other hand, a placement of the tongue at a point behind our designated position is called backing. Backing can be represented by [˘]. Thus, the symbol [k̠] refers to a voiceless stop produced somewhat in front of the designated velar point of articulation. This sound occurs in English *keep* [kʰip] and *ski* [ski], and is due to the following front vowel. The backing symbol may be added in words such as *cool* [kʰuɫ] and *school* [skuɫ], items in which the velar stop is followed by a back vowel. In some systems [˘] is also used to indicate retroflection. Retroflexion involves the bottom of the tongue tip as the articulator, and is restricted to alveolars and alveopalatals (e.g. [ṭ]). Although the tongue is curled in much the same way as it is in the retroflex *r*, in this case, there is actual contact at the point of articulation. In another system, fronting and backing are indicated by a different set of symbols, [˷] and [˴] respectively, so that the confusion with the use of [˘] is avoided. A backed *t* would be indicated by [t̢], distinguishing it from retroflex [ṭ].

Another type of modification involves the **devoicing** of a typically voiced sound segment, indicated by [˳], e.g. the voiceless nasal [m̥]. In English, laterals may also be devoiced in some contexts (e.g. [sl̥ip] 'sleep'). While our previous discussion of voicing assumed that segments were either completely voiced or voiceless, in reality voicing may only carry through part of the segment. If we listen carefully to the production of the final [z] in *rows*, we find that it fades into voicelessness after starting out as a voiced segment. We indicate this partial devoicing by adding an arrow to the devoicing symbol [˳→] (e.g. [roᵁz̥]).

It is also possible to recognize differences in the duration of various consonants. In some languages a **lengthened consonant** may contrast with an unlengthened consonant, but in English duration is restricted to a secondary role. There do, however, appear to be some special cases in which differences between words may be discernible only by the length of the consonants.

In casual speech style, some speakers of English pronounce final -sts clusters as a lengthened s (indicated here by [:]), producing [tɛs:] for *tests* or [rɛs:] for *rests*. For such speakers, a *guess* [gɛs] might be distinguished from *guests* [gɛs:] only by the phonetic length of the [s].

Another modification of stops and fricatives is the difference between **fortis** [ ] and **lenis** [ ]. Fortis sounds are produced with a greater degree of muscular tension and breath pressure; lenis sounds are produced with less. A lenis stop (actually a lenis dental unaspirated stop) is often produced for the [θ] in words like *think* and *thank* by non-mainstream speakers in New York City. The lenis production of the stop is an important aspect of maintaining the distinction between *thank* [tæŋk] and *tank* [tʰæŋk] in these varieties.

The chart which follows summarizes our discussion of the consonantal inventory. For the most part, the symbols used here follow the American tradition for transcription of English. Where other symbols are in current use, either from IPA or a different system within the American tradition, we have indicated the most common alternatives in parentheses. Although the presentation of various consonantal segments and their possible modifications may seem imposing to the reader with no background in articulatory phonetics, this account is actually quite selective. It is restricted largely to consonantal productions that we might expect a speaker of English to be familiar with. Continuing students of phonetics should refer to the more detailed sources listed at the end of the chapter to equip themselves with a framework adequate for detailed description of speech sounds.

Broad and Narrow Transcription

At the beginning of this chapter, we referred briefly to two different approaches to phonetic transcription: broad transcription, which excludes some of the finer phonetic detail in the representation of sounds, and narrow transcription, which includes more phonetic detail. Roughly speaking, we can say that the narrow transcription of English sounds tends to include many of the modifications described in the previous section, and that broad transcription tends to use only the primary phonetic symbols themselves. Thus, in a narrow transcription of English we would typically include the details of aspiration, unreleasing, different kinds of laterals, fronting and backing of velars, and devoicing. A broad transcription of the same utterance would exclude these details. Consider, for example, a broad and narrow transcription of the sentence *Eat proper food instead of vitamin pills* (we will ignore the vowels for now).

Narrow: [ʔit˺ pʰrapə fuɾ ɪnstɛɾ əvvaɪɾəmɪn pʰɪɫz]
Broad: [it prapə̊ fud ɪnstɛd əv vaɪtəmɪn pɪlz]

The narrowest transcription indicates every phonetic detail we can recognize, but in making a broader transcription it becomes difficult to decide which information to exclude. Clearly, it is a decision based heavily on our knowledge of the phonological structure of English, a matter to which we will return in Chapter 3. Degrees of narrowness are largely a matter of convenience. In the remainder of the book, we will use broad transcription except when it is necessary to focus on specific phonetic details which require narrow transcription. For example, in discussing the flap in forms like *patter*, we would transcribe the form as [pæɾə], but in discussing aspiration in the same form we would transcribe it as [pʰætə].

		Bilabial	Labiodental	Interdental	Alveolar	Alveopalatal	Velar	Uvular	Glottal
Stops	vl.	p			t		k		ʔ
	vd.	b			d		g		
Fricatives	vl.	p̄ (Φ)	f	θ			x		h
	vd.	b̄ (β)	v	ḏ (ð)			g̶ (ɣ)		ɦ
Sibilants	vl.				s	š (ʃ)			
	vd.				z	ž (ʒ)			
Affricates	vl.					tš (tʃ) (č)			
	vd.					dž (dʒ) (ǰ)			
Flaps					ɾ (ř)				
Trills					r̃			ʀ	
Nasals		m	ɱ		n	ñ	ŋ		
Liquids	lateral				l		ł (ɫ)		
	retroflex				r				
Glides	vl.					hy (y̥, hj)	hw (w̥)(ʍ)		
	vd.					y (j)	w		

Modification	Symbol	Illustrative sound
Aspirated	ʰ	[pʰ]
Unreleased	̚	[p̚]
Fronted	˅	[k̆]
Backed	˄	[k̂]
Retroflexed	·	[ṭ]
Lengthened	:	[s:]
Fortis	|	[t̪]
Lenis	|	[t̩]
Devoiced	̥	
Partially devoiced	̥̇	[z̥]

CONSONANT CHART

Exercise 9

Transcribe the consonants in the following English words in both broad and narrow transcription. Consider aspiration, unreleasing, backing, fronting, devoicing, and different kinds of *l*'s in your differentiation.

1.	lip	6.	please	11.	ease
2.	slip	7.	school	12.	tardy
3.	keep	8.	better	13.	cup
4.	easy	9.	kills	14.	loader
5.	acting	10.	rotten	15.	prone

Exercise 10

Give the descriptors for the following symbols. In adding modifications, the item is simply qualified appropriately, as in $[p^h]$, "a voiceless bilabial aspirated stop," or $[\underset{\scriptscriptstyle\smile}{t}^h]$ "a voiceless dental (fronted alveolar) aspirated stop."

1.	$[t^\daleth]$	5.	$[\underset{>}{\mathrm{k}}^\daleth]$
2.	$[x]$	6.	$[\underset{\smallsmile}{n}:]$
3.	$[\overset{<}{s}]$	7.	$[\bar{d}]$
4.	$[\underset{o\rightarrow}{\dot{z}}]$	8.	$[\underset{o}{\bar{m}}]$

VOWELS

While consonants are typically produced with some sort of constriction or stoppage in the oral cavity, vowels are produced without radical constriction. Rather, vowels take on their peculiar characteristics from changes in the size and shape of the oral cavity as a whole. This characterization is typical rather than definitive. As we have already seen, the distinction between vowels and consonants may come in some cases from the structure of the phonological system rather than clear-cut phonetic distinctions. The phonetic production of [y] and [i] may be quite similar, but the structure of consonant-vowel sequences in the phonological system will specify whether an occurrence is to be interpreted as vowel or as consonant.

Consonants are usually characterized by reference to distinct places and manners of articulation. In describing vowels, it is more convenient to make use of two continuous dimensions: tongue height (**vowel height**) and tongue retraction (**vowel backness**). The vowel height dimension refers to the relative location of the highest point of the body of the tongue on a vertical scale. The vowel backness dimension refers to the relative location of the highest part of the body of the tongue on a horizontal scale. To help clarify these notions, pronounce very slowly and deliberately the English word for the sound a cat makes: *meow*. Notice that the highest point of the tongue travels in something like an elliptical pattern, beginning near the palate, moving downward and backward in an arc and then changing directions and moving forward and upward until it stops just behind where it started. An impressionistic version of this path would be:

Notice that the jaw opens and then closes during the production of *meow*, and that the lips begin in a stretched (almost smiling) configuration and end in a pursed, protruding shape.

The point of sitting and *meowing* to yourself is to observe that the vowel quality of the word changes continuously as the tongue moves. The tongue does not move between specific places of articulation as it would in producing a series of consonants. This continuous characteristic of vowel quality makes it rather more difficult to describe vowels phonetically and to associate particular vowel qualities with phonetic symbols. Notice, however, that as you move your tongue around the elliptical path for *meow*, you hear vowels that sound like certain English vowels. If you were to stop moving your tongue at various places you might find vowels successively corresponding to those in *peat, pit, pet, pat, pot, bought, boat,* and *boot*. Of course, depending on how you pronounce *meow* and on how you pronounce these English words, you may not find all of them, but those that you do find should be in the same order on the ellipse. The area of the mouth in which vowels may be produced is divided into a grid, formed by three arbitrary divisions along the height and backness dimensions. Certain vowel symbols are associated with the sounds corresponding to each section of the grid. Vowel height is generally divided into **high, mid,** and **low;** backness is generally divided into **front, central,** and **back.**

In addition to the height and position of the tongue, other dimensions are needed to describe the articulatory processes for different vowels. One such dimension is **tenseness**—the degree to which the root of the tongue is pulled forward and bunched up. This parameter cannot be divorced completely from the height and backness dimensions, because tense vowels tend to be slightly higher than their lax counterparts. **Tense** vowels are typically found in English words like *beet* and *boot,* and their **lax** counterparts in *bit* and *put.*

Another dimension influencing vowel production is the involvement of the lips noted in pronouncing *meow*. During production of the vowel in *loop,* the lips tend to be **rounded** (i.e. slightly protruded), but there is no rounding in the vowel of *leap.* In English, the rounding of a vowel tends to correlate with its backness. Back vowels are typically rounded and front vowels are not. Many other languages, however, have both rounded and unrounded front and back vowels.

A vowel is described by reference to these four parameters. Thus, the vowel in *beat* [i] is called a "high, front, tense, unrounded vowel." A grid (sometimes referred to as a vowel quadrangle) containing the major vowels is shown below. Notice that the grid does not really reflect the elliptical nature of the vowel area. It is somewhat skewed to line up certain vowels which tend to group together in processes we will discuss later. The grid is intended to give a rough approximation of the position of the tongue in vowel production in terms of a cross-section of the tongue (front to back). There are, of course, slightly different schemes and opinions on the actual classification of some of the vowels in the grid. We shall not go into these differences here.[1]

Front Vowels. In the grid, we have distinguished a full set of six front vowels, including a pair of tense and lax vowels for each of three different height levels. The high front tense vowel [i] is typically found in *beat* [bit] and *keep* [kʰip], although English speakers often have a tendency to glide it slightly into another vowel. It may actually be produced as a combination of [i] and another vowel (e.g. [iⁱ]). In many European languages, it occurs without the glide. The high front lax vowel [ɪ] (or [ı] "iota") occurs in *bit* [bɪt] and *sit* [sɪt]. The mid front tense vowel [e] is used very rarely in English in its "pure" form, although it is associated with the vowel in *bait* and *late*. Usually the vowel of items like these consists of a glide from [e] into another vowel (e.g. [eᴵ], [eⁱ]). The [e] without a glide is found in German *geht*, French *été*, or Spanish *leche*. For some speakers of English, placing the tongue in position for the first part of the vowel in the word *gay*, and then lengthening the sound without moving the tongue, will produce the [e] vowel. Using a mirror to make sure the tongue and lower jaw do not rise can sometimes help the learner overcome the English tendency to glide [e] into the range of [i] or [ɪ].

The mid front lax vowel [ɛ] occurs in *bet* [bɛt] and *met* [mɛt]. The low front tense vowel [æ] occurs in *sat* [sæt] and *bat* [bæt] in many varieties of English, although there are some dialect variations. In many dialects of American English, [æ] is the lowest front vowel produced. There are, however, varieties which use a more lax (or lower) variety of front vowel which we symbolize here as [a]. The low front lax vowel [a] is sometimes heard in Eastern New England in items like *ask* [ask] or *path* [paθ]. In parts of the South and in some urban Black varieties, it may be heard as the vowel in items like *five* [fav] or *mine* [man]. In these varieties, the vowel ranges from [æ] to [a], and there is often no high front glide into [i] or [ɪ]. For the speaker to whom such a vowel is not native, starting with the high front vowel [i] and progressively working down the front vowels to a point lower than [æ] may help in producing this vowel.

Central Vowels. In the grid above, we have listed only four central vowels. The high central lax vowel [ɨ] is sometimes found in unstressed syllables of English. It may be found in *salad* [sælɨd] or *parted* [párɾɨd]. It can also occur in an unstressed position within a phrase, for example, *can* [kɨn] in a phrase like *I can do it* in casual speech style, or *just* [dʒɨs] in unstressed position as in *just a minute*. In stressed syllables, it is found in some Southern pronunciations of *sister* [sɨ́stə] or *dinner* [dɨ́nə]. To produce this vowel, start at the high front position and work backward toward the back vowels. Be careful, however, to distinguish it from [ɪ] and [ʊ].

In the mid range of central vowels, we distinguish the mid central tense vowel [ə], commonly referred to as "schwa," and the mid central lax vowel [ʌ], sometimes called a "caret." In some systems of classification [ʌ] is considered a mid or low back unrounded vowel, and the schwa a lax central vowel. The schwa very commonly occurs in unstressed positions in most dialects of English, e.g. *around* [əráʊnd], *telegraph* [tʰɛ́ləgræf], and *sofa* [sóʊfə]. It is sometimes difficult to perceive the difference between [ə] and [ʌ] in English, but [ʌ] typically occurs in stressed syllables such as *cup* [kʰʌp] or *cutting* [kʰʌ́ɾɪŋ]. *Above* [əbʌ́v] contains [ə] in the unstressed syllable and [ʌ] in the stressed syllable.

The mid central vowels may also be retroflexed (the articulatory basis of retroflexion was discussed above under consonants). In the production of vowels the front of the tongue may be slightly lower than that used in the production of consonantal [r]. Two types of retroflex vowels are often distinguished for English. The retroflex [ɝ] is commonly found in stressed syllables in items like *bird* [bɝd] and *third* [θɝd]. The retroflex [ɚ] is more frequently found in unstressed syllables such as in *mother* [mʌðɚ] and *runner* [rʌnɚ]. Although central vowels are the ones usually retroflexed in English, other languages retroflex the other vowels as well (indicated with a [ˆ] on the vowel, as in [uˆ]). In transcribing English, several different conventions have been used for indicating the retroflex segments. In one convention, [r] is always used, regardless of how the retroflex functions. In another, only [r] and [ɚ] are used. The system described in the previous paragraph, however, recognizes [r], [ɚ], and [ɝ]. Using these three different conventions, retroflex segments in representative contexts would be indicated in the following way.

Context	Example	[r]	[ɚ]	[ɚ] and [ɝ]
Stressed syllable	bird	[bɨrd]	[bəd]	[bɝd]
Unstressed syllable	mother	[mʌðɨr]	[mʌðɚ]	[mʌðɚ]
Before a vowel	rip	[rɪp]	[rɪp]	[rɪp]
After a non-central vowel	beer	[bir]	[bir]	[bir]

There are other conventions used by some linguists in transcribing English retroflex vowels, so that one must be careful to understand what particular convention is being used. Some of the differences are related to claims concerning different phonetic details of retroflexion. It may be claimed, for example, that [ɝ] is more retroflexed than [ɚ], or that [r] differs from both of these in phonetic substance. In actuality, however, differences often seem to be more related to the phonological structure of English than phonetic facts per se.

The other central vowel in the grid is commonly symbolized as [ɑ], but [a] is often used in its place because of the convenience of the latter symbol for the typewriter. Except where specifically indicated, we will use the symbol [a] in place of [ɑ] in the remainder of the book. In some treatments, it is considered a back vowel, and there is disagreement over whether it is tense or lax. We shall treat it here as a tense vowel, although phonetic evidence for this is not completely convincing. At any rate, this is the vowel found in items such as *father* [fɑðɚ] and *calm* [kʰaɨm] in many varieties of American English.

Back Vowels. In our treatment here, we distinguish four back vowels. All of these are produced with lip rounding in English, although the higher vowels tend to reveal more lip rounding than the lower ones. The high back tense vowel [u] is close to the vowel found in items like *too* [tʰu] or *boot* [but], although there may be slight differences in the actual position of the vowel among different speakers. Furthermore, there is a tendency to glide into another vowel (e.g. [uᵘ]), so English speakers usually do not produce a [u] without gliding. The high back lax vowel, represented as [ʊ] or [ʊ] (upsilon), is the typical vowel of *book* [bʊk] and *put* [pʰʊt]. The mid back tense vowel [o] is analogous to [e] in the sense that it is most frequently produced in a glided form in English. Items like *boat* [bo^{u}t] or *rope* [ro^{u}p] typically glide to the [ʊ] or [u] vowel. Many languages, however, use a form of the vowel without a glide, so that the German, Spanish, and French [o] sounds differ considerably from that found in English. When speaking these languages, the tendency of English speakers to glide these vowels contributes to their "foreign accent." Strategies similar to those we suggested for producing non-glided [e] may help in attempts to produce [o]. The low back tense vowel is [ɔ] (in some systems classified as a mid back lax vowel). The so-called "open-o" is used in the vowel of the items *caught* and *bought* in some varieties, but even there it is glided to a schwa [ɔ^ə], so that the [ɔ] is not usually found alone in English. Some varieties of English have a lower version of a back vowel, sometimes classified separately as [ɒ], while other varieties even use [ɑ] in these contexts. Compare your own [ɔ] to other versions in order to assess where in this spectrum your pronunciation falls.

Exercise 11

Transcribe the vowels in each of the following English words.

1. reap	8. late	15. nephew
2. boot	9. wrote	16. cousin
3. cut	10. look	17. daughter
4. lap	11. coffee	18. grandfather
5. left	12. lately	19. brother
6. call	13. mother	20. circumvent
7. cope	14. sister	

Diphthongs. In the previous section, we tried to restrict ourselves to vowel segments at particular points on the continuum. In taking our ability in English as a starting point, however, it was often difficult to limit ourselves to discussing single segments. This is due to the fact that many English vowel units start at one point in the vowel space and move to another, thereby creating sequences of vowels rather than single vowel sounds. A **diphthong** is a combination of two vowels in which one serves as the center of the syllable peak (the nucleus) and the other (the glide) moves into or away from it. Perceptually, the nucleus vowel of a diphthong has more prominence and typically a longer duration than the glide. The glide may occur either before the nucleus vowel or after it. The diphthongs we have mentioned so far are all **offgliding** diphthongs, that is, the glide occurs after the nucleus. Those in which the glide occurs first are called **ongliding** diphthongs. Ongliding diphthongs in English often involve either [ɪ] or [ʊ] as the glide. The semivowels [y] and [w] are often pronounced as onglides, e.g. *mule* [m^{ɪ}ul].

The offgliding diphthongs can be divided into three types. **Fronting** diphthongs glide into one of the front vowels, usually [i] or [ɪ] (but sometimes [e] or [ɛ]). The nucleus vowel of such diphthongs may be one of a variety of non-front vowels, including [æ], [a], [ɑ], [ɔ], and [ə]. Northern pronunciations of *bike* [ba^{ɪ}k] and *kite* [k^{h}a^{ɪ}t] use fronting diphthongs, although the status of the nucleus and the offglide vowels might vary. The nucleus may be [a], [ɑ], [ə], or [æ], depending on the dialect, and the offglide may be [i], [ɪ], or [e]. **Backing diphthongs** move to the range of [u], [ʊ], or [o]. Again, there is some variety in the combinations that are actually used in English dialects in items like *mouth* [ma^{ʊ}θ] or *out* [a^{ʊ}t]: [a], [ɑ], [æ], [ə], [o]. **Centralizing diphthongs** glide to a central vowel such as schwa.

The pronunciation of *ought* [ɔᵊt] or *man* [mɛᵊn] in some dialects of English uses a centralizing offglide. To cover the actual range of combinations utilized in English would require an extensive inventory of diphthongs. Rather than attempt to specify all these, we simply note that various combinations may be used. The phonetic transcriber must be careful to note the exact nature of the nucleus and offglide in narrow transcription. We can represent the approximate range of some of nuclei and offglides as follows:

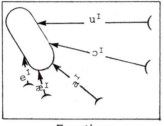

Fronting
diphthongs

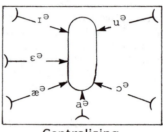

Centralizing
diphthongs

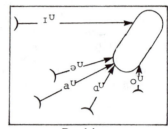

Backing
diphthongs

Among the more common diphthongs found in English varieties are:

Fronting	Backing	Centralizing
[aᴵ], e.g. *ride, bye* in Northern varieties	[aᵁ], e.g. *bout, mouth* in many varieties	[ɪᵊ], e.g. *hear, beer* in "*r*-less" varieties
[eᴵ], *late, eight* in most varieties	[æᵁ], *owl, bout* in some varieties	[ʊᵊ], *sure, pure* in "*r*-less" varieties
[ɔᴵ], *boy, toy* in Northern varieties	[oᵁ], *bow, boat* in many varieties	[ɔᵊ], *paw, caught* in many varieties
[əᴵ], "*r*-less" *bird* in New York City; *write* in more rapid, casual speech	[əᵁ], e.g. *boat* in Tidewater, some Canadian English varieties	[ɛᵊ], *man, fan* in many varieties

Even the brief list above must be taken with caution, since English diphthongs are so sensitive to variation. "Key words" used to identify certain diphthongs can be quite misleading. Serious students must learn to identify accurately the entire range of nuclei and glides.

There are several different transcription systems for vowel diphthongs. The one used here writes the offgliding or ongliding vowel above the nuclear vowel, as in [eᴵ] or [ᴵu]. Other systems place the nucleus and off- or onglide on the same line and indicate the glide through the use of a diacritic (e.g. [e̯ɪ], [ɪ̯u]). Whatever the convention, it is important to indicate the difference between a diphthong, which has one syllabic beat plus a glide, and a sequence of two vowels (a **vowel cluster**), each with its own syllabic beat. The nucleus and glide must also be distinguished from each other to differentiate ongliding and offgliding diphthongs. For example, in some *r*-less varieties in the North, an item like *here* [hɪᵊ] may have a centralizing diphthong, while speakers in some parts of the South produce this as a two vowel sequence [hɪə]. In one fairly popular convention introduced by Bloch and Trager (1942), fronting offglides are indicated by *y* ([bɔy] 'boy'), backing offglides by *w* ([bowt] 'boat'), and centralizing offglides as *h* ([bɔht] 'bought'). Obviously, such a system does not allow the same phonetic precision as that presented above. However, a number of American linguists have followed the Bloch and Trager convention, and the reader should be prepared to encounter it in descriptions of English phonology.

Exercise 12

Transcribe the vowels and consonants in the following English words. Be sure to transcribe them in the way you actually produce them.

1.	make	11.	pout	21.	phonetics
2.	fun	12.	clone	22.	phonology
3.	gate	13.	trough	23.	electricity
4.	shoot	14.	rapid	24.	photography
5.	caught	15.	today	25.	psychology
6.	right	16.	bounce	26.	photographic
7.	bled	17.	noisy	27.	telegraph
8.	pitch	18.	racer	28.	telegraphy
9.	throw	19.	gopher	29.	magnitude
10.	toy	20.	heed	30.	transcription

Detailed Vowel Descriptions

In the course of our discussion, we have already referred to special symbols that add detail to the basic vowels. As we have seen, retroflexion is one detail which can occur on any vowel. Another modification is **rounding**. Rounding usually accompanies back vowels in English and front vowels are usually unrounded, but this is not always the case with other languages. And, in fact, if we start to look at finer details of English, we find that the above statement has to be modified. For example, the [i] onglide in *beauty* [bi̯ṵɾi] and *puny* [pʰi̯ṵni] is typically rounded. There are several different conventions for indicating the rounding of front vowels and the unrounding of back vowels. Our system uses the subscript [ᵥ] to round front vowels (e.g. [i̯], [e̯]) and the symbol [ᴧ] to unround back vowels (e.g. [ṵ], [ǫ̰]). Another widely used convention employs an "umlaut" [¨] to shift the front vowels to the back and vice versa. Thus [ü] is a rounded high front tense vowel and [ï] is an unrounded high back tense vowel. Yet another convention uses distinct symbols for each vowel, such as [y] for rounded [i] and [ɯ] for unrounded [u].

One detail we have not yet mentioned is the **nasalization** of vowels. As with consonants, it is possible to keep open the nasal passage in the production of vowels. In some languages nasalized vowels (indicated by [~] above the vowel) may contrast with **oral** vowels to distinguish words. In all varieties of English, vowels preceding nasal consonants tend to be nasalized (e.g. [bɛ̃nd] 'bend'). In some varieties, the original nasal consonant may be lost completely, leaving only the nasalized vowel (e.g. [rɛ̃t] for *rent*). In some non-mainstream varieties of English, a sequence of a vowel and [n] occurring in an unstressed syllable may be realized simply as a nasalized vowel (e.g. [mɪ́tkmæ̃ə̃] 'milkman'). French uses nasalized vowels in a similar way, as in *bon* [bɔ̃].

Another modification of vowels involves slight adjustments in the backing or height of the tongue from those described in the basic vowel grid. For example, if we listened very closely to some pronunciations of *bat*, we would find that the vowel seems to be slightly higher than [æ], although it is not [ɛ]. In such cases, the phonetician may want to note that the vowel is slightly raised. This can be done by using a diacritic following the segment to indicate the direction in which it deviates from the position indicated in the grid. For example, slight raising would be indicated as [ˆ], lowering [ˇ], fronting by [‹], and backing by [›]. Students may be familiar with the fronted pronunciation of [ɑ] in an item like *Chicago* [šɪkʰá‹goᵁ], and the various modifications that accompany the [ɔə] of *coffee* in various dialects. Such details can be of considerable importance in looking at fine regional and social dialect differences.

One final aspect of transcribing vowels must be mentioned—the length or duration of a vowel. In English several different vowel lengths occur depending on the following segment. In the pronunciation of *but, Bud,* and *bun,* it can be observed that the [ʌ] is relatively short in *but,* longer in *Bud,* and longest in *bun.* Vowel length is indicated by [·] following the segment for slight lengthening and [:] for longer duration. In English, vowels before voiced consonants are longer than those before voiceless segments, and among voiced segments, they are longest before nasals (e.g. [bʌt] 'but', [bʌ·d] 'Bud,' [bʌ:n] 'bun'). For some speakers of English, the difference between *pom* [pʰa·m] and *palm* [pʰa:m] may be only in the length of the vowel. In German, vowel length is more significant in the distinction of items (e.g. [štat] *stadt* 'city,' [šta:t] *staat* 'state').

Exercise 13

Transcribe the following in both broad and narrow transcription of the English vowels and consonants. For vowels, details such as length, nasalization, and certain modifications in rounding and placement are considered part of the narrow transcription of English. For example, the broad transcription of *pun* is [pʌn] whereas the narrow transcription would be [pʰᴬ̃:n].

1.	bad	6.	closure	11.	found
2.	bull	7.	behind	12.	rapidly
3.	man	8.	breadth	13.	beautiful
4.	rich	9.	fantastic	14.	charity
5.	sang	10.	vestibule		

Exercise 14

In some broad transcriptions of English, certain predictable glides such as [eᴵ], [oᵁ], [ɔə], and [ɛə] or [æə] are transcribed as unglided [e], [o], [ɔ], [ɛ], and [æ], respectively. Notice that this does not include contrastive diphthongs such as [aᴵ] or [ɔᴵ]. Transcribe the following items in broad and narrow transcription according to this convention.

1.	late	6.	mail	11.	paid
2.	boat	7.	boy	12.	load
3.	behave	8.	ride	13.	shout
4.	bought	9.	coy	14.	loiter
5.	man	10.	ought		

Exercise 15

Provide the phonetic symbol which is represented by the following descriptors.

1. high front tense vowel
2. high front lax lengthened vowel
3. high back lax lowered vowel
4. low front tense nasalized vowel
5. mid central lax vowel
6. low central tense backed vowel
7. mid front tense rounded nasalized vowel
8. high back lax unrounded vowel
9. mid front lax lowered vowel
10. low front tense fronting diphthong
11. low front tense centralizing diphthong
12. low back tense fronting diphthong

SUPRASEGMENTAL ASPECTS OF PHONETICS

In addition to the many differences in sound segments mentioned above, a necessary aspect of speech involves variations in intensity, pitch, and timing. These aspects of phonetics are referred to as **suprasegmental** or **prosodic** elements of speech. Reference to certain aspects of suprasegmentals has been unavoidable in our previous discussion, because they may exert influence on the production of various sound segments. One suprasegmental is **stress,** which refers to the relative prominence of syllables. On one level, we may speak about various degrees of stress in isolated words. Thus, in *running* and *private* the first syllable of the word is given greater prominence than the second. If we extend this to a word of more than two syllables such as *telegraph* or *magnitude*, it is possible to identify more than two different levels of stress. In these words, the first syllable received the most prominent stress, referred to as **primary stress.** The final syllable, although not as prominent as the first, is more prominent than the middle syllable, so we say it carries **secondary stress.** The degrees of stress that phoneticians have identified for English vary, but typically they range from three to six different levels. Although degrees of stress seem to be relatively easy to identify impressionistically, recent studies have shown that stress does not correlate with a single articulatory gesture.

We can also look at the relative degrees of stress on a phrase level. A phrase like *John's not here* might have strong stress on the *here* and secondary stress on *John.* **Phrasal stress** may differ according to the syntactic units involved, or according to which particular items are emphasized in the utterance. In the sentence given above, it is possible to assign primary stress to *John*, but this implies a different interpretation of the sentence. Many different systems have been used to indicate stress. We will indicate primary stress by [ˊ] over the nucleus of the syllable (e.g. [rípə] 'reaper'), and secondary stress by [ˋ] (e.g. [tʰɛ̀ləgrǽf] 'telegraph').

We have seen that on the level of phonetics, the term "syllable" is used to refer to a group of consonants and vowels which have a maximum peak of resonance. From an acoustic perspective, the syllable may be viewed as a peak of acoustic energy, while from an articulatory perspective it has sometimes been seen as a thrust of the chest musculature. In the items *father* and *button*, we isolate two syllabic peaks. In other instances, the number of phonetically realized syllables may differ from one English variety to another. For example, some pronunciations of *generally* have three syllables [džɛ́nrəlì], while other pronunciations contain four [džɛ́nərəlì]. In most cases, a vowel serves as the peak of a syllable, but it is also possible for sonorant consonants to be syllabic peaks. These include the nasals, laterals, and the retroflex *r*. Syllabic consonants are represented by the addition of a subscript [ˌ] to the symbol for the consonant. Syllabic consonants occur in certain unstressed syllables in English. In many varieties, words like *mountain* [máᵁnʔn̩], *seven* [sɛ́vm̩], *button* [bʌ́ʔn̩], and *robin* [rábm̩] contain syllabic nasals. Similarly, laterals function as syllabic peaks in unstressed syllables of items like *table* [tʰéɪbl̩] and *nickel* [nɪ́kɫ̩] (only dark *l*'s can be syllabic in English). Parallel examples of syllabic *r* can be transcribed in forms like *under* [ʌ́ndr̩] and *finger* [fɪ́ŋgr̩]. Notice, however, the difficulty in distinguishing syllabic [r̩] from the retroflex [ɚ]. In most instances, it is simply a notational variant rather than an actual phonetic difference.

In discussing the syllables of a language, it is important to notice consonant-vowel sequences. For example, we may speak of a consonant-vowel pattern (usually abbreviated simply as *CV*), indicating that a syllable consists of a consonant followed by a vowel, or a consonant-consonant-vowel sequence (*CCV*), where a **consonant cluster** (two or more consonants in a sequence) precedes the vowel peak of the syllable. We shall have more to say about the patterning of consonant-vowel sequences in our discussion of phonotactics in Chapter 5.

Exercise 16

In the following English items, indicate the placement of primary and secondary stress and identify and transcribe syllabic consonants.

1. placement	5. stop 'n go	9. perpetuate
2. buttonhook	6. ridiculous	10. eleventh
3. telegraphic	7. Bible	11. troublesome
4. rattlesnake	8. reasonable	12. rock 'n roll

A notion related to the role of stress and syllables has traditionally been called **juncture**. Juncture refers to the transition between sounds. The lack of any real break between syllables of words is referred to as **close juncture**. We do not typically hear a break between syllables in words like *talking* or *money*. **Plus juncture**, or **open juncture**, is used to describe a break or pause between syllables in the same word or adjacent words. This can be represented by a space or a +. Several pairs of phrases have been used traditionally by linguists to demonstrate junctural differences: *a nice man* versus *an ice man*, *nitrate* versus *night rate*. We will see later that there are a number of fine phonetic differences that often coincide with junctural differences.

The last aspect of suprasegmental phonetics we will discuss here relates to pitch differences. The acoustic effect of pitch results from the speed of vibration of the vocal bands in the utterance: the faster the vibration, the higher the pitch. A practical approach to recognizing pitch is to think of the musical note associated with a particular vowel. Although pitch variation is to be found in all languages, its function may differ from language to language. In some languages, referred to as **tone languages**, pitch differences may be used to signify differences among words. Specifications of pitch may indicate a level, rising, or falling pattern for a given syllable. In English, pitch range differences are largely predictable, determined by stress patterns and the syntactic structures in which items occur. Pitch level is very individual, so the important aspect of pitch contours is a relative rather than an absolute matter. One person's lowest level may, for example, be considerably higher than another person's, but the hearer makes adjustments so that the perception of important differences is based on relative pitch contours.

Intonation refers to pitch contours as they occur in phrases and sentences. Contours may include sudden jumps in level or gradual rising and falling patterns. In some cases, understanding the content of a sentence may be dependent upon the intonational contour. If the sentence *He's a linguist* is used as an assertion, we might maintain a mid tone for *He's a*, raise the level for *ling-* and fall to a lower tone for *-guist*. Various techniques have been used to note intonational contours, including lines, numbers, and spacing:

2   3   1

He's a|lin|guist   He's a linguist   ling
He's a
                guist

Sudden changes in pitch contours are indicated by a vertical jump and more gradual changes by slanting lines (e.g. / or \ ). In the numerical system, the numbers generally progress from the lowest level (1) to the highest level (3). The number of actual levels and contours identified as significant in English is still somewhat open, although American linguists have traditionally identified four levels: low, mid, high, and extra high.

Intonational contours can signify differences in the content of sentences. The words of the sentence *He's a linguist* may start out with mid intonational contours, then rise to a higher level:

He's a | linguist.

This is interpreted as asking a question, or raising doubt about a person's status as a linguist. There are many potential contrasts of content and attitude that can be conveyed through intonational contours. An understanding of how language is used in social situations is required to go beyond relatively trivial observations about the nature of intonation in English. It can be difficult to perceive intonation reliably without assistance from instruments such as sound spectrographs.

Exercise 17

Compare the intonational contours at the end of each of the following 12 sentences. What are the contour differences between statements and questions? Do all questions have the same contour? If not, what is the difference between the types of questions with different contours?

1. Are you ready to go home?
2. He's ready to go home.
3. Why is he going home?
4. Here's the answer.
5. What's the answer?
6. Is there an answer?
7. Do you like transcribing sounds?
8. Students like transcribing sounds.
9. Where is your transcription?
10. Intonation is hard to transcribe.

---

11.   Is intonation hard to transcribe?
12.   Why is intonation hard to transcribe?

In the previous sections, we have specified some aspects of a phonetic base for phonology. Developing adequate skills in phonetics is essential to anyone who wishes to do phonological analysis. Understanding the symbols for transcription and the definition of various terms often used in articulatory phonetics is just a starting point. Considerable exercise in transcribing real speech is required to establish reliability in transcription. While specifically constructed laboratory exercises can be of benefit to students attempting to sharpen their transcription skills, students will need to spend considerable time developing abilities in phonetic perception by making the everyday world of speech their laboratory. There is one word of caution and encouragement on this point. Students may be dismayed if what they transcribe in listening to people actually speak does not match the isolated word pronunciations often found in phonetic workbooks (the so-called **citation forms**). The more we look at the phonetic production of citation forms and at the phonetic production of speech as it is used in the everyday world, the wider the gap between these two seems to become. When we get to the point where we can confidently transcribe exactly what we hear, instead of the citation form that we thought we were supposed to hear, we are on the way to becoming competent phoneticians. Developing skills in transcribing fine phonetic detail is something of an art, but the failure to record such detail reliably can often obscure the total picture of how phonological systems operate.

Exercise 18

Transcribe each of the following sentences twice. The first time, transcribe your pronunciation in a slow, deliberate style of speech. The second time speed it up into a rapid, normal, casual style of speaking. Note the changes in the two transcriptions of the sentences. For example, the segmented sounds of a sentence such as *Did you eat yet?* might be transcribed as [dɪd yu it yɛt] in slow, deliberate style, and [dʒɪityɛt] in a more rapid casual style.

1.   What did you want?
2.   He got you a present.
3.   He asked the instructor a question.
4.   Ed edited it.
5.   He wanted to study phonetics.
6.   I've had three tests since Tuesday.
7.   You can get comfortable doing transcription.
8.   Listen to how people talk.
9.   Write what you hear, not what you think you should hear.
10.   Did you get the point of the exercise?

Exercise 19

Choose several different speakers, elicit from them the words given below, and give a narrow transcription of their pronunciations. Try to choose speakers who represent different regions of the country or different social groups. Elicit the items without giving them as a part of the stimulus. For example, in order to elicit an item like *roof*, you might say, "The thing that covers a house so the rain can't get in is called a _____." What are some of the fine phonetic differences you observe from the various speakers?

1.	garage	6.	outside	11.	houses
2.	roof	7.	greasy	12.	merry
3.	coffee	8.	caught	13.	marry
4.	creek	9.	time	14.	Mary
5.	vegetables	10.	bottle	15.	mayonnaise

NOTES

1. In some treatments of vowel classification, the main dimensions are simply front and back vowels. As one gets to the lower vowels, the distinction between central and back and tense and lax is more difficult to make on articulatory grounds. For this reason, some writers consider the vowel grid as a triangle rather than a quadrangle or a trapezoid.

SUGGESTED READING

The interested reader should compare this chapter with the phonetics chapters found in standard introductory texts in descriptive linguistics. Introductions such as Gleason's *An Introduction to Descriptive Linguistics* (1961), Robins' *General Linguistics: An Introductory Survey* (1967), or Lehmann's *Descriptive Linguistics* (1976) emphasize phonetic detail from a variety of languages. Brosnahan and Malmberg's *Introduction to Phonetics* (1970) is a readable book, while Ladefoged's *A Course in Phonetics* (1975) includes many useful exercises in addition to the excellent presentation of phonetics. More comprehensive, and considerably more advanced, treatments of phonetics can be found in sources such as Abercrombie's *Elements of General Phonetics* (1967) or Heffner's *General Phonetics* (1949). There are discussions of phonetics relating specifically to English in Bronstein's *The Pronunciation of American English* (1960), and the chapter on phonetics in Francis' *The Structure of American English* (1958).

CHAPTER 3
Basic Units in Phonology: The Classical Phoneme

For the most part, phonetics is concerned with speech sounds independent of their function in particular language systems. Phonology, on the other hand, is concerned with how these sounds are put to use in a specific language system. The important question in phonology is how various sounds are organized so that they have the capability of distinguishing spoken messages from each other.

In our previous discussion of the phonetic base of sound systems, we have already anticipated the distinction between the actual phonetic realization of sounds and their organizational status. For one, we restricted our interest in phonetics to those aspects of phonetic detail that had the potential of taking on "significance" in one language or another. Minute aspects of physical phonetics which did not carry such potential were not covered. Our anticipation of phonology can also be seen in the distinction we made between "broad" and "narrow" phonetic transcription. Broad phonetics, for the most part, is concerned with transcribing the significant aspects of sounds, whereas narrow transcription includes phonetic detail regardless of its status. Thus, the broad transcription of an item like *pig as* /pɪg/ might eliminate the typical aspiration of [p^h] and the lengthening of the vowel [ɪ:] since these details do not contrast words in English. What is considered appropriate detail in the broad transcription in one language may, of course, be different from the aspects included in broad transcription for another language, since the significance of details may differ from language to language. As it turns out, traditional approaches to impressionistic phonetics often make it very difficult to avoid influence from the phonology of the transcriber's native language. So far, reference to the organization of phonology has been implicit in our discussion of phonetics. We now want to look explicitly at some of the significant units that must be recognized in discussing the phonology of a language.

Traditional treatments of phonology have usually recognized the unit termed the **phoneme** as the basic unit of contrast in phonology. The phoneme was originally defined shortly before 1900, but was prominent in phonology from the 1930's to the 1950's. During this time (generally called the American Structuralist period), a great deal of attention was given to the development of explicit principles and procedures for identifying the phonemes of a language. Although further developments in the 1960's challenged the traditional definition of the phoneme for reasons we shall discuss later, it is important to review this unit as it has been utilized in traditional treatments of phonology. The phoneme, as defined during this period, has been referred to as the "classical" or "taxonomic" phoneme.

Contrast

The most important aspect of the classical phoneme is its contrastive status in a language. When we speak of **contrast**, we are referring to the fact that different phonemes have the capability of distinguishing the words (actually, the **morphemes**) of a language from one another.[1] If a phonetic element does not have this contrastive capability in a particular language, then it is not considered to be a phoneme of that language. In English, the sounds represented by *p* and *b* have contrastive status because the difference in these sounds has the capability of signalling different words such as *pat* and *bat*. The phonetic details of these two words are identical except for *p* and *b*, so the contrastive function must be attributed solely to the difference between the sounds represented in spelling by *p* and *b*. Note that phonemes do not carry meaning in themselves. They are the stockpile from which the morphemes and words of a language are built up.

By convention, phonemes are written enclosed by slant lines—for example, /p/ and /b/—to distinguish phonemic transcriptions from phonetic ones. Phonetic transcriptions may indicate as much phonetic detail as it is possible to perceive reliably. Phonemic transcriptions, on the other hand, include only those units that have contrastive status in the language. The simplest procedure for discovering which sounds of a language are contrastive is to find words that differ by only one sound in one position in the word. The words *pat* and *bat* meet this criterion, as do *pat* and *pot*, and *sin* and *sing*. Such pairs of words are referred to as **minimal word pairs**. Using minimal word pairs is the most common technique linguists employ to determine the basic phonemic contrasts of a language system. Items like *sip* and *zip*, *fine* and *vine*, *though* and *dough* are minimal word pairs which establish phonemic contrast between the units /s/ and /z/, /f/ and /v/, and /ð/ and /d/, respectively. Although all of these examples involve minimal word pairs in which the contrastive units are found at the beginning of the word, contrasts may be found in any position. Minimal word pairs such as *rang* and *ran*, *pit* and *pet* demonstrate contrasts at the end and the middle of the word.

Exercise 1

Establish minimal word pairs in English for the following sounds in three different positions: (1) word-initial position, (2) word-final position, and (3) between vowels in the middle of a word. (You will be unable to find contrasts for some pairs in certain positions.) Example: initial, *pat*/*bat*; final, *rip*/*rib*; intervocalic, *ripping*/*ribbing*.

1.	p	b	6.	z	ž
2.	k	g	7.	š	ž
3.	m	n	8.	đ	θ
4.	p	f	9.	n	ŋ
5.	s	š	10.	ǰ	č

In many cases, it is not possible to find an exact minimal word pair. In such cases, potentially different phonemes may be established on the basis of a contrast in a "near minimal word pair." For example, /š/ and /ž/ may be said to contrast in a near minimal word pair such as *vision* and *fishin'*. The contrast of phonemes in minimal word pairs has also been referred to as contrast in **identical environment**, and that in near minimal word pairs as contrast in **analogous environment**. In the latter case, it is essential that the sounds which immediately surround the sounds in question are the same in the pairs of items, but more distant sounds may differ to some extent. Phonemes must be capable of contrasting with other phonemes to differentiate words and morphemes, but this does not prevent phonemes being used interchangeably in certain cases. For example, the fact that the same speaker might say both /vaz/ and /vez/ for *vase* does not mean that /a/ and /e/

do not contrast. In many other items they are used to contrast, e.g. *lot*, *late* and *rot*, *rate*. To be considered separate phonemes, the units must have the capability for contrasting words and morphemes in some linguistic contexts. The first characteristic of the phoneme, then, is its capability for establishing contrast.

Although we speak of the phoneme as a single unit, it is typically realized in actual speech by a set of alternative sounds rather than a single sound. The basic unit called /p/ in English is produced in at least three different ways phonetically. One of these is the aspirated [pʰ], which typically occurs at the beginning of a stressed syllable as in *pistol* [pʰístɨ] and *depart* [dɪpʰárt]. Another is the unaspirated [p], which occurs following another consonant, especially [s] (*spot* [spatˀ], *spat* [spætˀ]), and between vowels when the following vowel is unstressed (*rapid* [ræpɪd]). The third variant is the unreleased [pˀ], which may occur at the end of an utterance (*cup* [kʰʌpˀ]). All three of these phonetic variants are members of one phonemic class, which is represented simply as /p/. The number of actual different phonetic productions may differ from phoneme to phoneme, and depends to some extent on the fineness of the phonetic transcription, but it is important to recognize the phoneme is a category of actual speech sounds rather than a single sound itself.

Complementary Distribution

Because the phonemes of a language must have the capability of contrasting words, it stands to reason that the different phonetic realizations of a single phoneme cannot contrast with each other. The different phonetic realizations of the phoneme are usually referred to as **allophones** or **phonetic variants**. Just as the inventory of phonemes differs from one language to another, the allophones that comprise a particular phonemic class may differ from language to language. The Spanish phoneme represented by /b/ has the allophones [b] and [ƀ], whereas the English phoneme /b/ has only [b]. Two dialects of the same language often have the same phonemic inventory, but differ in the allophones that compose certain phonemes. In comparing dialects of English, we may find that one variety has [a<] (fronted [a]) as one allophone of /a/, whereas another dialect has only regular [a] (non-fronted).

Differences between the allophones of a particular phoneme do not have the capability of distinguishing words or morphemes under normal conditions. The three sounds that make up the phoneme /p/, are not capable of distinguishing words in English, and there are no words in English differentiated on the basis of the differences among these sounds. Each of them may contrast only with allophones from other phonemic classes. Thus, while there are no words [pɪtˀ] or [pˀɪtˀ] to contrast with the initial aspirated [pʰ] of [pʰɪtˀ] 'pit', allophones of other phonemes *do* contrast with [pʰ], e.g. [kʰɪtˀ] 'kit', [lɪtˀ] 'lit', and [sɪtˀ] 'sit'. However, this does not mean that the allophones of a phoneme can be used interchangeably wherever that phoneme is found in English, because each of these phonetic variants is restricted to particular positions in words. Any attempt to use one of the allophones where the other is typically found will make a word sound somewhat "distorted." For example, producing the word *spot* with an aspirated [pʰ] will sound strange.

The essential principle for grouping allophones as a single phoneme is **complementary distribution**. As used here, complementary distribution refers to the fact that different allophones of the same phoneme do not occur in the same linguistic environment. That is, each occurs in unique positions in words. More technically, they show mutually exclusive distributional characteristics. One way of specifying a relationship of complementary distribution is through an **only-never statement**. Unaspirated [p] only occurs following consonants such as [s], and between vowels when the following syllable is unstressed, while aspirated [pʰ] never occurs in these positions. This observation is a statement of complementary distribution: these two allophones of /p/ never occur in the same place.

Discovering complementary distribution between different sounds usually follows a simple procedure of trial and error. Sounds that look as if they might be in a complementary distribution are listed in an inventory, and a preliminary hypothesis about complementary distribution is offered. The hypothesis is then checked against the data at hand to see if it adequately accounts for them. For example, we may start with a list with the phonetic transcription of aspirated and unaspirated *p* as follows.

[pʰɪt]	'pit'	[rǽpɪd]	'rapid'
[spɪt]	'spit'	[spɛ́šəl]	'special'
[əpʰír]	'appear'	[rɪpʰít]	'repeat'
[pʰáɫɪš]	'polish'	[rǽpɚ]	'wrapper'
[ǽspɛkt]	'aspect'	[pʰɛ́pɚ]	'pepper'

In the first column unaspirated [p] follows [s], so our initial hypothesis may be that [p] only occurs following [s] and [pʰ] occurs elsewhere. However, while it is true that [pʰ] never occurs after [s], the second column reveals some items in which [p] occurs when it does not follow [s]. Our hypothesis thus must be revised. We might immediately suggest that unaspirated [p] also occurs between vowels, but this hypothesis is not confirmed by the data from *repeat* and *report*, where [pʰ] occurs between vowels. On looking closer, we see that [p] occurs only when the following vowel is unstressed, so we revise our hypothesis to account for all the observable data, and say [p] occurs between vowels (intervocalic position) when the following syllable is relatively unstressed. From this small base, we look for further data to see if our hypothesis can be rejected. Finding none, we assume that we have made an adequate observation about the complementary distribution of [pʰ] and [p]. Specifically, we conclude that [p] occurs after [s] and before an unstressed vowel, and [pʰ] occurs elsewhere. We continue to collect data, and if we find counter-examples to our statement of complementarity, we will refine the hypothesis so that it covers the new data. It is, in fact, not difficult to find English examples that require further refinement of our statement of distribution for the allophones of /p/.

Exercise 2

Consider the following data, all with /p/ in initial position. What role does stress play in determining the aspiration of the allophones of /p/ in initial positions? Revise the hypothesis about the allophones of /p/ according to your conclusions.

1.	[pʰəzíšɪn] 'position'	5.	[pʰrɪpʰǽr] 'prepare'
2.	[pʰɝ́pɪs] 'purpose'	6.	[pʰráspɚ] 'prosper'
3.	[pʰəlígəmi] 'polygamy'	7.	[pʰrəpʰóz] 'propose'
4.	[pʰásəm] 'possum'	8.	[pʰlɛ́zɪnt] 'pleasant'

The notion of complementary distribution in phonology is based on a basic principle of phonological systems: **sounds tend to be influenced by their linguistic environment.** "Linguistic environment" includes: (1) the effect of neighboring sounds; (2) the position of occurrence within larger units (such as the syllable, word, etc.); (3) the effect of suprasegmental

aspects of phonology (such as stress and pitch); and, in more recent treatments, (4) certain grammatical information about the word (such as whether
it is a compound, or if it is a noun or verb). The distribution of allophones
for the /p/ phoneme discussed above illustrates the first three of these types
of environmental conditioning. The limitation of the unaspirated [p] to a
position following [s] exemplifies the effect of a neighboring sound. Such
sounds are usually those immediately preceding or following the sound in
question, although there are cases where more distant sounds may be influencing factors.

In some cases, there seem to be fundamental physiological explanations
for the effect of neighboring sounds. We expect that a voiced allophone of
a given phoneme might be expected to occur next to other voiced segments,
that a neighboring front vowel would cause the occurrence of a fronted allophone [ḳ] for /k/; that a nasal segment would bring about the occurrence of
a nasalized allophone of a neighboring vowel phoneme ([bẽnd] 'bend' versus
[bɛd] 'bed').

Second, the realization of unreleased [p˺] as it occurs at the end of an
utterance is a case which illustrates the role of position in a larger unit.
The occurrence of [p˺] is related to word or syllable-final position at the
end of an utterance. In the case of *cup* cited above, we observe that a
phrase like a *cup of tea* [kʰʌpəvtʰi] would not have an unreleased [p˺],
whereas *He has the cup* [hihæzðəkʰʌp˺] would usually have this variant. As
with neighboring sound segments, this distribution appears to be physiologically natural, for the following silence does not require the immediate release
of the stop. Similarly, we might expect that segments followed by a silence
would be voiceless rather than voiced, since the following silence calls for
the voicing apparatus to be shut off.

Third, suprasegmental features of a word may also influence the distribution of allophones. In the case of /p/, we saw that stress was one factor
accounting for the complementary distribution of [p] and [pʰ]. Recall that
the [p] allophone of /p/ occurred intervocalically when the following vowel
was unstressed. The aspirated allophone occurred when the following vowel
was stressed. Thus, the stress of the surrounding environment helps to
account for complementary distribution. Note that in this case different kinds
of environmental influence contribute to complementarity.

A feature of allophones that allows us to group them together as a single
phonemic class is their **phonetic similarity**. Allophones of the same phoneme
must be phonetically similar. In fact, some pairs of sounds that stand in
complementary distribution are not grouped together because they are not
phonetically similar. Consider, for example, [h] and [ŋ] in English. It
turns out that these sounds are in complementary distribution. English /h/
(and its variant [ɦ]) occurs only at the beginning of a syllable, as in *hat*
[hæt] or *behind* [biɦaɪnd]. On the other hand [ŋ] does not occur in this
environment. It occurs only after the vocalic nucleus of a syllable as in *hang*
[hæŋ] or *rank* [ræŋk], where [h] never occurs. Although these sounds are
technically in complementary distribution, they are not considered members of
the same phoneme because they are phonetically quite dissimilar. Pairs like
[pʰ] and [p], [p] and [b], or [n] and [ŋ], which share properties of place
and/or manner of articulation, are much more likely to be allophones of the
same phoneme.

Sounds that are phonetically similar enough to be considered potential
members of the same phoneme have sometimes been referred to as **suspicious
pairs**. Although the criteria for defining a suspicious pair are somewhat
elusive, their identification constitutes the first stage in the phonemic analysis of a particular language. From that point, the analyst determines which
of the suspicious pairs must be separated as different phonemes because of
their contrastive potential, and which can be combined into a single phoneme.

The initial identification of suspicious pairs is critical to an analyst, because it narrows considerably the number of comparisons between sounds that need to be made. Non-suspicious pairs are phonetically dissimilar and can be ignored as candidates for membership in the same phonemic class.

Free Variation

Complementary distribution explains how many allophones are grouped within a phoneme. But there remain instances where phonetic variants are both non-contrastive and not in complementary distribution. In these cases, a speaker may use two or more of the allophones in the same environment. For example, speakers of American English may produce [p˥] in utterance-final position in one instance, and a released but unaspirated stop [p] in the same word in another instance. But these different phonetic segments do not have the capability of contrasting words and morphemes; they are simply interpreted as different pronunciations of the same phoneme. [stap] and [stap˥] are never interpreted as different words. This situation is called **free variation**. Recent studies show that each of the "free variants" does not necessarily have an equal chance of being realized. Social and linguistic factors may systematically determine which of the variants will be used more frequently, even though the phonetic variants may, in fact, occur in identical environments.

Sound Symmetry

In the previous paragraphs, we have considered only single phonemes, but some aspects of phonemic systems go beyond the individual units. In the overall system of contrasts, there are always interrelationships among phonemes. For example, in English there is a relationship between the pairs of phonemes /p/ and /b/, /t/ and /d/, and /k/ and /g/. This relationship is a symmetrical pattern of contrast between voiced and voiceless stops at three different places of articulation. Moreover, we find very symmetrical patterns of distribution of allophones for each of the voiceless stops, namely, an unreleased variant in utterance-final position, an unaspirated variant following [s] and intervocalically before an unstressed vowel, and an aspirated variant elsewhere.

All languages tend to be symmetrical in their arrangement of phonemic contrasts. So we would not expect a language with three vowels to have contrasts only between the front vowels /i/, /ɪ/, and /e/. Instead, we would expect a three vowel language to indicate contrast between front and back high vowels such as /i/ and /u/ and a low vowel such as /a/, revealing a more "even" distribution of the vowels in the vowel space. Pressure toward symmetrical systems of contrast is found in virtually all phonemic systems. From this perspective, phonemes may be seen as contrastive points in a system rather than randomly distributed sets of contrast. While there are certainly "holes" in the pattern of symmetry, there is little doubt that the phonemes of a language tend to pattern themselves in a symmetrical way. We can see this in the way languages change over time to realign certain non-symmetrical contrasts and to fill holes in the pattern. At one point in the recent history of English, the pattern of voiced and voiceless English fricatives and affricates looked like this:

$$\begin{array}{ccccc} f & \theta & s & š & č \\ v & ð & z & & ǰ \end{array}$$

Over time, however, English readily incorporated a number of forms with [ž], so that the pattern is now more symmetrical with a /ž/ phoneme filling the gap. In cases where the evidence for a particular analysis of phonemic status is marginal, the notion of symmetry is often cited as an argument for a particular solution.

Doing a Phonemic Analysis

We have already mentioned some of the procedures for establishing phonemes. Now we can turn to consideration of a fairly standard step-by-step procedure for traditional phonemic analysis. For the sake of our discussion, we will assume that we are working with a language that has never been analyzed phonemically, so our task is to identify the phonemes of the language in question.

Step 1:   Collect a representative corpus of items and transcribe them in reliable phonetic detail, together with glosses for the items. The first step in undertaking a phonemic analysis involves gathering a data base (generally referred to as a corpus). Establishing an adequate data base is an essential preliminary to the actual phonemic analysis. No phonological analysis can go beyond the accuracy of the phonetic material with which it has to work. If possible intra-transcriber and inter-transcriber reliability should be checked to eliminate errors due to transcriptional inconsistencies. If a preliminary check of phonetically similar sounds in a given position indicates inconsistency in the transcription, these should be rechecked to be sure that the transcription is accurate. In this way, we can make certain that those fluctuations which might appear as "free variation" are, in fact, attributable to the language system rather than the transcriber's inconsistent transcription.

The recording of glosses (approximate translations for the elicited items) is necessary in order to check various hypotheses of contrast. The ultimate basis of contrast between phonemes lies in their capability in distinguishing words or morphemes from each other. Knowing that two words "mean" different things is the simplest way of showing that they are different. Although some have maintained that it is possible to do a phonemic analysis without reference to meaning at all, it is quite clear that it is a much simpler procedure to work with contrast on the basis of the glosses for particular items.

Step 2:   Set up an inventory of the sounds, noting those that constitute suspicious pairs. The second step in phonemic analysis is a preliminary organization strategy. Extracting all the sounds represented in the corpus, the analyst should set up a phonetic chart of the sounds. Such a chart is drawn up on the basis of manners and places of articulation, as set forth in Chapter 2. The various sets of suspicious pairs are then listed, since they will serve as the basis for investigating contrast and complementarity. Suspicious pairs are pairs of sounds that are phonetically similar, and therefore have to be considered as potential allophones of the same phoneme. One sound may be included in several different suspicious pairs. Sounds which are so different phonetically that they cannot be considered as allophones need not be compared. This procedure would result in an inventory like the following chart (p. 47) of the sounds of a hypothetical language. Combinations of suspicious pairs are circled.

A number of dimensions have been considered in determining the suspicious pairs in the chart. Voiced and voiceless counterparts (e.g. [p] and [b], [s] and [z], are suspicious because they share so many aspects of their production (e.g. place of articulation, manner of articulation). Similarly, fricatives produced in adjacent places of articulation (e.g. [f] and [θ], [s] and [š]) are considered suspicious, as are adjacent vowels (e.g. [o] and [u], [i] and [e]). Major classes of sounds at similar places of articulation (e.g. [p] and [f], [t] and [θ]) may also be suspicious. And dimensions of fronting vs. backing (e.g. [ḳ] and [k]), and aspiration vs. non-aspiration

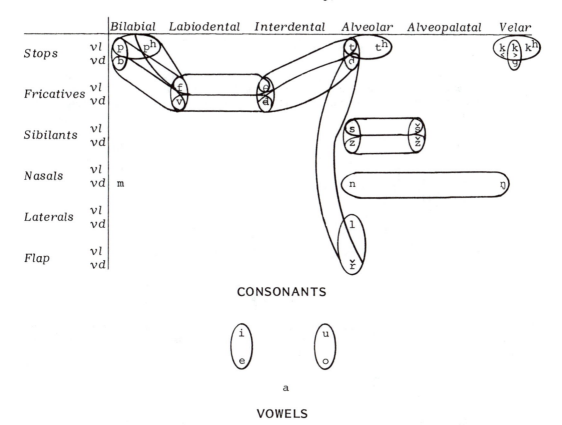

CONSONANTS

VOWELS

(e.g. [pʰ] and [p] are suspicious, as are most of the features indicated by diacritics. Although some general principles may guide the analyst in determining suspicious pairs (for example, suspicious pairs share a place and/or manner of articulation), there is often no hard and fast rule. [n] and [ŋ] are considered suspicious, but [m] and [n] are typically not, although the two sets of sounds seem quite parallel. The former pair is considered suspicious because there are so many languages in which they are allophones of the same phoneme, but the latter pair are not usually considered suspicious because virtually no languages have /m/ and /n/ as allophones of the same phoneme. Ultimately, the ability to determine suspicious pairs quickly involves partly experience with a number of phonological systems, and partly an intuitive "feel" for likely allophones. Certainly, it is preferable to overestimate the number of suspicious pairs rather than underestimate them, since subsequent analysis will determine the actual phonemic status of the sounds. Each of the suspicious pairs has to be considered in the analysis, although certain symmetrical patterns might suggest specific hypotheses that can eliminate the need to start from scratch every time. At this point, the phonetic data have been organized in a way that will enable the analysis to proceed in a systematic fashion.

Exercise 3

Which of the following pairs of sounds would you consider to be suspicious, and which would you consider non-suspicious? Give a reasonable phonetic basis for those sound pairs that you consider suspicious (that is, what phonetic characteristics do they share?).

1.	[t] , [d]	9.	[l] , [r]
2.	[i] , [ɪ]	10.	[w] , [ƀ]
3.	[i] , [a]	11.	[s] , [ǥ]
4.	[t] , [g]	12.	[b] , [v]
5.	[d] , [đ]	13.	[ŋ] , [n]
6.	[k] , [p]	14.	[l] , [s]
7.	[a] , [ə]	15.	[v] , [f]
8.	[m] , [ŋ]		

Exercise 4

Given the following data from a hypothetical language, make a phonetic chart of the inventory of sounds and circle the suspicious pairs. What is the phonetic basis for establishing each suspicious pair?

1.	[pubit]	'bird'	10.	[lapiƀ]	'go'
2.	[bʊkaš]	'dog'	11.	[wɪnbɪg]	'wine'
3.	[beƀɪm]	'cut'	12.	[sətəp]	'speak'
4.	[moɸɔk]	'man'	13.	[vako]	'fun'
5.	[zaǥʊt]	'run'	14.	[žakʊƀ]	'argue'
6.	[lañak]	'four'	15.	[palel]	'trap'
7.	[xʊlap̚]	'crazy'	16.	[šužəd]	'sing'
8.	[bɪndoǥ]	'woman'	17.	[gakʊ]	'walk'
9.	[kɔsɪp]	'come'			

Step 3:   Look at the elicited items (and their glosses) to decide if minimal word pairs can be readily established as a basis for contrasting phonemes. If minimal word pairs can be established for some suspicious pairs, these pairs can readily be assigned to different phonemes. Suppose that we had the following pairs in an elicited corpus of items:

[bot]	'cat'		[nuk]	'snake'
[pot]	'dog'		[ŋuk]	'father'
[pit]	'rake'		[lip]	'fight'
[pid]	'chicken'		[rip]	'mother'

Given forms such as these, we could conclude that at least /p/ and /b/, /t/ and /d/, /n/ and /ŋ/, and /l/ and /r/ are separate phonemes, since minimal word pairs exist for those sets of items. At this point, we might also propose that /k/ and /g/ will be separate phonemes because of the symmetrical nature of phonological systems. Then we would search the corpus for a minimal word pair for [k] and [g]. It we could not locate one, we might collect more data in an attempt to find minimal word pairs, or look for near-minimal word pairs. Given a word pair for [k] and [g] such as [kopan] 'boy' and [ɡopim] 'girl', we might conclude that /k/ and /ɡ/ are also separate phonemes, because both occur at the beginning of a word and are followed by [o]. The near-minimal word pair for [k] and [ɡ], coupled with the symmetry of a voiced-voiceless contrast in other stops, would probably be sufficient to establish that /k/ and /ɡ/ are members of different phonemes in this language. That is, they have the capability of contrasting items as found in minimal or near-minimal word pairs. Of course, in analyzing a real language, we would look for many such examples before making our final decision.

Exercise 5

Pick out the minimal and near-minimal word pairs that indicate contrast between phonemes. You will have to isolate suspicious pairs first.

1.	[vatok]	'gun'	9.	[pɪson]	'go'
2.	[bilog]	'car'	10.	[zantiɡ]	'free'
3.	[pison]	'joke'	11.	[naɡaŋ]	'cow'
4.	[santaɡ]	'smear'	12.	[piroɡ]	'milk'
5.	[naɡan]	'juice'	13.	[fatoɡ]	'mother'
6.	[kansɪr]	'sick'	14.	[rɪpel]	'orange'
7.	[pilog]	'anger'	15.	[fatok]	'talk'
8.	[fɪrfel]	'fall'	16.	[bason]	'bison'

Exercise 6

At one stage in the acquisition of English, a two-year-old child produced the following set of items. Based on these data alone, what is the phonological status of [l] and [l̥] at this particular stage? That is, are voiced [l] and voiceless [l̥] functioning as different phonemes in this child's phonological system? What is your evidence? Is this child's phonological system the same as that of an adult speaker of English?

1.	[lɪp]	'lip'	7.	[lɛt]	'let'
2.	[l̥ip]	'sleep'	8.	[l̥ápi]	'sloppy'
3.	[lʌv]	'love'	9.	[l̥oᵁ]	'slow'
4.	[sɪ́li]	'silly'	10.	[l̥æp]	'lap'
5.	[lɪp]	'slip'	11.	[loᵁ]	'low'
6.	[l̥iz]	'please'	12.	[l̥ɛᴵs]	'place'

Step 4: Examine the distribution of remaining suspicious pairs to formulate hypotheses on the complementarity of sounds which might be allophones of the same phoneme. We have established certain sound pairs as distinct phonemes on the basis of minimal or near-minimal word pairs. The next step is to see if other suspicious pairs may be classed as allophones under a single phoneme. In order to do this, we attempt to find a pattern of complementary distribution between the members of each suspicious pair. Using a trial-and-error method, we formulate a reasonable hypothesis on the influence of surrounding environment, and see if this hypothesis can account for all the data. Since we are essentially looking for environmental influences on various segments, we attempt to formulate hypotheses that might have some phonetic plausibility in terms of how sounds might be expected to influence other sounds. In

our formulation of the hypothesis to account for complementarity, we look for
potential influence from neighboring sounds, positions of occurrence, suprasegmental factors, or any combination of these. For example, given the
following items from a hypothetical language, we might make an initial hypothesis that [ɖ] occurs only between vowels, while [d] occurs at the beginning and the end of words.

[pid]	'chicken'	[kóɖaŋ]	'carry'
[dimó]	'shovel'	[píɖap]	'tractor'
[kod]	'fish'	[bíɖo]	'narcotic'
[dalú]	'bear'	[láɖin]	'dog'

As far as these data go, the hypothesis is supported. However, as we
examine more data, we find the following examples:

[kidíŋ]	'chief'
[radát]	'happy'
[pudél]	'water'

In order to account for these new forms, we must revise our hypothesis to
state that [ɖ] occurs intervocalically only when the following vowel is unstressed. In some cases, a number of such hypotheses may have to be formulated and rejected before we have one that handles all the data. The trial-
and-error approach is important in formulating these statements. Naturally,
a more experienced analyst has certain hypotheses which previous work in
phonemic analysis might suggest as a starting place, particularly given the
fact that we expect the influence of neighboring sounds to have some phonetic plausibility.

The distribution of the [d] and [ɖ] allophones above may be stated most
simply as follows: the allophone [ɖ] occurs intervocalically when the following
vowel is unstressed, and the allophone [d] occurs **elsewhere**. Such a statement implies the distribution of [d] rather than stating it explicitly. The
statement must predict all occurrences correctly, and must not predict their
occurrence in any place they cannot occur. Given the fact that we have
established [d] and [ɖ] to be members of the same phoneme on the basis of
their phonetic similarity and complementary distribution, we must decide on a
symbol to represent the phonemic class. The choice of a symbol to represent
the phoneme is arbitrary—it is simply the "name" of a category of sounds. In
many cases, the allophone with the widest distributional privilege is chosen to
represent the phoneme. In this case we would represent the phonemic class
as /d/, because [d] occurs most widely. However, established orthographic
conventions and ease of representation often enter into the choice of the allophone symbol used to represent the phoneme, so this is not a hard and fast
rule.

One of the early motivations for subjecting a language to phonemic analysis was to provide a means for developing orthographic systems for previously
unwritten languages. Such systems make explicit only those details that are
significant to the native speakers of the language. After completing the steps
for phonemic analysis outlined above, a **phonemic transcription** is achieved
simply by substituting the phonemic symbol for each allophone of the phonemic class. Thus, the phonemic representation of both [d] and [ɖ] would be
/d/ as in /kódaŋ/ 'carry' and /dalú/ 'bear' in our hypothetical language.

Exercise 7

The following data represent the distribution of dark and light *l* in one dialect of American English. Make a statement of complementary distribution,
based on the data (i.e. state where [l] and [ɫ] each occur). Which of the
types of environmental influences (neighboring sounds, position in larger
units, suprasegmental factors) is relevant in this distribution?

[lɪp]	'lip'		[ɫʌg]	'lug'
[lip]	'leap'		[ɫup]	'loop'
[læp]	'lap'		[ɫʊk]	'look'
[leᶦt]	'late'		[ɫɔᵊ]	'law'

Now consider the following additional data. How do the new data force you
to revise your statement of the distribution of [l] and [ɫ]? What types of
environmental influences now account for the distributional pattern?

[bʊɫ]	'bull'		[riɫi]	'really'
[bɛɫi]	'belly'		[fɪɫi]	'filly'
[bɪɫi]	'Billy'		[fɛɫoᵁ]	'fellow'
[diɫ]	'deal'		[bɪɫ]	'Bill'

Exercise 8

In Spanish, [b] and [ƀ], [d] and [đ], and [g] and [ɣ] are allophones of
/b/, /d/, and /g/ respectively. That is, they are suspicious pairs which
have been shown to be in complementary distribution. Based on the data
presented below, what is the complementary distribution of the allophones?

1.	[aɣusář]	'to sharpen'	9.	[př ɛndéř]	'to seize'
2.	[gříŋgo]	'foreigner'	10.	[bandído]	'bandit'
3.	[góřdo]	'fat'	11.	[ařdíya]	'squirrel'
4.	[paɣář]	'to pay'	12.	[ářbol]	'tree'
5.	[tiɛ́nda]	'store'	13.	[búřdo]	'rough'
6.	[tíɣre]	'tiger'	14.	[buskář]	'to look for'
7.	[taƀládo]	'flooring'	15.	[dɛƀéř]	'to owe'
8.	[taƀáko]	'tobacco'	16.	[dédo]	'finger, toe'

Based on your analysis above, predict the phonetic form of the following
items, written phonemically as: /doble/ 'double', and /bobada/ 'nonsense.'
Remember that a "phonemic rewrite" uses only one of the allophones of the
phoneme to represent the whole phonemic class.

Exercise 9

In a hypothetical language, the following vowel pairs are in complementary
distribution: [a] and [ə], [i] and [ɪ], and [u] and [ʊ]. What is the basis
for the complementarity? What type of environmental influence is operative?
How many different vowel phonemes are there?

Exercise 9 continued

1.	[gábə]	'dog'	7.	[gəbí]	'hip'
2.	[sísɪ]	'cow'	8.	[sábu]	'leaf'
3.	[bɪbú]	'fat'	9.	[zəzá]	'work'
4.	[dídɪ]	'tiger'	10.	[súsɪ]	'cold'
5.	[dágu]	'floor'	11.	[súku]	'ant'
6.	[bubí]	'hammer'	12.	[sʊgá]	'last'

Based on the data above, how would you rewrite items 1, 2, and 11 phonemically?

Exercise 10

Give a distributional statement of the phonetic variants [kʰ], [k] and [kˀ]
in English. Give specific items in English to illustrate your statement. How
does this distributional statement for /k/ compare with that given for /p/
earlier in this chapter?

Exercise 11

Make up a problem for a hypothetical language, showing complementary distribution of [p] and [b], [t] and [d], and [k] and [g]. Make sure the
problem demonstrates at least two of the three different kinds of environmental influences (neighboring sounds, position in words, or suprasegmental
influences).

*Step 5: Look for suspicious pairs that are in free variation, and assign them
as allophones of the same phoneme.* Careful instrumental analysis demonstrates
that it is virtually impossible to say a sound twice in precisely the same way.
While there is a certain amount of random variation in the repetition of a
sound, most cases will probably be clustered near a mean value so that they
are indistinguishable when transcribing impressionistically. There are, however, cases where an analyst may note two significantly different pronunciations of a sound in the same item in exactly the same linguistic context.
When such variation has no contrastive potential and cannot be captured by
any statement of complementary distribution, we can only note that the
allophones are in free variation. For example, we noted that unreleased [pˀ]
and released [p] may alternate in utterance-final position in /tɪp/, giving
[tʰɪpˀ] or [tʰɪp]. Variation of this sort is usually restricted to particular
environments where a phoneme occurs, and this is important to include in a
precise statement of allophonic distribution. For example, unreleased [pˀ]
and released [p] alternate only in utterance-final position. Suppose that in
analyzing a language we had transcribed the word for 'duck' as [botis] at one
point in our transcription, but on another occasion had transcribed it as
[botiz]. If we find no cases of [s] and [z] contrasting elsewhere, we simply
conclude that these two sounds are in free variation. This assumes, of
course, that we have transcribed them accurately in the first place.
    There can also be variation between different phonemes in a language.
One speaker of English might say both [ruf] and [rʊf] for 'roof' on different occasions. This is a different type of alternation, not to be included in

a phonemic analysis, since [u] and [ʊ] have contrastive status in English. Because free variation can exist between phonemes as well as between different allophones of a single phoneme, it is necessary to look at the whole range of variation before making any conclusions about its status. We would not want to say that [u] and [ʊ] are allophones of the same phoneme simply because English speakers say both [ɾuf] and [ɾʊf]. The same speakers do contrast *look* [ɫʊk] and *Luke* [ɫuk]. In the case of phonemic fluctuation such as /ɾuf/ and /ɾʊf/, a phonemic transcription would have to include both pronunciations. But in fluctuation between allophones such as [p] and [pʼ], phonemic transcription would not show the variation.

Exercise 12

Suppose a speaker of English fluctuates between the pronunciation of *either* as [aɪdə] and [idə]. Would you consider this to be a fluctuation between phonemes or allophones? Why?

Exercise 13

Consider the following pronunciations of [ɪ] and [ɛ] by a speaker of a Southern variety of English. What environmental influences determine when the fluctuations will occur? Is this fluctuation on a phonemic or allophonic level? Why?

1.	[pɪn] or [pɛn]	'pin'	6.	[θɪŋ] or [θɛŋ]	'thing'
2.	[pɛn] or [pɪn]	'pen'	7.	[pʰɪg]	'pig'
3.	[pɛt]	'pet'	8.	[pʰɛg]	'peg'
4.	[pɪt]	'pit'	9.	[hɪp]	'hip'
5.	[tʰɪm] or [tʰɛm]	'Tim'	10.	[stɛp]	'step'

The end result of our analysis will be an inventory of phonemes, together with a set of statements covering the distributional occurrences of the allophones of each phoneme. Illustrative examples supporting the statements are usually also included. Thus, we might have the following account to cover the description of the phoneme /p/ in English:

Phoneme	Allophones	Distribution
/p/	[pʰ]	occurs initially and when followed by a stressed vowel [ɾipʰít] 'repeat' [pʰǽnzi] 'Pansy'
		occurs word initially [pʰətʰéɾo] 'potato' [pʰɾɪpʰǽr] 'prepare'
	[p]	occurs when preceded by a sibilant [spat] 'spot' [ɾispɛ́kt] 'respect'
		occurs non-initially and followed by an unstressed vowel [ɾípɪŋ] 'ripping' [ɾǽpɪŋ] 'rapping'

Phoneme	Allophones	Distribution

occurs word-finally
[kʰip] 'keep' [lɪp] 'lip'

[p˥]   occurs in free variation with [p] at the end of an
utterance
[kʰip˥] or [kʰip] 'keep'
[lɪp˥] or [lɪp] 'lip'

Different linguists, of course, have different formats for presenting the inventory of phonemes in a language, but the essential information included is the same: (1) identification of the phonemes, (2) identification of the allophones, and (3) statements and examples giving the distributional privileges of the various allophones.

English Phonemes

The following are the main consonant phonemes typically recognized for English:

p		t	k	
b		d	g	
	f θ			h
v	đ			
		s š		
		z ž		
		č		
		ǰ		
m		n	ŋ	
		l		
		r		
		y w		

While there may be minor disputes concerning several phonemes, there is fairly widespread agreement among phonologists about these 24 consonant phonemes. There are some dialect differences in the distribution of allophones, but the status of the phonemes does not appear to differ much from one American English dialect to another. Some phonologists would not include the /đ/ phoneme for some non-mainstream dialects, but our own research suggests that it does have contrastive status. Other phonologists include /hw/ as a single unit phoneme in dialects that distinguish *which* from *witch*, or /hy/ in dialects that distinguish *you* from *Hugh*. However, many consider /hw/ and /hy/ simply as sequences of two phonemes rather than a single phonemic unit.

The identification of vowel phonemes is a much more controversial matter. Quite divergent phonemic classifications of the vowel phonemes of English have been proposed, depending on the goals or theoretical orientation of the linguist. Those systems most closely related to the phonetic facts may recognize up to 12 vowels (usually /i, ɪ, e, ɛ, æ, ɨ, ə, a, u, ʊ, o, ɔ/), and at least three diphthongs (/aᴵ/, /ɔᴵ/, aᵁ/), depending on the dialect in question. Many American structural phonologists, however, have followed a phonemic analysis originally proposed by Trager and Smith in *An Outline of English Structure* (1951). This system reduces the inventory of vowel phonemes to a symmetrical set of nine vowels and three main glides which can combine with these vowels:

i	ɨ	u
e	ə	o
æ	a	ɔ

In order to account for the contrasts between vocalic units, three main glide phonemes are recognized in this system: /y/, /w/, and /h/. The semivowel /y/ is used for front gliding vowels, /w/ for back gliding vowels, and /h/ for centralizing glides. In this framework, the transcription of *beet* would be /biyt/ and *bit* /bit/. Analogously, *boot* is interpreted phonemically as /buwt/ and *put* as /put/. *Paw* as produced by midwestern dialects would be transcribed phonemically as /pɔh/. In this system, the phonetic value of /h/ is usually a schwa-type of sound, so that the symbol is quite distant from the actual phonetic production with which *h* is usually associated. One important motivation for this system is the desire to account for various dialects of English without altering the basic symmetrical inventory of vowel nuclei and glides. Differences among dialects are represented in the combinations of vowels with glides. Thus, for example, the word *house* might be transcribed as /haws/ in the Midwest, /hæws/ in Philadelphia, and /həws/ in Eastern Canada, where the phonetic realizations are [haᵁs], [hæᵁs], and [həᵁs], respectively. Whereas the combinations of vowels and glides vary considerably from dialect to dialect, the basic inventory of nine symmetrical vowels and three glides should remain relatively constant.

The Trager and Smith analysis has not been accepted without question, even by other structural phonologists. The motivation for a phonemic analysis in terms of an "overall" phonemic pattern as opposed to a phonemic analysis of each dialect as an entity in its own right is one major area of controversy. Another concerns the departure from the phonetic facts, particularly in the interpretation of schwa-like glides as /h/. There are also questions concerning the applicability of this classification to the range of dialects that it is intended to include. Although we do not use this system in this book, it is still accepted by many as the most adequate classification scheme of English vowels.

Five factors have been cited (Gleason 1961:313) to account for differences among the various phonemic analyses and resultant phonemic transcriptions of English. These include: (1) differences in symbols, (2) differences in the data included, (3) differences in the interpretation of data, (4) differences in the concept of the phoneme, and (5) differences in the state of linguistic research. Some of these factors are more significant than others. The use of different symbols, while causing some practical confusion, is not a serious problem. On the other hand, differences in the concept of the phoneme and interpretation of data may lead to significant differences among phonological analyses of English.

The Reality of the Phoneme

Up to this point, we have been concerned with a definition of the phoneme within the tradition of American structuralism. This view emphasized the methodological procedures for determining phonemes, rather than establishing the theoretical validity of the phoneme as a construct. This emphasis is clearly seen in Gleason's *Workbook in Descriptive Linguistics* (1955:2):

> ...Descriptive linguistics is necessarily a system of analytic techniques more than it is a body of concepts. Even such units as the phoneme and the morpheme can perhaps best be viewed as devices to be used in language analysis, to be redefined and reinterpreted to fit the needs of any particular language structure.

Earlier attempts to define the phoneme, however, often appealed to the phoneme as a construct to which mental or psychological reality could be
attributed.   At the turn of the century, Baudouin de Courtenay (one of
the original definers of the phoneme) viewed it as a mental reality related to
the intention of the speaker, or impression of the hearer, or both.   In the
1920's, Edward Sapir also attributed psychological reality to the status of the
phoneme:

> Each member of this system is not only characterized by a distinc-
> tive and slightly variable articulation and a corresponding acoustic
> image, but also--*and this is crucial*--by a psychological aloofness
> from all other members of the system.
>
> (Sapir, in Makkai, 1972:14)

Sapir's claim for the psychological reality of the phoneme is clear in his observation that it is necessary to get "behind the sense data of any type of
expression in order to grasp the intuitively felt and communicated forms which
alone give significance to such expression" (Sapir, in Makkai, 1972:21).

With the development of American structuralism, the appeal to defining
the phoneme in terms of its psychological reality was rejected out of hand.
This approach derived largely from the commitment during the 1930's to the
scientific philosophy of behaviorism, which posited a very mechanical view of
language behavior, and was therefore limited to the analysis of observable
data.

> (1) we have no right to guess about the linguistic workings of an
> inaccessible "mind," and (2) we can secure no advantage from such
> guesses.   The linguistic processes of the "mind" as such are simply
> unobservable; and introspection about linguistic processes is
> notoriously a fire in a wooden stove.
>
> (Twaddell, in Joos, 1957:57)

Despite this rejection, many American structuralists observed that "their
non-psychological phonemic systems have some psychological validity for the
speakers" (Hyman, 1975:73).   This reality was most readily demonstrated by
the fact that the speakers of a given language tended to view the different
allophones of a phoneme as the same.   That is, a speaker of English views
[pʰ], [p], and [pˈ] as the same unit despite their phonetic differences.
Furthermore, the imposition of a speaker's own system of phonological contrast on that of another language in situations of "second" language acquisition suggests that there are perceptual correlates of the phonemic concept.
As it turns out, the anti-behaviorist reaction within linguistics in the late
1950's and 1960's resurrected the mental basis as the most valid criterion for
defining basic units such as the phoneme.   We shall return to this notion
later in our treatment of the systematic phoneme.

NOTES

1.   Morphemes have been defined by Hockett (1958:123) as "the smallest
     individually meaningful elements in the utterances of a language."   Mor-
     phemes may be a whole word or part of a word.   For example, the item
     boy consists of one morpheme, while the item *boys* consists of two mor-
     phemes, one represented by the spelling of *boy* and the other repre-
     sented in spelling as *s*, indicating plurality.   The lexicon of a language
     includes the inventory of morphemes in that language.

SUGGESTED READING

Discussions of the classical phoneme in structural phonology can be found in most introductory linguistic texts such as Gleason's *An Introduction to Descriptive Linguistics* (1961), Hockett's *A Course in Modern Linguistics* (1958), and Robins' *General Linguistics: An Introductory Survey* (1967). A relatively detailed summary of the phonemes of English and their various allophones can be found in Francis' *The Structure of American English* (1958). See also Trager and Smith's *An Outline of English Structure* (1951). Pike's *Phonemics* (1947b) still offers the best introduction to step-by-step procedures for analyzing the phonemic structure of a language. Problems in phonemics may be found in Pike's book, Robinson's *Workbook for Phonological Analysis* (1975), and Gleason's *Workbook in Descriptive Linguistics* (1955). For a discussion of some of the basic considerations in the structural definition of the phoneme, see Twaddell's "On Defining the Phoneme," originally published in 1935, but also found reprinted in a number of collections (e.g. Joos, 1957). Sapir's "Sound Patterns in Language" (1925) and "The Psychological Reality of Phonemes" (both reprinted in Makkai, 1972) are important for their historical significance. Makkai's *Phonological Theory: Evolution and Current Practice* (1972) contains additional articles of historical importance in the development of the notion of the phoneme.

CHAPTER 4
Properties of Sounds: Distinctive Features

Why Features?

In Chapter 3, we discussed the units of the phonological system of a language only from the perspective of whole sound segments. While traditional approaches to phonology have considered whole sound segments to be the smallest contrastive units in a language, there is considerable evidence suggesting that it is various properties of sounds rather than whole segments that are the ultimate units of contrast in phonology.

We have seen that there are several phonetic realizations of the contrastive unit we identified as English /p/, including the aspirated stop [p^h], the unaspirated stop [p], and the unreleased stop [p^1] Despite these different phonetic forms or allophones, /p/ is consistently maintained as different from /b/ by the fact that the various phonetic variants for /p/ are always voiceless while the variants for /b/ are voiced. Other properties of /p/ and /b/ are quite similar. Both share the bilabial place of articulation and the stop manner of production, but are consistently differentiated by the property of voicing. Voicing is a widespread contrastive unit in the English consonantal system, as illustrated by its role in differentiating the following pairs of items:

Voiceless	*Voiced*
tip	dip
Kate	gate
fine	vine
sip	zip
pill	Bill
chug	jug

Thus, the property of voicing provides not only a means of describing one aspect of the phonetic production of individual sounds, but also accounts for one aspect of the contrastive status of phonemes. We refer to such properties as **features**.

In the list above, just one feature provides the basis for an entire series of contrasts between pairs of English words. However, there is a whole set of features that characterize each sound segment and also have the potential for contrasting words. Thus, additional features differentiate the sound pair /p/ and /b/ from /t/ and /d/, or from /k/ and /g/. In these cases, the features describing place of articulation account for contrast, so that the bilabial production of /p/ and /b/ distinguishes them from the alveolar production of /t/ and /d/, and from the velar production of /k/ and /g/. The features of voicing and place of articulation discriminate the stop consonants of English. When we consider sounds produced with other manners of articulation, other contrastive features become necessary. For example, we see that the feature of stopness (or more technically, that feature which characterizes plosives) becomes significant when we add sound segments like /m/, /n/, and /ŋ/ to our inventory. The nasals are all voiced and produced

58

at the same three points of articulation as the voiced stops discussed above, but they are not plosives. We will identify them by a feature we call *nasal*. We can summarize the properties that have some contrastive status for the voiced and voiceless stops and the nasals at three different places of articulation like this:

p	*t*	*k*
voiceless	voiceless	voiceless
bilabial	alveolar	velar
stop	stop	stop
b	*d*	*g*
voiced	voiced	voiced
bilabial	alveolar	velar
stop	stop	stop
m	*n*	ŋ
voiced	voiced	voiced
bilabial	alveolar	velar
nasal	nasal	nasal

Exercise 1

Using the phonetic descriptors in Chapter 2, indicate the feature or features by which the following parts of sound segments are distinguished. For example, *t* and *p* are distinguished by place of articulation, *k* and *g* by voicing.

1. t,d	5. č,ǰ	9. o,e
2. m,n	6. t,s	10. m,b
3. k,t	7. u,ʊ	11. ŋ,b
4. g,p	8. v,z	12. d,l

A complete description of English phonology would require many more features to specify contrasts for the entire inventory of sounds. The important point is that the most systematic understanding of phonological contrast is one in which contrastive phonemes are viewed as divisible into sets of features rather than as individual entities. Thus, we have a system in which the sound segments have certain types of internal phonetic relationships with one another. The recognition of features of sounds allows us to capture the systematic nature of these internal relationships and to demonstrate that these features are the ultimate basis for phonological contrasts.

There are several ways in which we can demonstrate that the contrast between features of segments is more important than contrast between segments taken as whole units. Certain regularities of phonological systems are found within sets of segments that all share particular features. The regularities seem to relate to the features themselves rather than the whole segments. We shall discuss these processes more completely in the following chapters, but we can anticipate by considering the basis for capturing certain regularities. Consider the fact that the regular plural in English takes three forms, depending on the final segment of the noun to which it is attached. Although we think of the form *boys* as a single word, it is composed of two morphemes, the noun *boy* and the regular plural suffix, written *-s*. It is significant that the morpheme PLURAL takes several different phonetic shapes. Each of the following forms is composed of a noun and the plural morpheme: *books, rods, buses.* These three forms are examples of the regular plural. All three words contain the same plural morpheme, but it is pronounced differently in each case: first as [s], then as [z], and then something like [ɪz].

Exercise 2

Broadly transcribe the following regular English plurals. Assign each example to one of the three realizations of the regular plural. List the segments which occur just before the plural form.

races	days	hips	curves
ingots	churches	ashes	ties
rocks	thumbs	garages	pads
ripoffs	tons	laws	salamanders
badges	flues	phases	girls
tabs	peas	eggs	eighths
toes	cows		

If phonological patterns related to whole segments rather than to their parts, we would have to specify the distribution of plural forms according to large lists of preceding segments such as those derived in Exercise 2. But upon examining the three sets of segments in the distributions, we find that which form of the plural occurs is not random. All the sounds in each of the sets share some phonetic properties that determine which of the plural forms will occur. The form [ɪz], for example, only occurs following sounds defined by the property of sibilancy. This set includes the fricatives *s, z, š, ž,* and the affricates *č* and *ǰ.* The [z] form follows those non-sibilant sounds that are characterized by the property of voicing. The [s] variant follows non-sibilant sounds that share the property of voicelessness. There is an obvious relationship between the presence or absence of voicing in the preceding segment and the distribution of voiced [z] and voiceless [s] as realizations of the plural form, as well as a relationship between sibilancy and the [ɪz] realization. These observations are charted below:

Preceding segments: Sibilant sounds   take plural *ɪz*
s,z,š,ž,č,ǰ

Non-sibilant, voiced sounds   take plural *z*
b,d,g,v,đ,m,n,ŋ,r,l,y,w,
all vowels

Non-sibilant, non-voiced sounds   take plural *s*
p,t,k,f,θ

It appears that shared features or characteristics of certain sets of sounds determine which form of the plural occurs. The groups of sounds that call for a given plural form are not just random groupings. Rather, they share certain articulatory characteristics with one another and with the plural form that occurs.

Consider another phonological pattern from some Southern varieties of American English. Here the standard contrast between /ɪ/ and /ɛ/ is not found before *m, n,* and *ŋ.* Thus, the words *pin* and *pen* are both pronounced as [pɪn], and *tin* and *ten* as [tɪn]. This happens only where the segment following the vowel is *m, n,* or *ŋ. Pit* and *pet,* and *pick* and *peck,* are pronounced with contrasting vowels. The group of sounds *m*, *n*, and ŋ specifies the relevant phonological environment, but an essential regularity is lost if we consider them just as a random list of segments. Clearly, the property of nasality is the important aspect of the environment in which /ɛ/ becomes [ɪ]. If we do not admit units smaller than segments, we are unable to capture this regularity.

Use of phonological features allows us to state phonological patterns explicitly and concisely in terms of the phonetic details that may account for them. A relatively small set of features utilized in various combinations should be able to account for a wide range of contrasts among phonetic segments. For example, if we have an inventory of just 12 binary feature distinctions (with either a plus or minus value), the various combinations of these features theoretically result in 2^{12} different segmental units of contrast. While no language needs to use all possible combinations of properties in its system of contrasts, it is clear how a small inventory of features can account for a wide variety of different contrasts. Appealing to phonetic features allows us to capture important regularities in the composition of units and in the processes that operate on them as a part of the rules of a language.

PHONOLOGICAL FEATURES

The recognition of features as the contrastive base of phonological systems has led to the development of a series of special phonetic feature systems. There have been a number of attempts to arrive at a set of contrastive features for phonology. These range from attempts to isolate the various features following the manners and places of articulation we discussed in Chapter 2, to an acoustically based feature system.

Although beginning students may be somewhat confused when confronted with different interpretations of feature systems, the variety of attempts to define features should not be attributed to the basic whimsical nature of linguists. There are theoretical goals which motivate the attempts to define or revise distinctive feature parameters. One of the goals is to arrive at a limited set of universal features that is adequate for describing the phonological contrasts of all languages of the world. This set should also efficiently and naturally account for the types of sound classes that are important in the phonological organization of any language. The features should ideally fit data from an articulatory, acoustic, and perceptual base as closely as possible. With such high goals for a theory of phonological features, it is understandable that they are still in need of considerable refinement and revision as our knowledge of language systems increases.

Like our phonetic descriptions in Chapter 2, the features we use here refer to specific articulatory characteristics of phonetic segments. As we have seen, they are at once **descriptive** and **contrastive**: descriptive because they express some detail of the production of a sound, and contrastive because they permit one sound to be distinguished from another. In order to accomplish both goals effectively, each feature must refer to one of a number of explicitly defined articulatory characteristics of sounds. Features may specify which major sound class a segment belongs to (for example, whether it is a vowel or consonant), manner of articulation (for example, whether it is a stop, fricative, or nasal), place of articulation, voicing, or suprasegmental characteristics. A segment is characterized or described by the combination of all such features.

In most cases, it is assumed that features can be assigned binary values, that is, that we can specify them by indicating whether a given attribute is present. Rather than having two separate labels, such as *voiced* and *voiceless*, we set up the single label [voice] and simply indicate voiced as [+voice] and voiceless as [-voice].[1] In this way, natural oppositions are established, and sets of sounds are differentiated by the plus or minus value. Thus, the segments [p], [t], [f], and [s] will all be specified as [-voice], and [b], [d], [v], and [z] as [+voice].

Many of the important distinctions of place and manner of articulation that we demonstrated in Chapter 2 were not binary. A binary system of features exploits a number of different dimensions, but ultimately arrives at the same set of places and manners of articulation described through combinations of features. For example, we will introduce a feature called *coronal* which assigns the value [+coronal] to all the sounds made with the tongue blade raised, and [-coronal] to all those made without raising the tongue blade. Coronal sounds include [t], [d], [s], and [z], while non-coronal sounds include [p], [b], [f], and [v]. Although [coronal] does not indicate an exact place of articulation, all sounds made by raising the tongue blade are made at some point in between the interdental and alveopalatal places of articulation. Thus, [+coronal] sounds are restricted to a zone of articulation, as are their opposites [-coronal], which are not made in this zone. Other features will distinguish one [+coronal] sound from another.

While features usually have binary values, more detailed phonetic specifications may be achieved by a continuous-valued or multi-valued scale rather than a simple binary one. For example, stops may be articulated with different degrees of aspiration, and nasalized vowels may have different degrees of nasalization. Representations with more phonetic detail must specify such continuous dimensions, even though the basic phonological contrasts are made by binary values. The binary value of some features refers to the simple absence or presence of a particular characteristic such as voicing. Other binary features are intended to reflect opposite sides of an articulatory boundary or place of articulation. Thus, the feature *anterior* sets a boundary at the alveolar ridge. Sounds articulated in front of this boundary are [+anterior], and those behind it are [-anterior]. While there is still considerable debate concerning linguists' use of binary values for features, particularly in specifying aspects of phonetic detail, we shall assume here that the features used to represent phonological contrasts are essentially binary and can be specified by plus or minus values.

Below, we present definitions of a set of phonological features that are essential in identifying the contrastive segmental units of English. They are called **distinctive features** because of their ability to distinguish the sounds of a language from one another. This list of features is a subset of the universal inventory of features. Such an inventory usually consists of 25 to 35 basic feature contrasts, from which each language selects a few to contrast the segments in its phonological inventory. The list of phonological features presented here is taken primarily from Chomsky and Halle (1968), with some more recent modifications. There are still many unsettled issues about the most natural and economical list of distinctive features for English, so this list of features may differ slightly from those presented by other phonologists. (A chart specifying distinctive features for the sounds of English appears on p. 66.)

Major Class Features

Major class features distinguish basic categories such as vowels, obstruents, and glides.

Syllabic (syl): Segments that constitute a syllable peak are syllabic [+syl], while those that do not constitute a syllable peak are non-syllabic [-syl]. Typically, nucleus vowels are [+syl] and the non-vowels are [-syl]. When non-vowels constitute a syllable peak (e.g. [l] in *riddle* [rɪdl̩] and [n̩] in *button* [bʌʔn̩]), they are specified as [+syl].[2]

Sonorant (son): Sonorant sounds are typically produced without an extreme degree of oral cavity constriction. Vowels, nasals, oral glides (*w* and *y*), and liquids (*r, l*) are usually considered [+son], while sounds with more radical cavity constriction, such as stops and fricatives (obstruents), are specified as [-son].

Consonantal (cons): Consonantal sounds are produced with obstruction along the center line of the oral cavity. In most cases, the classification of consonantal sounds tends to match the traditional designations discussed in Chapter 2. The only non-consonantal sounds in English are the vowels and the oral glides *w* and *y*.[3]

The matrix below shows how these three features distinguish the major sound classes.

	Vowels	Non-syllabic liquids & nasals	Syllabic liquids & nasals	Oral glides	Obstruents
syl	+	−	+	−	−
son	+	+	+	+	−
cons	−	+	+	−	+

Manner of Articulation Features

Five features distinguish segments according to their manner of articulation.

Continuant (cont): Continuant sounds are characterized by continued air movement through the oral cavity during the production of the sound. Non-continuants are produced with complete obstruction in the oral cavity. Thus, stops are [-cont], while fricatives, glides, and so forth are [+cont]. The feature [+cont] does not refer to sounds of extended duration. Because the nasals *m, n,* and ŋ are produced with complete obstruction of air passage through the mouth, they are considered to be [-cont] even though the sound produced is of some duration. Distinctive feature analyses before Chomsky and Halle (1968) generally treated nasals as continuants.

Strident (str): Strident sounds are produced with an obstruction in the oral cavity which allows air to come through a relatively narrow constriction. As the air escapes, the turbulence produces "white" noise (a hissing sound). Many, but not all, of the sounds traditionally classified as fricatives are considered to be strident. In English, the fricatives *s, z, f, v,* and the affricates ǰ and č are [+str]. The affricates are distinguished from the strident fricatives by the specification [-continuant] because of the stop onset. English [θ] and [ð] are [-str]. The feature [strident] tends to be more acoustically than articulatorily based, and there is still some discussion concerning its validity.

Delayed Release (d.r.): Delayed release specifies the manner in which consonants are released. Stops are released instantaneously; affricates, fricatives, and other sounds are released gradually. This feature is important in distinguishing stops from affricates. Thus, in English č and ǰ are [+d.r.], and *t* and *d* [-d.r.], although they share the specification [-cont].

Nasal (nas): Nasal sounds are characterized by the opening of the velum so that air can escape through the nasal passage. Non-nasal sounds are produced with the velum closed so that air can escape only through the oral cavity. The definition of this feature parameter matches the traditional phonetic definition of nasal consonants and nasalized vowels.

Lateral (lat): Lateral sounds are characterized by a lowering of one side of the tongue (or both sides, but not the middle) so that the air moves through the side of the oral cavity. This feature corresponds to the definition of lateral sounds in Chapter 2. In English, only *l* is normally lateral.

The following matrix demonstrates the manner in which the features *cont*, *str*, and *d.r.* distinguish among stops, strident affricates (such as č and ǰ), non-strident affricates (such as tθ, which occurs in some varieties of American English), strident fricatives (s, f, š), and non-strident fricatives (θ and đ).

	Stops	Non-strident affricates	Strident affricates	Strident fricatives	Non-strident fricatives
cons	+	+	+	+	+
cont	–	–	–	+	+
str	–	–	+	+	–
d.r.	–	+	+	+	+

Oral Articulation

The following features relate to some aspect of oral articulation and, for the most part, distinguish the major places of articulation. They express such aspects of articulation as point of articulation, shape of tongue, location of the tongue, and lip rounding.

Anterior (ant): Anterior sounds are produced with a primary obstruction located at or in front of the alveolar region of the mouth. Sounds produced at or behind the alveopalatal region are non-anterior. Labial, dental, and alveolar sounds are [+ant]; alveopalatal, palatal, and velar sounds are all [-ant]. Notice that this feature incorporates several more traditional points of articulation. Traditional phonetic parameters such as bilabial, alveolar, and velar are distinguished by combinations of features.

Coronal (cor): Coronal sounds are produced with the front (tip or blade) of the tongue raised from neutral position. This includes articulations from the interdental through the alveopalatal positions. Sounds that are produced without raising the front of the tongue are [-cor]. They involve the back of the tongue or no primary tongue placement. The features [cor] and [ant] distinguish among labials, alveolars, alveopalatals, and velars:

labials	[-cor, +ant]
alveolars	[+cor, +ant]
alveopalatals	[+cor, -ant]
velars	[-cor, -ant]

High (hi): High sounds involve the raising of the body of the tongue from the neutral position. Tongue placement for the vowel ɛ is generally considered to be the neutral position. In English, the vowels *i, ɪ, u,* and *ʊ* are all [+hi], while all vowels produced at a lower position are [-hi]. Alveopalatal and velar consonants, and the glides *y* and *w*, are also [+hi], while alveolar, dental, and labial consonants are [-hi].

Low (lo): Low sounds are produced with a lowering of the body of the tongue from the neutral position. The English vowels æ, a, and ɔ are [+lo]. The three height positions we discussed in Chapter 2 are accounted for by these two pairings in the distinctive feature matrix. Mid vowels are uniquely characterized by being simultaneously [-hi] and [-lo]. With the exception of the glottal fricative *h*, all the consonants of English are considered to be

[-lo], so this parameter is most relevant for the vowels.[4]

Back (bk): Back sounds are produced with the body of the tongue moved back (and usually slightly raised) from the neutral position. If a sound is produced at or in front of the neutral position, it is considered to be [-bk]. Thus, the English vowels, *i, e,* and *æ* are [-bk], while *u, o, ə,* and *ɔ* are [+bk]. Notice that the three positions we discussed in our descriptive matrix of vowels in Chapter 2 have been collapsed into just one parameter of backness, so that *ʌ* and *ə* are [+bk]. Distinctions between central and back vowels will be made by other features. Velar consonants are also considered to be [+bk], as is the oral glide *w,* which is phonetically similar to the back vowels *u* or *ʊ*.
    Features pertaining to place of articulation are prominent in distinguishing contrasts for both consonants and vowels. The following matrix shows how these features distinguish the major places of articulation for consonants.

	Labiodental	Alveolar	Alveopalatal	Velar	Laryngeal
ant	+	+	–	–	–
cor	–	+	+	–	–
hi	–	–	+	+	–
bk	–	–	–	+	–
lo	–	–	–	–	+

In this matrix, the bilabial and labiodental places of articulation are not distinguished by these features. The dental and alveolar places of articulation are also combined. When contrasting sounds do occur in these places, they can be distinguished by other features (usually by manner of articulation features).
    The following matrix demonstrates how the features pertaining to the body of the tongue distinguish English vowels.[5] The features *coronal* and *anterior* are not included here, since they are not relevant for the vowel system. English vowels are always [-cor] and [+ant].

i ɪ		ʊ u		[+hi]
				[-hi]
e ɛ		ə	o	[-lo]
				[+lo]
æ			a ɔ	
	[-bk]	[+bk]		

Tense (tns): Tense sounds are produced with a more deliberate gesture that involves considerable muscular activity at the base of the tongue. Non-tense sounds are produced with less muscle activity. There is still a need for research on the actual articulatory basis for this feature, although [+tns] vowels such as *i, e,* and *u* are usually distinguished from their [-tns] counterparts *ɪ, ɛ,* and *ʊ* by this feature.
    In addition to the aspects of tongue position we have specified above, we also need a feature to describe lip configuration:

Round (rd): Sounds produced with a protrusion of the lips are considered to be rounded. The vowels *u, ʊ, o,* and *ɔ* are typically [+rd] in English, while the other English vowels are [-rd]. In some interpretations of distinctive features for English, a vowel pair like *a* and *ɔ* is distinguished only on the basis of this feature (*a* is [-rd], and *ɔ* is [+rd]).

Laryngeal Features

So far we have dealt only with place and manner features within the oral cavity. There are additional features that relate to aspects of the vocal bands or glottal opening in some way. Other languages apply several dimensions of the glottal opening in contrastive ways. The only dimension utilized contrastively by English is voicing.

Voiced (vd): Voiced sounds are produced with a vibration of the vocal bands in the larynx. Voiceless sounds are produced without such vibration. The sounds *t, p, s,* and *š* are [-vd], while their counterparts *d, b, z,* and *ž* are [+vd]. In certain cases, this parameter is really a continuum. Then the distinctive aspect is really between "more voiced" and "less voiced" sounds, although we continue to represent voicing as a binary feature.

FEATURE MATRICES FOR ENGLISH SEGMENTS

Below is a matrix of the contrastive segmental units of English. Notice that certain non-contrastive segments, such as aspirated stops and nasalized vowels, do not appear in the matrix. Specifications of these details are predictable by phonological rules. Notice also that the vowel matrix lacks certain specifications which are contrastive only for consonants. These specifications will be predicted by redundancy conditions (which will be explained later in this chapter).

	y	w	m	n	ŋ	r	l	p	b	f	v	θ	đ	t	d	s	z	š	ž	č	ǰ	k	g	h
syl	-	-	-	-	-	-	-	-	-	-	-	-	-	-	-	-	-	-	-	-	-	-	-	-
son	+	+	+	+	+	+	+	-	-	-	-	-	-	-	-	-	-	-	-	-	-	-	-	-
cons	-	-	+	+	+	+	+	+	+	+	+	+	+	+	+	+	+	+	+	+	+	+	+	+
ant	-	-	+	+	-	-	+	+	+	+	+	+	+	+	+	+	+	-	-	-	-	-	-	-
cor	-	-	-	+	-	+	+	-	-	-	-	+	+	+	+	+	+	+	+	+	+	-	-	-
hi	+	+	-	-	+	-	-	-	-	-	-	-	-	-	-	-	-	+	+	+	+	+	+	-
lo	-	-	-	-	-	-	-	-	-	-	-	-	-	-	-	-	-	-	-	-	-	-	-	+
bk	-	+	-	-	+	-	-	-	-	-	-	-	-	-	-	-	-	-	-	-	-	+	+	-
cont	+	+	-	-	-	+	+	-	-	+	+	+	+	-	-	+	+	+	+	-	-	-	-	+
str	-	-	-	-	-	-	-	-	-	+	+	-	-	-	-	+	+	+	+	+	+	-	-	-
d.r.	+	+	+	+	+	+	+	-	-	+	+	+	+	-	-	+	+	+	+	+	+	-	-	+
vd	+	+	+	+	+	+	+	-	+	-	+	-	+	-	+	-	+	-	+	-	+	-	+	-
nas	-	-	+	+	+	-	-	-	-	-	-	-	-	-	-	-	-	-	-	-	-	-	-	-
lat	-	-	-	-	-	-	+	-	-	-	-	-	-	-	-	-	-	-	-	-	-	-	-	-
rd	-	+	-	-	-	-	-	-	-	-	-	-	-	-	-	-	-	-	-	-	-	-	-	-

CONSONANTS

	i	ɪ	e	ɛ	æ	u	ʊ	o	ə	a	ɔ
syl	+	+	+	+	+	+	+	+	+	+	+
son	+	+	+	+	+	+	+	+	+	+	+
cons	−	−	−	−	−	−	−	−	−	−	−
hi	+	+	−	−	−	+	+	−	−	−	−
lo	−	−	−	−	+	−	−	−	−	+	+
bk	−	−	−	−	−	+	+	+	+	+	+
tns	+	−	+	−	−	+	−	+	−	+	+
rd	−	−	−	−	−	+	+	+	−	−	+

VOWELS

Exercise 3

Based on the distinctive feature matrix for English given above, list all those features that the following pairs of sound segments share:

1.	p,b	6.	z,ž	11.	f,θ
2.	m,n	7.	č,š	12.	m,b
3.	g,ŋ	8.	k,s	13.	k,ŋ
4.	t,l	9.	w,y	14.	e,ɛ
5.	l,r	10.	i,ɪ	15.	u,i

The matrix of features for a given language, such as that given above for English, should have the capability of uniquely identifying all those segments (and, of course, suprasegmental aspects where relevant) that hold potential for contrast in the language.   Thus, they are usually referred to as **distinctive feature matrices.**   As mentioned previously, this distinctiveness is achieved through various combinations of features.   If a distinctive feature matrix does not allow each of the contrasting segments to be uniquely identified, then it is inadequate.   Distinctive feature matrices should also allow for

---

Exercise 4

For the following pairs of items, give only the features by which the sounds are differentiated from each other:

1.	p,b	6.	k,s	11.	k,n
2.	n,ŋ	7.	v,d	12.	i,y
3.	i,ɪ	8.	ə,o	13.	w,p
4.	a,ɔ	9.	r,l	14.	š,z
5.	t,d	10.	w,y	15.	b,m

---

the identification of natural similarities that various segments may have with one another.   Thus, there is a minimal feature distinction (only one feature [voiced]), between the units *p* and *b*, which are very similar.   Between dissimilar pairs like *p* and *h*, or *p* and *i*, there are differences in the values for a number of features.

While the set of features we have presented here distinguishes all the contrastive segments of English, this is not the only subset of features that will account for the contrasts among English segments. It is possible another analysis would choose different features from the universal inventory. For example, in our analysis the only contrast in English vowels entirely dependent on the feature [round] is that between *a* and *ɔ*. All other contrasts of vowels, while specified phonetically for the feature [round], can be distinguished by other features. In particular, combinations of tenseness and roundness account for the contrasts among back vowels. If *a* were considered to be [-tns], as it is in some interpretations (it is [+tns] in our matrix), the contrast between *a* and *ɔ* would not be on the basis of rounding alone, so the feature [round] could be eliminated as a distinctive feature for English segments. That is, roundness would not be distinctive for that analysis of English because it would not uniquely account for the difference between any two segments. The contrast would now be covered by the difference in tenseness (*a* would now be [-tns] and *ɔ* [+tns]), a feature which is required to make several other distinctions. The following matrices demonstrate these two alternatives.

Our specifications			Alternative specifications			Distinguishing function of our feature
	a	ɔ		a	ɔ	
syl	+	+	syl	+	+	Distinct from non-vowels, which are all [-syl].
bk	+	+	bk	+	+	Distinct from *i*, *ɪ*, *e*, *ɛ*, *æ*, which are all [-bk].
hi	-	-	hi	-	-	Distinct from *u*, *ʊ*, which are [+hi].
lo	+	+	lo	+	+	Distinct from *ə*, *o*, which are [-lo].
rd	-	+	tns	-	+	Distinct from each other.
tns	+	+	rd	-	+	Not distinctive for these two segments, because they may be distinguished from each other and every other segment of the language without using this feature. [Round] can be eliminated from the alternative specification because it makes no other contrasts in this analysis of English, but it must be retained in our specification.

Notice that in each matrix above, even though a particular feature does not function to distinguish two sounds, the specifications for that feature are nevertheless a part of the phonetic makeup of that sound. Although [tense] is non-distinctive for *a* and *ɔ* in our analysis, they both must still be considered as [+tns] vowels.

We should stress again that different interpretations such as those presented above cannot simply be dismissed as meaningless idiosyncrasies of particular analyses. Different interpretations may be based on two fundamental considerations. One is **economy**. Other things being equal, that distinctive feature analysis which uses the smallest set of features is preferred. The desire to eliminate rounding as a distinctive feature rather than a completely predictable one in some analyses may be motivated by such considerations of economy. But differing analyses may also be based on the desire to arrive at a classification that can account for similarities or internal relationships in a **natural** manner. For example, it is possible to exclude the feature [nasal] as a distinctive feature of English. In the chart above, only *m*, *n*, and ŋ are [+son] and [-cont], so that the additional feature [nasal] is not distinctive. If we eliminate [nasal], however, then we have eliminated a feature that is important in various patterns of English phonology. In other words, we feel that the feature [nasal] rather than the combination of [+son] and [-cont] triggers certain phonological patterns of English. Both the natural basis for understanding certain patterns within a language, and the matter of economy, must be considered in arriving at the most reasonable inventory of distinctive features for a given language.

Exercise 5

For the following combinations, give *all but only* those English segments that are included in the class of sounds covered by feature values in the matrix.

1. $\begin{bmatrix} +\text{nas} \\ +\text{ant} \end{bmatrix}$

2. $\begin{bmatrix} +\text{cons} \\ +\text{vd} \end{bmatrix}$

3. $\begin{bmatrix} +\text{cons} \\ -\text{ant} \\ -\text{cor} \end{bmatrix}$

4. $\begin{bmatrix} -\text{d.r.} \\ -\text{vd} \end{bmatrix}$

5. $\begin{bmatrix} +\text{cons} \\ +\text{cont} \\ +\text{cor} \\ -\text{str} \end{bmatrix}$

6. $\begin{bmatrix} -\text{d.r.} \\ +\text{ant} \end{bmatrix}$

7. $\begin{bmatrix} +\text{syl} \\ +\text{tns} \end{bmatrix}$

8. $\begin{bmatrix} +\text{syl} \\ -\text{hi} \\ -\text{lo} \end{bmatrix}$

9. $\begin{bmatrix} +\text{syl} \\ +\text{rd} \end{bmatrix}$

10. $\begin{bmatrix} -\text{d.r.} \\ +\text{cor} \end{bmatrix}$

11. $\begin{bmatrix} +\text{syl} \\ +\text{hi} \\ -\text{bk} \end{bmatrix}$

12. $\begin{bmatrix} +\text{syl} \\ +\text{lo} \\ -\text{bk} \end{bmatrix}$

13. $\begin{bmatrix} +\text{syl} \\ +\text{lo} \\ +\text{bk} \end{bmatrix}$

14. $\begin{bmatrix} -\text{cont} \\ +\text{cor} \\ -\text{nas} \end{bmatrix}$

Natural Classes

At various points in our previous discussion, we have referred to sounds that tend to group together. We saw that the plural form [s] only occurs when the preceding consonant is a voiceless, non-sibilant sound. When such a group of sounds can be uniquely specified by a relatively small set of shared features, we refer to it as a **natural class**. The set of features used to characterize a natural class should be capable of including all those sounds that are in the set, at the same time as it excludes all those not in the set. Accordingly, the set of sounds in English referred to as vowels is uniquely specified by the feature specification [+syl], because all the vowels are specified as [+syl]. Similarly, the feature specification [+nas] characterizes that class of segments which includes *m*, *n*, and ŋ. The characterization of sets may require more features than one, so that the combination [-son, +cont] includes all sounds in the English inventory which are *both* non-sonorant and continuant. This includes *f*, *v*, θ, ð, *s*, *z*, š, ž, and *h*—all the fricatives.

Feature characterizations of classes specify groups of segments that are inherently related. It would be impossible to discover a combination of features that uniquely specified the set *k*, *b*, and *n*, since there is no simple combination of feature specifications which would include all but only these

segments. Whatever combinations of features we tried, we would find ourselves including sounds other than those in this group. Thus, we would conclude that this set of sounds does not constitute a natural class, because our
feature system does not predict an inherent relationship between them. This
conclusion matches our intuitions about sound systems. In general, we may
say that natural classes can be uniquely specified by fewer feature specifications than are required to specify any individual member of the set. Features, then, provide a basis for defining what constitutes a natural class of
sounds in a language.

Exercise 6

Some of the following sets of sounds appear to constitute natural classes
while others do not. In cases of natural classes, what are the features that
uniquely distinguish them? In cases where the set does not appear to constitute a natural class, eliminate the sound that does not fit with the other
sounds, and then specify the remaining class. Explain why the eliminated
sound does not belong.

1.	t,d	6.	p,b,m,f,v	11.	i,e,u
2.	m,n,ŋ,k	7.	f,v,s,z	12.	č,ǰ,k
3.	e,ɛ,æ,a	8.	t,θ,d̶	13.	y,w,u,ʊ
4.	s,z,š,ž	9.	u,ʊ,o,a,ɔ	14.	t,d,n
5.	i,ɪ,e	10.	ŋ,k,g		

FEATURE REDUNDANCY

In the distinctive feature matrix for English given earlier, segments were
assigned a value for most of the features. However, this does not mean that
all the features function independently of each other. As it turns out, the
values of some features are completely predictable from the values of other
features. There is a certain amount of feature redundancy within segments.
This sort of **segmental redundancy** will be the topic of the rest of this chapter. In the next chapter we will examine the redundancy that results from
predictable sequences of segments.

Segmental Redundancy

In segmental redundancy, some aspects of the total bundle of features charac-
terizing a segment are predictable from the values of other features within
the bundle. We have already anticipated this predictability in failing to
specify for vowels many of the distinctive features we used for consonants.
We could do this because these features are completely predictable on the
basis of the specification [+syl] for vowels. That is, all vowels share a number of features, so we may say that those values are predictable (or redundant) if we know that a particular segment is a vowel. If the values of
features are always predictable, it seems needless to specify these values
every time the segment is characterized. Thus, we state this observation as
a regularity in terms of features in a **segmental redundancy condition**, as below.

[+syl]
↓

$$\begin{bmatrix} +son \\ -cons \\ -ant \\ -cor \\ +cont \\ -str \\ +d.r. \\ +vd \\ -nas \\ -lat \end{bmatrix}$$

This condition should be read: If a segment is specified as [+syl], then we know that it will also have the specifications indicated for the features below the arrow. Put differently, we might say that the specification [+syl] implies the other feature values within a segment.[6] If we worked through the feature specifications for the vowels, we would find that every [+syl] segment also has the values indicated for the features above.

While a relatively full matrix of features was listed for the consonants in the chart, many of those features are also redundant. For example, the feature *round* is predictable for those sounds classified as obstruents ([-son]), as indicated below:

[-son]
↓
[-r̄d]

This means that every segment specified as [-son] in the matrix is also specified as [-rd]. Similarly, the nasals imply an entire set of redundant features in the matrix:

[+nas]
↓

$$\begin{bmatrix} -syl \\ +son \\ +cons \\ -lo \\ -cont \\ -str \\ +d.r. \\ +vd \\ -lat \\ -rd \end{bmatrix}$$

In the instances above, the value of one particular feature implies the specification of values for other features. There are also cases where a combination of features in a matrix, rather than a single feature, serves as the basis for predictability. Consider how the feature of rounding can be predicted for the glides *y* and *w*.

$$\begin{matrix} y & & w \\ \begin{bmatrix} -syl \\ -cons \\ -bk \end{bmatrix} & & \begin{bmatrix} -syl \\ -cons \\ +bk \end{bmatrix} \\ \downarrow & & \downarrow \\ [-r̄d] & & [+r̄d] \end{matrix}$$

None of the features uniquely specifying *y* or *w* is sufficient by itself to predict the value of rounding, but the combination of [+bk] with [-syl] and [-cons] implies the value of [+rd]. The combination of [-bk] with [-syl] and [-cons] implies the value [-rd]. (The glides *y* and *w* are the only English segments which are both [-syl] and [-cons].) Many such examples can be found in English.

In examining redundant features within a cross-section of languages, some types of redundancies prove to be **universal**, while others are **language-specific**. That is, some redundancies exist regardless of the language in question, whereas others exist only because of the organization of a particular language. The following condition is an example of universal redundancy:

$$[+\text{hi}]$$
$$\downarrow$$
$$[-\text{lo}]$$

This type of universal predictability is understandable because of the limitations of the human tongue, which cannot be both high and low at the same time. Many universal redundancies have a natural explanation of this sort. On the other hand, there are cases of redundancy that result entirely from the specific language's unique inventory of sounds. The feature [+rd] for English vowels necessarily implies [+bk], and the feature [-bk] implies [-rd]:

$$\begin{bmatrix} +\text{syl} \\ +\text{rd} \end{bmatrix} \qquad \begin{bmatrix} +\text{syl} \\ -\text{bk} \end{bmatrix}$$
$$\downarrow \qquad\qquad \downarrow$$
$$[+\text{bk}] \qquad\quad [-\text{rd}]$$

These redundancies occur because English has not chosen to use rounded, front vowels. On the other hand, French and German employ contrastive differences between non-back round and unrounded vowels (e.g. /i/ versus /ɨ̞/), and so do not have a predictable relationship of this type.

So far, we have limited the discussion to redundancies among the features that are used contrastively in the language system in question. Ultimately, however, in order to arrive at a complete phonetic specification for each segment, it is necessary to specify non-contrastive phonetic detail.

In an efficient description of a phonological system, it seems most economical to separate the predictable feature specifications from those that are utilized in a distinctive capacity. A single set of segmental redundancy conditions can supply the redundant values. This permits segments to be characterized by only the non-redundant feature specifications necessary to distinguish one segment from another. Although it is essential to differentiate redundant from non-redundant value specifications in discussing the phonology of a language, this does not mean that the values of redundant features are of no interest. For one thing, redundant features may be essential in formally referring to natural classes. Thus, even though the value [+rd] is redundant for /u/ and /ʊ/, they are still in the natural class of rounded vowels. Moreover, as we mentioned above, redundant values are important in eventually describing the systematic phonetic detail that is necessary as part of a complete phonological description. Redundant feature value specifications are therefore an important part of a total language description.

Exercise 7

The following feature matrices include some features which are redundant for the identification of English segments. Indicate the features in each matrix that are redundant, and the distinctive features in the matrix from which these redundancies can be predicted. For example, if we represent the segments *m*, *n*, and ŋ as [+nas, -str, +vd], we observe that the features [-strident] and [+voiced] are redundant. Both are predicted by [+nas].

1. $\begin{bmatrix} +\text{ant} \\ -\text{cor} \\ -\text{nas} \\ -\text{bk} \\ -\text{str} \\ -\text{d.r.} \end{bmatrix}$ p,b

2. $\begin{bmatrix} +\text{syl} \\ +\text{hi} \\ -\text{lo} \\ -\text{bk} \\ -\text{rd} \end{bmatrix}$ i, ɪ

3. $\begin{bmatrix} -\text{cons} \\ -\text{syl} \\ +\text{cont} \\ -\text{nas} \end{bmatrix}$ y, w

4. $\begin{bmatrix} -\text{cont} \\ -\text{nas} \\ -\text{d.r.} \\ +\text{ant} \\ +\text{cor} \\ -\text{str} \\ -\text{son} \end{bmatrix}$ t, d

5. $\begin{bmatrix} -\text{cont} \\ -\text{nas} \\ +\text{str} \\ +\text{hi} \\ +\text{d.r.} \end{bmatrix}$ č, ǰ

6. $\begin{bmatrix} +\text{syl} \\ -\text{hi} \\ -\text{lo} \\ -\text{bk} \\ -\text{nas} \\ +\text{son} \end{bmatrix}$ e, ɛ

7. $\begin{bmatrix} +\text{cont} \\ -\text{str} \\ -\text{son} \\ +\text{ant} \\ +\text{cor} \\ -\text{nas} \end{bmatrix}$ θ, d

8. $\begin{bmatrix} +\text{str} \\ +\text{cont} \\ -\text{lo} \\ +\text{cor} \\ -\text{bk} \end{bmatrix}$ s, z, š, ž

9. $\begin{bmatrix} -\text{syl} \\ +\text{son} \\ +\text{cons} \\ +\text{cont} \\ -\text{nas} \\ +\text{vd} \end{bmatrix}$ r, l

10. $\begin{bmatrix} -\text{cont} \\ -\text{ant} \\ -\text{cor} \\ +\text{hi} \end{bmatrix}$ k, g, ŋ

Exercise 8

For the following classes of sounds, give the *minimal* number of features that characterize the class as it is distinguished from all other classes of sounds in English. In other words, give just enough features to uniquely specify the class by eliminating the redundant feature values for the class. (This exercise is most effectively done by using as a guide the complete matrix given earlier.)

Start by looking for a feature that includes the relevant class of sounds and at the same time excludes the largest number of other segments. Suppose that the class we want to specify is *s*, *z*, *š*, and *ž*. By starting with the feature [+str], we can immediately eliminate many sounds, since only *f*, *v*, *s*, *z*, *š*, *ž*, *č*, and *ǰ* are [+str]. The next task is to eliminate the *f*, *v*, *č*, and *ǰ* from inclusion in the set. The *f* and *v* can be eliminated by specifying [+cor], since *s*, *z*, *š*, and *ž* are all [+cor] but *f* and *v* are not. We now need to eliminate the *č* and *ǰ*. Several options may be possible, but the specification of [+cont] will exclude *č* and *ǰ*, leaving only *s*, *z*, *š*, and *ž*. The minimal specification, then, is: [+str, +cont, +cor]. All other feature values are predictable on the basis of the combination of these features.

Exercise 8 continued

1.	č,ǰ,k,g	5.	θ,d̶	9.	e,o
2.	s,z	6.	i,ɪ,u,ʊ	10.	æ,a
3.	f,v	7.	p,b	11.	p,b,m
4.	t,d	8.	ŋ,k,g	12.	r,l

NOTES

1. Notice that square brackets are now being used to enclose distinctive feature specifications. Up to this point, we have used them only to enclose phonetic segments.
2. This parameter replaces the earlier designation of *vocalic*, because vocalic does not permit the natural specification of the syllabic nasals and liquids.
3. Some treatments of the feature *consonantal* insist that only sounds produced within the oral cavity itself may be considered [+cons]. Thus, they specify the laryngeal glides *h* and *ʔ* as [-cons]. In our system, *h* and *ʔ* are [+cons].
4. Because *h* often takes the tongue features of the segment either preceding or following it, some treatments do not consider *h* to be [+lo].
5. The distinction between [ʌ] and [ə], which we have generally maintained in broad phonetic transcription, is not indicated here since there is no phonemic distinction between these items in English. In reference to the contrastive units of English, we typically use /ə/ to represent both [ə] and [ʌ].
6. The use of vertical arrows should be clearly distinguished from the horizontal arrow which changes feature specifications (discussed in Chapter 8).

SUGGESTED READING

There are a number of different works which should be consulted on distinctive features. More detail on the feature distinctions can be found in Chapter 7 of Chomsky and Halle's *The Sound Pattern of English* (1968). Ladefoged's *Preliminaries to Linguistic Phonetics* (1971) is an excellent critical discussion of the phonetic base of distinctive features, drawn from an investigation of a wide range of data. One of the earlier justifications for the formal inclusion of distinctive features in a phonological description is Halle's "On the Bases of Phonology" (1964). Elaboration on aspects of phonological redundancy can be found in Stanley's "Redundancy Rules in Phonology" (1967). This article also explicates in an insightful manner many of the problems of previous conceptions of redundancy relations. The interested reader might also compare the discussion of distinctive features in this chapter with Chapters 3 and 4 of Schane's *Generative Phonology* (1973).

CHAPTER 5
Sequences of Sounds: Phonotactics

In previous chapters, we discussed the phonological units of language systems with reference to patterns of contrast among sounds. There are also patterns that govern the sequences of sounds. In American English, we can derive six actual words by combining the three phonemes /p/, /t/, and /a/.

/pa/	'pa'	/pap/	'pop'
/apt/	'opt'	/tat/	'tot'
/tap/	'top'	/pat/	'pot'

It is significant that only six of the many possible arrangements of these phonemes actually are used in the construction of English words. Moreover, it is not simply accidental that our lexicon does not include such combinations as */atp/ and */pta/.[1] If, for example, we were to ask speakers of English if */atp/ and */pta/ could be used as words in English, we would get almost complete agreement that they could not. Obviously, the phonetic segments of English are not combined in random order, and somehow speakers of the language know this. We find that in every language there are regular patterns of permissible sequences of phonemic units as they combine to form the larger units of the language—morphemes and words. The regular patterns for combining the sounds of a language in a sequence are called the **phonotactics** of the language. As with phonemic analysis, we want the generalizations we propose about phonotactics to represent the knowledge native speakers have about the sound patterns of their language. This is the reason we may ask native speakers to judge the acceptability of sequences of sounds.

Phonological vs. Phonetic Units

Sound sequences of the type illustrated above may appear fairly straightforward, but further investigation indicates a number of problems in arriving at a system to describe them. One such problem involves sequences that contain a "transitional" sound, such as the affricates [tʃ] or [dʒ]. The English affricates [tʃ] of *church* and [dʒ] of *judge* have long presented a problem for linguists. The difficulty is that affricates are phonetically a sequence of a stop and a fricative. Arguments might be made both for treating the stop and sibilant as one unit, /č/ and /ǰ/, and for maintaining them as separate phonemes that simply combine in a sequence, such as /t/ followed by /ʃ/ and /d/ followed by /ʒ/. Because the units /t/, /d/, /ʃ/, and /ʒ/ must all be recognized as phonemes in their own right, treating [tʃ] and [dʒ] as combinations of separate phonemes would reduce the number of phonological categories in the basic inventory of phonemes. In the absence of other types of conflicting evidence, "economy" in the system is a strong argument for a particular solution in phonological analysis.

An argument for treating these as single phonemes comes from the consideration of other types of word-initial consonant sequences. We know that languages tend to pattern in terms of sets rather than individual items, yet there are no word-initial stop plus fricative phoneme sequences in English. If we examined a large corpus of English words, we would discover that clusters of /t/ plus fricative are extremely rare, except for [tʃ] and [dʒ]. The sequences of /tf/, /dv/, /tθ/, and /dd̪/ do not appear initially in English words, and occur medially and finally only across syllables (as in *advance*) or across morphemes (as in *eighth*). Similarly, [ts] is extremely rare, occurring only in a handful of imported morphemes like *tsetse*. Thus, there appears to be no regular pattern of /t/ plus fricative clusters except for the two cases we are considering. This evidence can be taken as an argument for the treatment of [tʃ] and [dʒ] as single phonemic units, /č/ and /ǰ/. Economy of the system argues *against* them as a single unit, while pressure from other patterns argues *for* treating them as a single unit.

Recent evidence acquired from native speakers of English suggests that these sequences are intuitively treated as one phonological unit. One type of evidence comes from the study of performance errors (slips of the tongue) such as Spoonerisms (in which parts of two words are interchanged). Studies of this phenomenon (Fromkin, 1971;1973) suggest that even though something has gone wrong with our speech production mechanisms when our tongues slip, we nevertheless tend to maintain our use of phonemes as if they were in real words. Consider these actual Spoonerisms:

top notch	became [tatʃ nap]
pretty chilly	became [tʃɪti prɪli]
key chain	became [tʃi ken]
cream cheese	became [tʃim kriz]
blue jay	became [dʒu ble]

In each of these examples, a [tʃ] or [dʒ] is exchanged with a segment (or two) from the other word. In such cases the [t] and [ʃ], or [d] and [ʒ] are never divided between words, so that forms like *[tat napʃ] (from *top notch*) do not occur. This pattern of errors suggests that speakers of English actually treat /č/ and /ǰ/ as phonological units. If they were clusters of two units, we would expect to find them broken apart in some performance errors, and we have found no such examples.

Exercise 1

Consider the following actual slips of the tongue recorded by Fromkin (1973).

pedal steel guitar	became *steadel peel guitar*
make a long story short	became ... *shorey stort*
official dressing taster	became ... *dresting taser*
steak and potatoes	became *spake and tomatoes*
there's a pest in every class	became ... *a pess in every clatt*
stick in the mud	became *smuck in the tid*
deep structure	became *steep dructure*
streak of bad luck	became *steak of brad luck*

Applying the kinds of arguments described above, attempt to determine whether the sequence *s* + *t* is a phonological unit or a sequence of two phonemes.

Exercise 2

The following list of actual performance errors contains a number of sequences of consonant plus [r]. Sequences of this sort (and those containing a consonant and an [l]) might be treated as if they were either one or two units. In your estimation, what is the phonological status of such sequences—that is, do they function as one unit or two?

little island in Brittany	became *brittle island in litany*
brake fluid	became *blake fruid*
if Bill Bright comes	became *... Brill Bite....*
drop a bomb	became *bop a dromb*
fresh clear water	became *flesh queer water*
fish grotto	became *frish gotto*
fricaseed chicken	became *chickaseed fricken*
from Pounds to Franks	became *from Prounds to Fanks*
trees are pretty	became *prees are tritty*
stick around and try to see	became *sick around and tie to tree ... I mean ... trick around and sigh to tea ... oh, you know what I mean.*
tongue tip trill	became *tongue trip till*

List three speech errors which would strengthen your argument about whether these sequences are one unit or two.

Sequential Phonological Structure

Unlike /č/ and /ǰ/, most sequences of consonants in English words cannot be considered together as phonological units. Rather, they must be treated as clusters of independent phonemes which are combined according to a speaker's knowledge of the regular patterns for word formation. In order to discover what some of these patterns might be for English speakers, we will reconsider a few of the speech errors from the exercises above.

First, it is clear that even though slips of the tongue are errors in speech, they are quite predictable. They follow general patterns. Notice especially that the forms actually uttered are ones which any native speaker of English might have made and could probably decode. However, there are some combinations which would never occur. For example, *streak of bad luck* actually became *steak of brad luck*, but might also have become *beak of strad luck* or even *breek of stad luck*. But we can be certain that a native speaker of English would never utter **treek of sbad luck* or **btreek of sad luck*. In these cases, the disallowed recombinations produce forms containing combinations of phonemes which do not occur in English words. The prohibition may, in fact, be so strong that a speech error progressing toward a Spoonerism will be altered to conform to the English pattern, as in the following examples:

sphynx in moonlight	became *minks in spoonlight* rather than the expected **sfoonlight.*
play the victor	became *flay the pictor* rather than the expected **vlay.*

In these cases, sequences not found in English, such as word-initial **/sf/* and **/vl/*, may not even occur in a slip of the tongue. This observation suggests that there are strong constraints on how a word may be formed, specifying what may and may not be a permissible word in English. The determination of the patterns of these **permissible words** is an important part of speakers' knowledge about their language. Given a sample of actual items from a language, we can describe its phonotactic structure in terms of specifications (called **restrictions or constraints**) for combining its sound units. The set of restrictions should account for all the actual words observed, as well as those permissible sequences not currently used in actual words of the language. By the same token, the restrictions should disallow the formation of non-permissible sequences.

Exercise 3

Below are some combinations of English segments. Although they do not occur as actual English words, some of them would be acceptable English items if they were assigned a meaning. List those that could not be English items, and explain why they would be unacceptable sequences.

1.	/splarb/	6.	/pruks/	11.	/blarč/
2.	/fnɪp/	7.	/fagzau/	12.	/ðɛrk/
3.	/gnot/	8.	/nifɪr/	13.	/čɛǰ/
4.	/kugən/	9.	/tθɔb/	14.	/gzub/
5.	/ksæk/	10.	/bɪtθ/		

In some cases, we may decide that the phonotactic constraints of a language exclude certain sequences which occur in recently imported forms. For example, although the vocabulary of many speakers of American English includes the words *schlock, schnook,* and *schmaltz,* the sequential constraints of English might prohibit the initial sequences /ʃm/, /ʃl/, and /ʃn/, because they occur almost exclusively in unassimilated forms derived from Yiddish or German. Similarly, we exclude the initial /ts/ sequence from consideration because it occurs only in the borrowed form *tsetse fly.* That initial /ts/ is not a permissible English sequence is demonstrated by the tendency of many English speakers to pronounce *tsetse* as /titsi/, which is an acceptable English sequence. If we wanted to claim that the importation of disallowed sequences changed English sequential constraints, we might expect to find initial /ts/ occurring in newly invented words—perhaps, for example, a new brand of cereal called *Tsik-Tsak.* Until such combinations are used widely in the creation of English words, they must be considered as unproductive and excluded from the set of regular sequential constraints.

In Chapter 4, we discussed the notion of segmental redundancy, in which some specifications for the features of a sound segment were predictable on the basis of other feature specifications for the segment. A similar type of redundancy exists on the basis of other segments in a sequence. In this case, the predictability relates to the sequential organization of segments within morphemes or words rather than to the total inventory of segments used in the language. The difference between segmental and sequential redundancy is shown in the figure on page 79.

As with segmental redundancy, some aspects of sequential redundancy may be universal in nature, whereas others are quite language-specific. For example, we would not normally expect a language to have word-initial clusters of five obstruents, because of the physiological complexity involved in such a production. Accordingly, we would say that some of the feature specifications for a segment following four obstruent consonants in word-initial position are

Segmental Redundancy   *Sequential Redundancy*

Segment 1   Segment 2

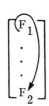   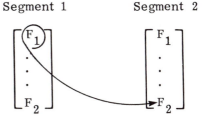

redundant in all languages, because we can predict that it will not be another
obstruent.   More often, we are able to derive redundant information from
language-specific sequential restrictions. For example, English does not allow
word-initial sequences of a nasal plus another consonant (e.g. *mb* or *nt*),
whereas other languages in the world do. We are interested here in discovering restrictions specific to English, although we must bear in mind that some
of these details may correspond to universal restrictions.

Sequential Morpheme Structure Conditions

There are two aspects of the sequential structure of morphemes that need to
be represented. First, there are aspects that relate to the number of consonant and vowel sequences permissible in a morpheme or syllable.[2] For example, we quickly discover that English has a limit on the number of segments
in a word-initial consonant cluster. We find many examples of two-consonant
clusters such as *stone, scab, blue, twin,* and *small*. There are also a number
of three-consonant clusters such as *streak, splash, scream,* and *skew* (/skyu/).
But we do not find an English word with four initial consonants. Thus, we
may propose a **syllable structure condition** which restricts initial consonant
clusters to a maximum of three members. For now, we may state this condition thusly:

(a) Syllable structure condition on initial consonant clusters:
    A string of segments will be accepted as a permissible English syllable
    only if it is initiated with three or fewer non-vowels.

Examining the combinations of consonants within the clusters permitted by
condition (a), we discover again that only certain combinations of segments
may occur at the beginning of English words. This is the second aspect of
the sequential structure of morphemes. The words *spring, strike, scramble,
split, spew, skewer,* and *squeeze* illustrate the possibilities for initial three-
consonant clusters.[3]   In the examples, we recognize that English is limited to
the combinations /spr/, /str/, /skr/, /spl/, /spy/, /sky/, /skw/. These kinds
of restrictions are typically referred to as **sequential morpheme structure conditions.**

Exercise 4

What regularities can you find for initial clusters of three consonants in English? Organize your investigation by answering the following questions for
each position within the cluster, first for the initial segment, then for the
second segment, and then for the third.

Exercise 4 continued

(1) Can the segments that may occur in this position be defined as some natural class?

(2) Does the presence of a segment (or class of segments) in this position depend upon which segment occurs in one of the other positions?

In doing Exercise 4, we discover the following facts about English, which we will state as Condition (b):

(b) *Sequential morpheme structure condition on word-initial clusters of three consonants:*
  (1) The initial segment must be /s/;
  (2) The second segment must be a voiceless stop (/p/, /t/, or /k/);
  (3) The third segment must be either a liquid (/l/, or /r/) or glide (/y/ or /w/); *and* if the second segment is /t/, then only /r/ may occur; or if the second segment is /k/, then only /r/, /y/, or /w/ may occur; or if the second segment is /p/, then /r/, /y/, or /l/ may occur.

Assume that these conditions act as monitors which let pass any string of segments which is acceptable in English and block any string which violates acceptable English form. Clearly, if our conditions are valid generalizations about the linguistic knowledge of native English speakers, then forms that are accepted by all of the conditions will be permissible words, while those that do not meet the conditions will be non-permissible words.

Suppose we subject the strings /strom/, /stwom/, and /stryom/ to Conditions (a) and (b) stated above. We find, first, that /strom/ and /stwom/ are acceptable in their syllable structure because they are accepted by Condition (a), which states that they should contain no more than three non-vowels before the first vowel. The string */stryom/ does not meet this condition. It contains four initial non-vowels and is judged to be non-permissible. Condition (b) will allow only /strom/ to pass, for, although */stwom/ contains an initial /s/ followed by a /t/, only an /r/ may follow /st/ in initial three-consonant clusters.

As with the inventory of phonological units, statements about sequences are often most economically stated in terms of feature specifications. Thus, we may rewrite Condition (a) as Condition (1) below.

(1) +## ([-syl]) ([-syl]) ([-syl]) [+syl]

The form of Condition (1) is significant. First, the plus-sign (+) at the beginning indicates that it is a **positive condition**, which will accept only those strings with features matching those of the condition. Secondly, the symbol ## indicates the beginning of a word (which for our purposes also corresponds to the beginning of a syllable), and the order of the segments to the right of the ## indicates the order of the segments in the word. Third, parentheses around a segment indicate that its presence is optional; it may or may not occur in the string. Fourth, the feature specifications within the segments are represented as natural classes, so that they reflect regularities about the language. Condition (1) should be read as: A string of initial segments will be accepted if it consists of one of the following combinations: ##CCCV, ##CCV, ##CV, or ##V.

Condition (b) may also be represented in features, although that is complicated because it is composed of several statements of regularities. First, we may state the observation that if there are three initial consonants, then the first one must be /s/, the second a voiceless stop, and so on. This requires another kind of morpheme structure condition: an if-then condition. If-then conditions state that a preliminary condition must be met in order for another condition to apply. A condition does not apply to every string, but only to those which match its "if" component.

(2) If: ## [-syl]   [-syl]   [-syl]

Then:
$$\begin{bmatrix} +ant \\ +cor \\ +str \\ -vd \end{bmatrix} \quad \begin{bmatrix} -vd \\ -d.r. \end{bmatrix} \quad \begin{bmatrix} +son \\ -nas \end{bmatrix}$$

         (s)   (p,t,k)   (r,l,y,w)

Condition (2) pertains only to initial, three-consonant clusters and restricts the classes of segments that may occur in each position of the cluster. It expresses combinations in terms of general classes of segments. We observed in Condition (b), however, that not every combination of voiceless stop and liquid or glide could occur. Rather, the occurrence of a segment in the second position excludes the occurrence of particular segments in the third position. But this fact presents a difficulty in stating the remainder of the condition, for, although we have expressed Condition (b) from the point of view of the second segment, it might be said just as reliably that the third segment was responsible for the presence of the second. For example, we might say that if the third segment is /w/, then the second segment must be /k/, just as easily as if the second segment is /k/, then the third segment is /w/. Presently we have no way of determining the direction in which these conditions should operate, so we will state them as simply as possible without regard for the direction in which they operate.

Reorganizing the combinations expressed by Condition (b), we will find that three consonant clusters ending with /r/ may contain any of the voiceless stops, but that those ending with /l/ may contain only /p/. Condition (3) expresses this observation.

(3) If: ## [-syl]   [-syl] $\begin{bmatrix} +cons \\ +lat \end{bmatrix}$

Then: $\begin{bmatrix} +ant \\ -cor \end{bmatrix}$

              (p)   (l)

Condition (3) states only that if the final segment is /l/, then the second segment must be /p/. We need only two features here to distinguish the /p/, because we already know from Condition (2) that the middle segment must be a voiceless stop. The occurrence of /r/ need not be stated in this condition, because it is not restricted in this way.

Similarly, we know that if a glide occurs in the third position, then the second segment must be a /p/ or /k/, which is stated in Condition (4).

(4) If: ## [-syl]   [-syl] $\begin{bmatrix} -syl \\ -cons \end{bmatrix}$

Then: [-cor]

              (p,k)   (w,y)

However, if the glide is /y/, either /p/ or /k/ may occur, but if the glide is /w/, then only /k/ may occur. Again stating the most restrictive case, /w/ following /k/, we produce Condition (5).

(5) If: ## [-syl]   [-syl] $\begin{bmatrix} -syl \\ -cons \\ +bk \end{bmatrix}$

Then: [+bk]

            (k)   (w)

Let us now examine these five conditions as they apply to an illustrative sequence of segments. The clusters /spr/ and /skw/ occur in such common words as *spring, spray, spruce,* and *squat, squelch, squash,* so our conditions should accept them. Below are the distinctive feature specifications of these segments, and the way in which the conditions apply:

	/## sprV/	/## skwV/
syl	---+	---+
son	--+	--+
cons	+++	++-
ant	++-	+--
cor	+--	+--
bk	---	-++
cont	+-+	+-+
str	+--	+--
d.r.	+-+	+-+
vd	--+	--+
nas	---	---
lat	---	---

Condition (1) accepts both forms because it permits three [-syl] segments initially.

Condition (2) accepts both forms because they contain a voiceless stop ([-d.r.] [-vd]) in second position, and r, l, y, or w ([+son] [-nas]) in third position.

Condition (3) does not apply to either because the third segment is not *l* ([+lat]), so we ignore it.

Condition (4) does not apply to *spr* but accepts *skw* because the third consonant is w or y ([-syl] [-cons]) and the second is k or p ([-d.r.] [-vd] [-cor]).

Condition (5) does not apply to *spr* but accepts *skw* because the third segment is w ([-syl] [-cons] [+bk]) and the second is k ([-d.r.] [-vd] [+bk]).

Because these items are accepted by every condition that applies to them, they are judged to be acceptable English sequences. If we repeat this procedure for every possible combination of initial three-consonant cluster sequences in English, we will find that our conditions specify the permissible sequences. Furthermore, it will eliminate all non-permissible sequences. We claim that such conditions represent accurate generalizations about the knowledge of native speakers of English.

Exercise 5

From the following nonsense items, pick out those initial consonant clusters that are permissible sequences in English. Compare these items with the ones that are not acceptable as initial clusters in English, and attempt to make statements which can cover all initial two-consonant sequences in English. Notice that this list does not contain examples of all the combinations of English consonants, so you may need to look for other permissible sequences. Also, be sure to distinguish between the spelling and the phonemic representation of the words. Provide examples of acceptable and unacceptable sequences from actual English words that justify your conclusions.

1.	/prʊm/	13.	/drɪp/	25.	/trʊp/
2.	/plɪp/	14.	/snop/	26.	/grap/
3.	/pmat/	15.	/gnap/	27.	/spot/
4.	/zrot/	16.	/kræt/	28.	/glɪd/
5.	/fnol/	17.	/bdog/	29.	/θlon/
6.	/stot/	18.	/tvin/	30.	/skip/
7.	/smæt/	19.	/dnop/	31.	/slug/
8.	/tlap/	20.	/klæb/	32.	/brit/
9.	/θrɪk/	21.	/drok/	33.	/from/
10.	/twɪf/	22.	/flen/	34.	/šrɪp/
11.	/dwap/	23.	/blin/	35.	/swek/
12.	/kwæt/	24.	/dwaf/	36.	/ktopt/

Exercise 5 should result in a fairly extensive list of initial two-consonant clusters. It is important to recognize that for speakers of many English varieties, certain combinations other than those found in Exercise 5 may be permissible. Some people may use /hw/ and /hy/, while others may have a range of permissible combinations with /y/ as the second consonant. In the following discussion of CCV sequences, we eliminate those combinations containing a /w/ or /y/.

Two immediate observations may be made about the inventory represented in Exercise 5: (a) the first segment must be an obstruent (stop or fricative), and (b) the second segment must be a nasal, a liquid, or a voiceless stop. Of course, it is possible to formalize conditions for two-consonant clusters just as we did for the three-consonant sequences, but we will not do so here. Looking for co-occurrence relations between segments, we find that if the second segment is anything but /r/ or /l/, then the first segment must be /s/. We have /sp/, /st/, /sk/, /sm/, and /sn/, but not */kt/ or */fn/. We find words such as *spill, stew, skip, small,* and *snooze* representing the permissible sequences in English, but no words such as */ktop/ or */fnol/.

The inventory of segments that can occur with /r/ in ##CC clusters is: /p, b, t, d, k, g, f, θ, š/, as in *proud, brown, trip, droll, cream, gross, frank, throw, shrink.* There are no ##Cr sequences such as */drip/ or */zrot/. Those initial segments that can occur with /l/ are /p, b, k, g, f, s/, as in *place, bloom, clue, gloat, flop, slim.* There are no sequences such as */tlap/ and */θlon/. The segments that can occur with /r/ and /l/ represent a fairly complex natural class.

Exercise 6

The following is a list of nonsense words, each of which contains a word-final cluster involving stops. From this list, pick out those forms which would be permissible as English *nouns*, and those permissible as past tense forms of *verbs*. Provide an actual English word demonstrating this acceptability. State a condition that accounts for the permissible cluster.

1.	/ræpb/	9.	/lɪdg/	17.	/bʊbp/
2.	/kotk/	10.	/takg/	18.	/lɪgd/
3.	/gokt/	11.	/bɪgp/	19.	/hapk/
4.	/gadt/	12.	/sɪtb/	20.	/kɪtd/
5.	/bokb/	13.	/sɪbd/	21.	/sæbk/
6.	/rædp/	14.	/batg/	22.	/rʊtp/
7.	/lʊpt/	15.	/sæpd/		
8.	/ræpg/	16.	/bokp/		

Some classes of words in English may allow more combinations of final stops than do other classes, but the differences do not result simply from the fact that one word is a noun and another a verb. Rather, they come about because verbs add /d/ and /t/ forms of the past tense morpheme, and nouns do not (*sag* + PAST = /sægd/, *pluck* + PAST = /plʌkt/).

The combinations which result from joining two morphemes are accounted for by a special set of phonological rules, which we will discuss in Chapter 8. These rules apply to acceptable combinations of morphemes, like *sag* + PAST, and modify them according to the general patterns of the language. For example, in Exercise 6, there are certain restrictions on which stops may occur before either /d/ or /t/. Specifically, /t/ occurs after [-vd] stops and /d/ after [+vd] stops (other than alveolars). The regular past tense suffix follows a general phonological pattern in English: to agree in voicing with the segment which precedes it.

In the following chapters, we will follow an approach to phonology that distinguishes the phonological patterning governing the combinations of morphemes from morpheme structure conditions such as those discussed above. However, an increasing number of phonologists feel that the syllable, rather than the morpheme, should be the basis for determining the acceptability of sound sequences and for understanding phonological patterns. The details of such an approach are beyond the scope of this discussion, but we must examine some characteristics of syllables that pertain to our discussion of phonotactics.

The Syllable: A Phonological Perspective

In Chapter 2, we discussed the phonetic base of the syllable as a unit within the sound system. We mentioned that the nucleus of the syllable was the maximum peak of sonority, and that this peak could be surrounded by an onset (initiating segment or segments) and a coda (terminating segment or segments). We often find syllables composed of consonants initially, a vowel at the peak, and then consonants finally. While this approach to the syllable is impressionistically valid, the difficulty in defining degrees of sonority among segments sometimes makes it difficult to apply to our understanding of syllable structure.

Attending to finer phonetic detail, we can observe that it is difficult to pronounce a syllable without any onset. Thus, the finely tuned ear will discover that a syllable such as [at] in isolation is usually pronounced with an initiating glottal stop, as [ʔat]. A sequence such as [at] can be produced (although often with an initiating preaspiration such as [^{h}at]), but only with fairly intense concentration. This seems to be evidence for the fact that syllables are more generally initiated with a consonant onset. Interestingly, our view of phonetics reflects this observation. For example, we treat the glides [w] and [y] as consonants, not because their production is unlike vowels, but because they are usually associated with rapid movement to or from another position. In reality, [w] and [y] are phonetically quite like [ʊ] and [ɪ], respectively. These segments are, however, interpreted as glides [w] and [y] in items such as English *win* and *yes*. These segments occur as the onsetting element of syllables. The onset of syllables is typically a consonant, so we consider [y] and [w] to be consonants in initial position. Thus, the dominant consonant-vowel (CV) syllable pattern of English may be the influential factor in the assignment of certain supposedly phonetic classifications.

While syllables have a strong tendency to begin with a consonant, they may or may not terminate with one. Syllables without a consonantal coda are called **open syllables**; syllables with a consonantal coda are called **closed syllables**. Whether a syllable is open or closed may be an important factor in the occurrence of certain phonotactic patterns.

Exercise 7

The following is a list of monosyllabic English words.

(a) Mark which are open syllables with *CV* and those which are closed syllables with *CVC*. Do not trust the spelling; determine their syllabicity on the basis of how they are pronounced. Treat final offglides (e.g. [pe^ɪ] 'pay', as a part of the vowel ([pe]).

(b) State which vowels can occur in open syllables. Capture the pattern through the use of distinctive feature specifications.

do	fee	nook	toe
cot	feat	pen	new
toad	caught	though	claw
fat	nude	pun	pay

	i	ɪ	e	ɛ	æ	u	ʊ	o	ə	a	ɔ
hi	+	+	-	-	-	+	+	-	-	-	-
lo	-	-	-	-	+	-	-	-	-	+	+
bk	-	-	-	-	-	+	+	+	+	+	+
tns	+	-	+	-	-	+	-	+	-	+	+
rd	-	-	-	-	-	+	+	+	-	-	+

Syllabification

While it seems relatively simple to determine whether monosyllabic words are composed of open or closed syllables, it is sometimes more difficult to determine the syllable structure of multisyllabic words. One approach to this problem has been to allow syllable breaks only where the resultant syllables conform to permissible combinations in monosyllabic words. For example, *anger* /æŋgɚ/ may be broken between the /ŋ/ and /g/ because /ŋg/ as a sequence does not normally occur either word-initially or word-finally in English. Aside from the fact that this solution ignores the variety of English spoken in Long Island (where *long* may be [lɔŋg]), the approach is unable to provide a definitive judgment for some words.

A more useful approach for English combines the criterion of acceptable sequences with two principles of syllable structure (Pulgram, 1970). They are: (1) if possible, every syllable should be an open syllable, and (2) if a syllable cannot be an open syllable, then its coda should be as short as possible. Combining these principles with the criterion that syllables should conform to acceptable sequential patterns, we can divide the word *extra* as follows. First, we want as many open syllables as possible, so we break it as /ɛ$kstrə/, where $ indicates a syllable break. This division creates two non-permissible sequences. First, our morpheme structure conditions prohibit the sequence */kstr/ initially. Second, stressed lax vowels (like /ɛ/) may not end syllables in English, so the first syllable may not be open. Then according to the second principle, we attach as little as possible to the first syllable, yielding /ɛk$strə/, which is now composed of acceptable sequences. Applying the same procedures, we assign the following **syllabifications** (also referred to as **syllabication**), where the offglide semivowels again are considered to be a part of the syllable peak, and syllabic consonants sometimes carry the syllable peak alone.

		Principle 1	*Principle 2*
rotation	/roteʃən/	/ro$teʃ$ən/	
toaster	/tostɚ/	/to$stɚ/	
sister	/sɪstɚ/	/sɪ$stɚ/	/sɪs$tɚ/
inscribe	/ɪnskraɪb/	/ɪ$nskraɪb/	/ɪn$skraɪb/

The first two syllabify simply by assigning open syllables. *Sister* must have a closed first syllable because /ɪ/ is stressed, and *inscribe* must have a closed first syllable because */nskr/ is not a permissible initial sequence in English.

Exercise 8

Syllabify the following words according to the principles discussed above: *person, mainstay, syllable, plaintiff, explain, broadloom.* Show the steps you used to arrive at your solutions.

The syllabification of some English words according to these criteria will still be indeterminate. For example, syllabifying *examine* /ɛgzæmɪn/ provides, first, /ɛ$gzæmɪn/, then, getting rid of the */gz/ sequence, /ɛg$zæmɪn/. But it still retains the stressed, lax vowel /æ/ in an open syllable, which is unacceptable. If we use the /m/ to close the second syllable, we leave the final syllable without an onset /ɛgzæm$ɪn/, which is also unacceptable. The simplest way to avoid this difficulty is to assign /m/ to both syllables simultaneously, which we indicate by a raised syllable boundary symbol:

$$\text{/ɛg\$zæm}^{\$}\text{ɪn/}$$

Exercise 9

The following are some words as spoken by a two-and-a-half-year-old child. What do they tell you about the structure of syllables for this child? That is, what permissible syllable structure does her grammar have, and which sequences of consonants are permissible within those syllables?

Exercise 9 continued

[twa]	'straw'	[no]	'snow'
[glæs]	'glass'	[slip]	'sleep'
[tap]	'stop'	[blæki]	'Blacky' (her dog)
[tap]	'top'	[bwaɪn]	'Brian'
[twen]	'train'	[pʊn]	'spoon'
[kaɪ]	'sky'	[twit]	'street'

NOTES

1. The asterisk is used here to indicate a non-permissible form. This is a traditional convention for *, although it is more commonly used in grammatical than phonological descriptions.
2. Although we have discussed sequential constraints in terms of basic lexical forms or morphemes, it appears that the syllable rather than the morpheme should be considered the basic unit for describing such sequences.
3. The word *sclerosis* (/skl/) also occurs, but this is a restricted importation from Greek, much like the /ʃm/ cited above. Therefore, we do not consider /skl/ a productive English cluster.

SUGGESTED READING

A more complete discussion of the role of speech errors in substantiating linguistic hypotheses can be found in Fromkin's *Speech Errors as Linguistic Evidence* (1973). She and other authors provide evidence that supports not only claims about phonotactics but also the existence of distinctive features, the reality of phonological rules, and the reality of segmentation.

Chomsky and Halle (1968), Stanley (1967), and Hyman (1975) all discuss in detail the theoretical basis for morpheme structure conditions. Stanley's paper "Redundancy Rules in Phonology" is particularly useful reading for people who intend to study more phonology. Harms (1968) is useful for understanding the specialized formalisms that often appear in studies of phonotactics and phonology. Detailed analyses of English phonotactics may be found in Trager and Smith's *Outline of English Structure* (1951), and in Trnka's *Phonological Analysis of Present Day Standard English* (1966). Rockey's *Phonetic Lexicon* (1973) provides tables of English words organized by sequential combinations, and is useful for compiling lists to exemplify English phonotactic restrictions. Her organization is based largely on British pronunciation, however, so it should be used carefully when making claims about American English.

Abercrombie's *Elements of General Phonetics* (1967) provides a clear and thorough discussion of syllable phonetics and airstream mechanisms. A more technical discussion appears in Stetson, *Motor Phonetics* (1951). The clearest discussions of the syllable from a phonological perspective are in Hyman (1975) and Pulgram (1970). More recently, the range of issues concerning the syllable has been discussed in Bell and Hooper, *Syllable and Segments* (1978). Arguments in favor of using the syllable rather than the morpheme as the basis of phonotactics may be found in Vennemann (1972) and Hooper (1972).

CHAPTER 6
Phonological Processes

Phonology is not a static system in which an established unit remains unchanged in all its occurrences. Rather, it is a dynamic system in which units change as they come into contact with other units in the system. We refer to such changes as **phonological processes**. The examination of a phonological system at a given point in time will reveal many such processes. Although our concern here is not with the historical dimensions of a language system, we will show later that the operation of various phonological processes through time changes the shape of the language in many ways.

As explained in Chapter 3, there is a universal principle that applies to all sound systems, namely, that sound units tend to be influenced by their environment. "Environment" as used here refers specifically to the influence of neighboring units–the position in which a sound occurs in larger units such as a syllable, morpheme, or word, and the occurrence of certain suprasegmental units such as stress and intonation. In this chapter, we are most concerned with the various changes that take place when certain sound sequences are juxtaposed through the combination of morphemes into words, and words into sentences.

Ultimately, the modification of sounds seems to follow natural principles related to physiological and psychological strategies. Some phonological processes may be explained as muscle coordination within the vocal mechanism. Others may be due to perceptual strategies that enhance effective communication. The understanding of these natural principles is one of the areas phonologists are most actively pursuing at this time as they attempt to explain the nature of phonological systems. We shall return to them in Chapter 9. A number of different processes can be identified in phonological systems. Our examples are primarily from English, but similar illustrations exist in many languages. In several cases, processes not clearly revealed in English are illustrated from other languages.

Assimilation

One of the most common types of processes found in language is **assimilation**, in which a sound takes on the characteristics of a neighboring sound. From the perspective of a feature analysis, we observe that various features of a sound become identical to that of a neighboring sound. There are two necessary components that define assimilation: first, a sound that changes (the **assimilating sound**) and second, the sound that causes the change (the **conditioning sound**).

In terms of the traditional classification of phonological changes, one of the ways in which a sound may assimilate relates to the **place of articulation** of a neighboring sound. A sound may change to take on the position of a preceding or following sound. One of the most widely cited cases of assimilation to the place of articulation in English is the negative prefix:

[ɪndərɛ́kt]	'indirect'
[ɪndɪ́gnɪti]	'indignity'
[ɪ́mpətɪnt]	'impotent'
[ɪmmətšǔr]	'immature'
[ɪŋkənklúsɪv]	'inconclusive'
[ɪŋgrǽtətud]	'ingratitude'

Assuming that the original form of the negative prefix is /ɪn-/, we note that the nasal changes its place of articulation according to the position of the following sound. Thus, the nasal is the assimilated segment, and the first segment of the word base is the conditioning segment. In the case of a following bilabial sound, such as *p* or *m*, the pronunciation of the nasal is *m*. Here the actual phonetic change is represented by a change in the spelling system of English. When the nasal is followed by a velar sound—*g* or *k*—it typically becomes the velar ŋ. In this case, the change is not matched in the spelling, but the speaker simply makes the change automatically because of the phonological context which determines the form of the nasal segment. Do not be thrown off by the orthographic system of English, which does not indicate many of the phonetic forms resulting from the operation of various phonological processes.

A sound may also take on the **manner of articulation** from an adjacent sound. When we looked in Chapter 4 at how certain plurals were formed in English, we observed the assimilation of the voicing specification from the preceding sound. Recall the /s/ and /z/ forms of the plural as found in the following examples:

[kæts]	'cats'
[tæps]	'taps'
[pæks]	'packs'
[kæbz]	'cabs'
[lɪdz]	'lids'
[tægz]	'tags'

The list illustrates that the voicing of the plural suffix is dependent on the voicing of the preceding segment. This aspect of plural formation is but one part of a more general rule for suffix formation in English. In this rule, the initial consonant in a suffix matches the voicing specification of the final consonant of the base. This rule also applies to the regular past tense suffix in English, spelled -*ed*. The process accounts for the /t/ or /d/ forms in:

[pɪkt]	'picked'
[ræpt]	'rapped'
[pæst]	'passed'
[brægd]	'bragged'
[ræzd]	'razzed'
[rɪbd]	'ribbed'

In these cases, the voiceless stop is used when the preceding segment is voiceless, and the voiced stop when the preceding segment is voiced. The conditioning factor for the process is obviously the voicing specification of the preceding segment. Assimilation processes such as these reflect a physiological principle in which the phonetic distance of successive sound segments is minimized.

Regular assimilation processes such as those given above are productive. That is, they are highly predictable and automatically applied by native speakers. On the basis of such productive processes, we may predict how a native speaker of English would add suffixes to new items. Given some nonsense verb forms such as *blick, blag, fup,* or *feb,* and nonsense noun forms like *wuck, wug, stap,* or *weeb,* we would expect the past tense and plural forms of these items to be as follows:

[blɪkt]	'blicked'
[blægd]	'blagged'
[fʌpt]	'fupped'
[fɛbd]	'febbed'
[wʌks]	'wucks'
[wʌgz]	'wugs'
[stæps]	'staps'
[wibz]	'weebs'

The occurrence of these forms demonstrates that the operation of the assimilation process is a regular part of the English sound system.

Exercise 1

Invent nine nonsense nouns like those given above. Three should end with voiceless, non-sibilant sounds, three with voiced, non-sibilant sounds, and three with sibilant sounds. Give the list to an adult, native speaker of English, and explain that each word is the name of a little-known animal. Ask how they would refer to more than one of each animal, and record the responses. Do the responses support the contention that native English speakers apply the assimilation process as described above?

Traditionally, two kinds of assimilation have been distinguished. In progressive assimilation, the assimilated sound follows the conditioning sound. The case of plural and past tense suffixes cited above is an example of progressive assimilation, since the final segment of the word base conditions the form of the following segment. In regressive assimilation, the assimilated segment precedes the conditioning item. The case of the assimilated nasal prefix cited previously is regressive assimilation, since the following segment conditions the shape of the preceding one. The difference between progressive and regressive assimilation may be illustrated as follows:

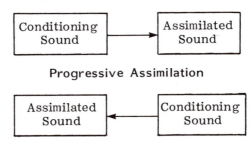

Progressive Assimilation

Regressive Assimilation

Most commonly, assimilation takes place when the conditioning sound and the assimilated sound are immediately adjacent, as in all the examples given above. Sometimes, however, a sound may condition assimilation in a non-adjacent sound. Although such cases have been observed for both consonantal and vowel segments, it is more common for the vowel of one syllable to take on the quality of a vowel in another syllable. Vowel assimilation in different syllables is typically referred to as **vowel harmony**. One of the most commonly cited cases of vowel harmony is found in Turkish, where the vowel of a suffix takes on some of the characteristics of the vowel in the preceding syllable. For example, when the vowel in the base form is a back vowel, the vowel of the plural suffix is /a/:

/ok/	'arrow'	/oklar/	'arrows'
/pul/	'postage stamp'	/pullar/	'postage stamps'
/baš/	'head'	/bašlar/	'heads'

If the vowel of the base form is a front unrounded vowel, the vowel of the plural suffix is /e/:

/iz/	'footprint'	/izler/	'footprints'
/el/	'hand'	/eller/	'hands'

One subcategory of vowel harmony is commonly referred to as **umlaut**. Umlaut is a process in which the vowel of the base is fronted before certain suffixes which contain a high front vowel, a specialized case of regressive assimilation. For example, in an early stage of the development of German, the plural suffix *-i* caused back vowels of the base to become front vowels:

/gast/	'guest'	/gɛsti/	'guests'
/fus/	'foot'	/fi̯si/	'feet'

Although the phonetic form of the suffix has changed to *-ə* in modern German, the effect of the umlauting process on the base vowels has been preserved to a large extent: /gɛstə/ 'guests', and /fi̯sə/ 'feet'. Similarly, though umlauting is no longer a productive process in English, there is an indication that certain irregular plurals have resulted historically from this process: *foot/feet*, *goose/geese*, *tooth/teeth*, and *mouse/mice*. At one point in the development of the English language, there was an *-i* plural suffix which caused the vowel in the base word to take on the fronting characteristics of the suffix vowel. In time, however, the *-i* plural form was lost, so that the vowel change itself remains as the sole indicator of plurality.

Consonant harmony, a process not found in adult English phonological systems, occurs quite frequently in the phonologies of young children acquiring English. Children who pronounce *dog* as [gɔg], *yellow* as [lɛlo], or *sun* as [nʌn] do so because the initial consonant is changed to the form of the following consonant. This is a type of non-contiguous regressive consonant assimilation.

Assimilation involves the change of phonological features rather than the change of an entire segment. When a sound assimilates to another one, a range of resulting sounds is possible, depending on which and how many features assimilate. Consider some of the ways in which an *n* might assimilate to the conditioning environment of a *p*.

Original Segment	*Conditioning Segment*	*Assimilated Segment*

$\begin{bmatrix} +\text{voiced} \\ +\text{coronal} \\ +\text{nasal} \\ +\text{delayed} \\ \text{release} \end{bmatrix}$	$\begin{bmatrix} -\text{voiced} \\ -\text{coronal} \\ -\text{nasal} \\ -\text{delayed} \\ \text{release} \end{bmatrix}$

Original Segment	Conditioning Segment	Assimilated Segment
n	p	ŋ [-vd]
n	p	m [-cor]
n	p	d [-nas] [-d.r.]
n	p	ɱ [-vd] [-cor]
n	p	t [-vd] [-nas] [-d.r.]
n	p	p [-vd] [-nas] [-cor] [-d.r.]

In the first two cases, only one feature is assimilated. In the next two cases, two features are assimilated. While this results in a closer approximation to the conditioning segment, the assimilation is still only partial. For /t/ to occur, three features must be changed. The final case shows four assimilated features, and assimilation is complete.

When an assimilation process results in contiguous identical consonants, it is called gemination. There are a number of cases of gemination in English which typically take place in more casual and rapid speech styles (the style of speech in which phonological processes are most numerous). Some of these are fairly well known, as in /gɪmmi/ for *give me* and /lɛmmi/ for *let me*. Other cases are not as well known, but can be observed with careful attention to more rapid speech styles. There is an interesting case of gemination in English in which alveolar stops may assimilate to a following labial or velar stop. This process can occur across words when the words occur within the same phonological phrase, resulting in items such as /gʊbbaɪ/ for *good bye*, /raɪppɔr/ for *right poor*, /raɪkkɔrnə/ for *right corner*, and /bæggɛs/ for *bad guess*. As we shall see in our discussion of coalescence, there are many cases of gemination which are subsequently reduced to a single segment (e.g. /lɛmmi/ to /lɛmi/, or /gʊbbaɪ/ to /gʊbaɪ/). Once assimilation has resulted in geminate forms, such reductions are to be expected.

Exercise 2

For the following examples of assimilation, indicate the significant feature or features involved in the change. Show the relevant features of the original segment, the conditioning segment, and the assimilated segment. Use the distinctive features discussed in Chapter 4 as the basis for your answers.

1. *s* becomes *z*, conditioned by *g*
2. *f* becomes *p*, conditioned by *m*
3. *k* becomes *t* , conditioned by *n*
4. *i* becomes *e* , conditioned by *æ*
5. *i* becomes *u*, conditioned by *o*
6. *v* becomes *m*, conditioned by *m*
7. *z* becomes *t* , conditioned by *k*
8. *t* becomes *p*, conditioned by *p*
9. *θ* becomes *s* , conditioned by *s*
10. *s* becomes *š*, conditioned by *i*
11. *d* becomes *ǰ* , conditioned by *y*
12. *f* becomes *z* , conditioned by *z*

All of the types of assimilation discussed so far involve the effect of consonants on other consonants or vowels on other vowels. However, vowels may also condition consonants and vice versa. For example, in everyday

American English, it is common for a final alveolar stop to assimilate to an initial high front vowel /i/ or glide /y/ of the following word. Thus, it is not unusual to hear *meet you* as /mičyə/, *what are you doing* as /wəčyəduɪn/, *got you* as /gačyə/, and *did you* as /dɪǰyə/. Assimilation processes in which a consonant sound takes on the qualities of a high front vowel or glide are typically referred to as **palatalization**. There are a number of ways in which vowels may assimilate to consonants. One of the most common involves the assimilation of a vowel with a neighboring nasal consonant, a process known as **nasalization**. We explained in Chapter 2 that English vowels are often nasalized before nasal consonants: [bǽnd] 'band', [mɛ̃nd] 'mend'. Vowels in other languages may assimilate other features of consonants, such as backing and fronting or even voicelessness.

The fact that we can identify a number of different subclasses attests to the widespread nature of assimilation as a process in phonological systems. There are other subtypes which we might have added, but it is sufficient here to observe how frequently this phenomenon occurs.

Exercise 3

Using distinctive feature specifications, explain why palatalization is an example of assimilation. What features seem to be particularly crucial in accounting for this assimilation?

Dissimilation

Whereas assimilation refers to the process in which segments take on the character of neighboring segments, **dissimilation** refers to the process in which segments change to become less like a neighboring segment. On the whole, dissimilation is much rarer than assimilation, although there are some well-known instances, such as the "deaspiration" of stops in ancient Greek. In this case, when two aspirated stops (e.g. /tʰ/ and /kʰ/) stand in initial position in successive syllables, then the first one is dissimilated to an unaspirated stop. Thus, the aspirated /tʰ/ in /tʰriks/ 'hair' (nominative) becomes unaspirated /t/ when the following syllable begins with aspirated /kʰ/: /trikʰos/ 'hair' (genitive).

There are several cases of words which have apparently developed into their current form through dissimilation. The word *pilgrim* is sometimes cited as a case of dissimilation. It was derived from the Latin form *peregrius* by changing the first *r* to *l*. Similarly, in non-mainstream varieties where *chimley* corresponds to the standard form *chimney*, the change from *n* to the non-nasal *l* may also be viewed as a dissimilation. In some varieties of English, the deletion of *r* may be accounted for in terms of a dissimilation process. Cases such as *suprise* for *surprise*, *libary* for *library*, and *govenor* for *governor* involve a deletion of *r* in one syllable because an *r* is present in the following syllable. For the most part, however, cases such as these are relatively isolated and do not appear to be productive in English.

Neutralization

Particular processes that result in the cancellation of contrasts between phonological units are often described by the term **neutralization**. That is, two or more units that ordinarily contrast lose that contrast in certain environments. Normally, the process changes the form of one unit to that of the other, as represented below.

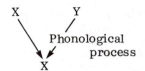

Contrasting phonological units

Phonological
process

Surface phonetic form

One of the most commonly cited cases of neutralization is that of word-final
stops in German. In initial and medial word positions, German maintains a
contrast between /p/ and /b/, /t/ and /d/, and /k/ and /g/. In word-final
position, however, only the voiceless stop occurs, e.g.: [dibə] 'thieves' and
[dip] 'thief'; [todə] 'deaths' and [tot] 'death'; [tagə] 'days' and [tak] 'day'.
The phonological process whereby voiced segments become voiceless is referred
to as **devoicing**. The neutralization resulting from this devoicing process is
shown below.

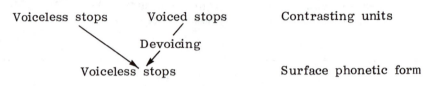

Voiceless stops   Voiced stops   Contrasting units

Devoicing

Voiceless stops   Surface phonetic form

Exercise 4

Standard English does not have a devoicing process like the one in German.
There are, however, some non-mainstream varieties that reveal a limited devoicing process. Based on the following examples, give the conditions under
which *d* is devoiced to *t*. Phonetically, the *t* may be a glottal stop [ʔ] or
unreleased [t˺].

1.	[sǽlɪt]	'salad'	8.	[bæts]	'bats'
2.	[sǽlɪdz]	'salads'	9.	[rǽbɪt]	'rabbit'
3.	[bɛd]	'bed'	10.	[rǽbɪts]	'rabbits'
4.	[bɛdz]	'beds'	11.	[bæd]	'bad'
5.	[stúpɪt]	'stupid'	12.	[bǽdnɪs]	'badness'
6.	[stúpɪdnɪs]	'stupidness'	13.	[rǽpɪt]	'rapid'
7.	[bæt]	'bat'	14.	[rǽpɪdz]	'rapids'

In English, a great deal of neutralization is found in the vowel system,
where a number of different vowels take on a schwa-like quality in an unstressed syllable. In *telegraph* and *photograph*, the first syllable receives
primary stress, the second syllable is unstressed, and the third syllable receives secondary stress. These items are usually pronounced something like
[téləgræ̀f] and [fótəgræ̀f], with a schwa-like vowel in the unstressed syllable.
But if we add a -*y* suffix, changing the stress pattern, we get something like
[təlɛ́grəfì] and [fətágrəfì]. Note that the first and third syllables are now
relatively unstressed; consequently /ɛ/, /æ/, and /o/ are reduced to schwa.
Although there are elaborate rules for assigning stress in English words, the
important point to note here is the systematic process of **vowel reduction** in
which vowels in unstressed syllables may become a schwa. The vowels will
automatically be neutralized according to the stress patterns, despite the
different vowels that are produced when they occur in a stressed syllable.
    Other types of neutralization between vowel contrasts in English may be
peculiar to specific regional and social varieties. We have already mentioned
that the contrast between /ɪ/ and /ɛ/ may be neutralized before nasals in
some Southern varieties. Similarly, in some varieties the contrast between
/ɛ/ and /æ/ may be neutralized before *r*. Thus, items such as *merry* and

---

Exercise 5

For each underlined schwa-like vowel in the words below, determine what contrastive vowel has been reduced. Examine a related word in which the stress pattern shifts in order to find the vowel. For example, *telegraphy* contains two such schwas: /tə/ and /grəf/. The related word *telegraph* [tέləgræf] demonstrates that the unreduced form of the first schwa is ε, and that of the second is æ.

1.	telegraphic	6.	preparation
2.	imposition	7.	pornographic
3.	beautiful	8.	revelation
4.	contrastive	9.	indicative
5.	relative	10.	regalia

---

marry, or *berry* and *Barry*, may be produced identically. In other environments, these vowel differences will be retained (*bet, bat*), since the neutralization is restricted to the phonological context of following *r*.

Neutralization seems somewhat different from other processes discussed in this chapter. It is a more general designation that technically might be used for any instance in which a contrast between units is cancelled. Thus, assimilation might be considered an instance of neutralization if it resulted in the elimination of a contrast in a particular phonological environment. Nonetheless, there remain processes cancelling out contrasts which are not covered by other designations, so neutralization can usefully cover these cases. (Note: some phonologists prefer not to use this term for phonological processes.)

Deletion

In the phonological process of **deletion**, units which occur in some contexts are lost in others. In many cases, deletion processes change the syllable structure of a word, thereby creating preferred types of syllable patterns. For example, deletion processes may break up clusters of consonants or vowels in order to arrive at the more universally preferred CV pattern. Thus, if we look at the alternation of the indefinite article forms *a* and *an*, we note the article *a* occurs before items beginning with a consonant and *an* before items beginning with a vowel (*a pear* versus *an apple*). This distribution prevents the occurrence of *CC* and *VV* sequences. If we posit *an* as the basic form, we can explain the distribution through the deletion of the *n*.

Another widely recognized case of deletion in English involves "contracted" forms such as *He's made it, He'd fallen,* and *He'd come,* from *He has made it, He had fallen,* and *He would come.* In certain relatively unstressed contexts, the initial /h/ and /w/ of auxiliaries (*have, had, will, would*) are deleted. Then, in a second deletion process, the vowel nucleus is also eliminated. This second deletion applies also to the vowels of *is* and *are* in contracted forms, resulting in forms like *He's ugly* and *You're ugly*.

There are many other deletion processes in English. Some of these are readily noticeable; others are simply forms that we automatically apply but may not be aware of until they are pointed out. Consider the following forms as they might be pronounced in casual conversation by many speakers of standard English.

[wεs saɪd]	'west side'
[wεst εnd]	'west end'
[blaɪn mæn]	'blind man'

　　　　　　　　[bla^{I}nd a^I] 　'blind eye'
　　　　　　　　[wa^{I}l gus] 　'wild goose'
　　　　　　　　[wa^{I}ld ɛnd] 　'wild end'

In these examples of **cluster reduction**, the final segment of a word-final consonant cluster is deleted when the following word begins with a consonant. If the following word begins with a vowel, however, this process usually does not apply. The effect of the process is that the number of successive consonants is reduced from three to two. This change makes the consonant sequences more compatible with preferred types of syllable sequences in English. Deletion processes of this type are relatively common in casual styles.

Exercise 6

Based on the following examples, identify the class(es) of final segments that can undergo the cluster reduction process discussed above.

1.	[wɛs]	'west'	9.	[bʌlǰ]	'bulge'
2.	[lats]	'lots'	10.	[wɪn]	'wind'
3.	[dɛs]	'desk'	11.	[lʌnč]	'lunch'
4.	[faks]	'fox'	12.	[sɛns]	'sense'
5.	[was]	'wasp'	13.	[la^{U}nǰ]	'lounge'
6.	[læps]	'lapse'	14.	[rɛs]	'rest'
7.	[æk]	'act'	15.	[baks]	'box'
8.	[wa^{I}l]	'wild'			

To show that a deletion process takes place, it is first necessary to demonstrate that the deleted sound actually occurs in some context. There are some types of deletion processes proposed for English which may not be recognized as easily as those above, since their recognition is dependent on understanding the relationship between certain pairs of words. In these cases, comparing two lexical items suggests that a deletion process has operated on one of the items. For example, consider the relationship between these forms:

　　　　[sa^{I}n] 　'sign' 　　　　　　　[sɪgnətšur] 　'signature'
　　　　[rɪza^{I}n] 　'resign' 　　　　　　[rɛzɪgnešən] 　'resignation'

If these pairs are related in the lexicon of English, then we observe that *g* occurs when a suffix like *-ature* or *-ation* is added. Without these suffixes, however, the *g* is not pronounced. If we propose that *g* actually exists in an item like *sign*, then it must be deleted when these types of suffixes are not added.

There are a number of more specific subtypes of deletion processes, one of which is **haplology**. In haplology, an entire syllable is lost when it is identical to another syllable. One example sometimes identified in English as haplology applies to adjectives ending in *-ly*, such as *lively* or *friendly* (*He is is a lively/friendly person*). When these are used as adverbs, the addition of the normal adverbial suffix *-ly* (e.g. *nice/nicely*) results in two identical syllables, *-lyly*. One of these is deleted, however, for we do not use adverbial forms such as *livelyly* but would rather say *He stepped lively*. Another case of haplology occurs in some non-mainstream varieties of English, when *-ing* is added to a verb that ends in an unstressed *-n*, such as *listen* and *open*. If casual pronunciation of the *-ing* /ɪn/ occurs, the verb ends in two syllables that are identical ([lísɪnɪn], [ópɪnɪn]). In these varieties we might get *He was listen'* [lísɪn] *to it,* or *He is open'* [opɪn] *the can.* Haplology is a process that causes two identical syllables to become different, in the sense that one remains intact while the other is lost, so the process is sometimes classified as a specialized type of dissimilation.

There are also several processes referring to the deletion of a vowel or a syllable when it is unstressed. **Aphesis** refers to the loss of an unstressed initial vowel or syllable. **Syncope** is the loss of a medial vowel or syllable, and **apocope** the loss of a final vowel or syllable. Aphesis is a relatively common phenomenon in casual styles of English, accounting for items such as *'bout* for *about,* *'round* for *around,* and *'cause* for *because.* In standard varieties, it is most common in unstressed syllables of prepositions, conjunctions, and adverbs. In some non-mainstream varieties of English, aphesis can be extended to other word classes, accounting for *'lectrician, 'tato, 'member,* and *'posta* for *electrician, potato, remember,* and *supposed to.*

Syncope is observed quite often in the casual style of English speakers when the medial syllable of polysyllabic words is unstressed, as in *choc'late, ev'ning, batt'ry,* and *ev'ry.* This kind of syncope is fairly productive in American English. On the other hand, apocope is not a particularly productive process in the English language at present, although it was active in earlier stages of its development. Derivation of *sing* from Old English *singan* or *find* from *finde* results from apocope. In some languages apocope is a fully productive phonological process.

As suggested above, there are many different deletion processes that have taken part in the historical development of the English language, particularly affecting segments which occur in relatively unstressed syllables. Deletion as a process is much more likely to occur in unstressed than in stressed syllables, although it is not necessarily restricted to this environment. A number of the dialect differences currently found in English can be traced to a deletion process that operates in one variety but has not yet spread to another. At one point in the history of English, there was an initial *h* in some pronouns (*hit* for present-day *it*), and certain auxiliaries (*hain't* for present-day *ain't*). In some varieties of English, this *h* is deleted. Those varieties which still have the *h* (Appalachian English, for example) simply do not apply this process.

Coalescence

In a specialized process which involves both assimilation and deletion, two or more segments can be replaced by one segment that shares characteristics of each of the original segments. A typical case of such **coalescence** in English is found in the attachment of the *-ion* suffix. Consider the following pairs:

Base form		Base with *-ion* suffix	
[rəbέl]	'rebel'	[rəbέlyən]	'rebellion'
[domén]	'domain'	[dəmínyən]	'dominion'
[dέmənstrèt]	'demonstrate'	[dὲmənstréšən]	'demonstration'
[ɛród]	'erode'	[əróžən]	'erosion'
[kənfέs]	'confess'	[kənfέšən]	'confession'
[kənfyúz]	'confuse'	[kənfyúžən]	'confusion'

The first two examples in this list end in *l* and *n*, and the suffix contains the palatal segment *y*; the form of the suffix is [yən]. But when this suffix is added to items ending in *t, d, s,* or *z,* the final segment combines with the *y* to form an alveopalatal sibilant. Thus, /t/ + /y/ and /s/ + /y/ become /š/, and /d/ + /y/ and /z/ + /y/ become /ž/. In these cases, some features from each segment combine, resulting in a segment different from both. From our viewpoint, this is interpreted most realistically as the result of two processes.

The palatalization process we described above operates first, resulting in the alveopalatal /š/ or /ž/. This produces sequences such as /šy/ and /žy/. Then, /y/ is deleted, leaving simply /š/ and /ž/. In effect, then, coalescence is a process of both assimilation and deletion.

A different sort of coalescence involves reduction of geminate consonants (degemination). In one such case, the assimilation of the negative prefix *in-* to the bases *legal* and *responsible* results in geminate consonants: *illegal* and *irresponsible*. In normal usage one of these consonants is deleted, so that only a single segment is produced. Similarly, in the form *useta* [yustə], the original /zd/ of *used* [yuzd] assimilates the voicelessness of the following /t/ of *to*. This results in geminate *t*'s [yusttə] which may then be coalesced into one segment. This process is fairly common in some languages, especially in more casual speech styles where it is quite difficult to maintain distinctiveness between identical contiguous segments.

Epenthesis

Inserting a sound segment into a form is called epenthesis. Although it seems to occur less frequently than deletion, epenthesis is by no means uncommon as a phonological process. Both vowels and consonants may be inserted in epenthetic processes. One process often considered to be epenthetic involves plural forms in English. In our discussion above, we noted that two different realizations of the regular plural /s/ and /z/ were dependent on the voicing specification of the previous sound segment. We have also seen that a third form of the plural occurs after sibilants ([bʌsɪz] 'buses', [dɪšɪz] 'dishes', [ǰʌǰɪz] 'judges'). The vowel of /ɪz/ in these examples is inserted between sibilants. From the standpoint of perception, this insertion is understandable since the addition of /s/ or /z/ to an item already ending in a sibilant would result in a doubled or lengthened segment. This might be difficult to perceive as a plural form (e.g. [rozz] 'roses', or [bʌss] 'buses'). Adding the vowel makes the plural formation easier to perceive.

The insertion of the vowel in plurals is actually part of a more general process which applies when the first consonant of a suffix is similar to the one in which the base form ends. Thus, we find a similar kind of epenthesis with the regular past tense. The consonants involved are different, but the general principle is the same: [wetɪd] 'waited', [redɪd] 'raided', [plæntɪd] 'planted', [maɪndɪd] 'minded'. If the base form ends in /t/ or /d/, then the vowel will be inserted to keep two alveolar stops from occurring next to each other.

Another instance of epenthesis concerns the automatic insertion of voiceless stops. The [p] which sometimes occurs in items like *attempt* [ətɛmpt] and *comfort* [kʌmpfət] results from a process which inserts a voiceless stop following a nasal and preceding another voiceless consonant. The same epenthetic process accounts for some English speakers' production of *since* as [sɪnts] and *tense* as [tɛnts]. The epenthetic stop matches the place of articulation of the nasal. Similarly, the insertion of a *b* between *m* and *l* seems to be a reasonable way to account for the nonstandard English pronunciations of *family* and *chimney* as *fambly* and *chimbly*. An epenthetic process may also be used to account for the presence of a schwa ə before an *l* in certain contexts: [æ̀θəlɛ́tɪk] for *athletic,* [bəlo] for *blow.*

Sometimes a particular formation seems describable as either an epenthetic or a deletion process. The possible alternatives depend on the interpretation of the base form of the word. Some interpretations of the plural formation of English start with a vowel in the base form (/ɪz/), then simply delete the vowel. Our interpretation posits a base form without the vowel, which is inserted through an epenthetic process. In Chapter 7, we will present arguments for choosing between these interpretations.

Metathesis

Processes such as deletion and epenthesis may result in the redistribution of consonants and vowels. It is also possible to change the linear order of segments by permutations of one type or another. When two segments reverse positions, the process is known as **metathesis**. Pronouncing *ask* as *aks* (in some nonmainstream varieties) represents the remnants of this process. We know that, historically, the older form contained the sequence *aks*. This means that the metathesis originally took place among speakers of standard English varieties when the form changed to *ask*. In some varieties of English, the following examples of *r* plus a vowel are interpreted as metathesis:

[prɪskraɪb]	or	[pɪrskraɪb]	'prescribe'
[hʌndrɪd]	or	[hʌndɪrd]	'hundred'
[prɪzɪrv]	or	[pɪrzɪrv]	'preserve'
[prənaᵘns]	or	[pɪrnaᵘns]	'pronounce'

All these examples concern the metathesis of contiguous segments. However, it is possible to observe metathesis in which the order of non-contiguous elements is involved, such as the pronunciation of *relevant* and *irrelevant* as *revelant* and *irrevelant*. Many of the spoonerisms we discussed in Chapter 5 involved metathesis of segments from different words. Although the permutation of elements is quite common in the grammatical system of English (e.g. *He put the garbage out* or *He put out the garbage*), it is much more restricted in the phonological system. Metathesis is fairly well documented as a process accounting for changes in the historical development of languages, but some linguists do not consider it to be a legitimate, productive phonological process.

Exercise 7

Label the phonological processes which account for the types of changes indicated below. Be sure to give the specific subcategory (e.g. particular type of assimilation) of a process where appropriate.

1. *s* becomes *z* when followed by voiced sound
2. *k* is added when preceded by a nasal and followed by *s*
3. the vowel ɪ is inserted between two sibilants
4. *i, ɪ, u,* and ʊ become ə in unstressed syllables
5. *ps* becomes *sp* at the end of the word
6. *t* becomes *p* when the following sound is *p*
7. *o* becomes *u* when *i* occurs in the preceding syllable
8. ɪr is lost when the preceding syllable is ɪr
9. *r* becomes *l* when *l* occurs in the next syllable
10. *t* becomes *s* when followed by *s*
11. *t* and *ts* are both produced as *tš* when the following sound is *i*
12. *d* is not produced when it is followed by *z*
13. ə is lost when it is in unstressed word-initial position
14. *t* becomes *k* when following an *s*
15. *t* and *p* become *p* when preceding a *p*
16. word-final ə is lost when in an unstressed syllable
17. ʊ becomes *i* when followed by a syllable containing *i*
18. *d* becomes ž when followed by an *i*
19. word-medial ə in an unstressed syllable is lost
20. *b* becomes *p* when preceded by a voiceless sound
21. *d* and *y* in a sequence become ž

Exercise 7 continued

22. *l* becomes ʊ when following a vowel
23. *tk* becomes *kt* at the end of a word
24. *t* and *d* are both produced as *t* at the end of a word
25. *o* becomes *i* when an *i* occurs in the following syllable
26. *t* is inserted when preceded by *n* and followed by *s*
27. *s* becomes *z* between vowels
28. θ becomes *s* when followed by *s*

Exercise 8

Based on a comparison of the English items given in Columns *A* and *B* below, label the process which may account for the form of the item in *B* when compared with that in *A*. As with Exercise 7, be sure to label the specific subcategory of the process where appropriate. For the purpose of this exercise, we are assuming that the items in *A* are the base forms.

	A	*B*	
1.	[bɛst kæt]	[bɛs kæt]	'best cat'
2.	[əraʊnd]	[raʊnd]	'around'
3.	[prɪzm̩]	[prɪzəm]	'prism'
4.	[gat yə]	[gatšə]	'got you'
5.	[prabəbli]	[prabli]	'probably'
6.	[sɛkrətɛri]	[sɛkɨrtɛri]	'secretary'
7.	[sɛkrətɛri]	[sɛktɛri]	'secretary'
8.	[ɛləvet]	[ɛvəlet]	'elevate'
9.	[laɪbrɛri]	[laɪbɛri]	'library'
10.	[æn ðɛn]	[æn nɛn]	'and then'
11.	[strɛŋgθ]	[strɛŋkθ]	'strength'
12.	[kʌmfət]	[kʌmpfət]	'comfort'
13.	[grændpa]	[græmpa]	'grandpa'
14.	[grændma]	[græma]	'grandma'
15.	[hævtu]	[hæftə]	'have to'
16.	[tuθ]	[tuf]	'tooth'
17.	[maʊθ šʌt]	[maʊ šʌt]	'mouth shut'
18.	[stupɪd]	[stupɪt]	'stupid'
19.	[kɛnt]	[kɛ̃t]	'Kent'
20.	[ætɪtud]	[ætətud]	'attitude'

SUGGESTED READING

Most introductory textbooks in descriptive linguistics contain a section in which the processes discussed above are presented. Since many of these accounts are more illustrative than complete, it is advisable to look at several different texts, such as Francis' *The Structure of American English* (1958), Lehmann's *Descriptive Linguistics* (1976), and Gleason's *An Introduction to Descriptive Linguistics* (1961). More complete accounts are given in Schane's *Generative Phonology* (1973), Sloat, Taylor, and Hoard's *Introduction to Phonology* (1978), and Kenstowicz and Kisseberth's *Topics in Phonological Theory* (1977). Remember that the author's theoretical orientation may influence the delimitation of various processes. The first three references cited present more of a traditional explanation of phonological processes. Compare carefully the traditional approaches to these processes with those set forth from a generative point of view. Chomsky and Halle's *The Sound Pattern of English* (1968) gives the most complete account of the processes as applied to English words – although this is not easy reading for the beginning student.

CHAPTER 7
The Systematic Phoneme

We have seen that the phoneme as a unit of contrast has practical usefulness in phonological analysis. It has become increasingly apparent, however, that the classical phoneme as presented in Chapter 3 is inadequate to account for many of the phenomena that we can observe in language. In this chapter, we shall examine several attempts to account in a satisfying way for such phenomena.

As the concept of the phoneme was presented earlier, the most important aspect of phonological analysis was the assignment of the phones of a language to phonemic units. This categorization was based strictly on contrasts and complementarity observable in the phonetic record. Underlying this approach was the assumption that all significant phonological information about an utterance is directly observable in the phonetic form of that utterance. More precisely, our approach there assumed that (1) all phonemic contrasts would be observable as phonetic contrasts in identical or analogous environments, and (2) that adequate phonemic analysis could be achieved without reference to the grammatical information provided by the morphology and syntax of a language. Because of these characteristic assumptions, this approach to phonology has become known as **taxonomic phonemics**, referring to its emphasis on the segmentation and classification of observable phonetic contrasts into phonemes. Another label is **autonomous phonemics**, emphasizing the independence of phonology from other levels of a language system such as morphology and syntax.

Grammatical Information in Phonemic Analysis

In actuality, numbers of languages exhibit patterns which appear to violate one or the other of the assumptions mentioned above. Patterns of stress assignment in certain English words, such as those presented in Exercise 1 below, depend to some extent on information about the grammatical category of the word. While such violations have been tacitly recognized for years, until recently there have been few attempts to bring the theory into conformity with the details found in actual language organization.

Exercise 1

Each of the following written words corresponds to two spoken forms, one with the stress on the first syllable, and the other with the stress on the second syllable. Explain what sort of grammatical information is required to specify which syllable receives the stress in the spoken version of these words. That is, with what grammatical class is stress assigned to the first syllable, and with what class is it assigned to the second syllable?

Exercise 1 continued

1.	project	5.	subject
2.	convert	6.	conduct
3.	affect	7.	pervert
4.	produce	8.	reject

Exercise 1 indicates that grammatical information is sometimes necessary in understanding phonological patterning. These data suggest that two-syllable nouns in English are generally stressed on the first syllable, while two-syllable verbs are generally stressed on the second. Although the situation is much more complex than that, this condition tends to hold for two-syllable noun-verb pairs as well as for many other two-syllable nouns and verbs that are not paired in this way.

The observations above present obvious difficulties for the orientation of autonomous phonemics, because stress cannot be predicted simply on the basis of the phonetic facts. If a phonology is to account for such regularities, it must have access to certain types of grammatical information, such as part of speech. The autonomous approach to phonology would have to claim that the nouns and verbs of the pairs presented above were essentially unrelated and, by extension, that stress in English is phonemic. An alternative to this approach is to incorporate into the grammar the connection between such pairs by setting up one form and assigning stress according to the stress patterns appropriate for nouns and verbs. Thus, we see that a phonology appealing to grammatical information may end up with an analysis considerably different from one that appeals simply to phonetic facts.

Phonemic Neutralization

There are also situations in which languages seem to violate the requirement of phonemic contrasts being directly observable in phonetic forms. In the examples in Chapter 3, this issue did not arise, because in each case clearcut surface phonetic facts permitted us to see plausible phonemic categories easily. That is, the allophones of each phoneme were unique to that phoneme. When each sound was examined in terms of its distribution, it was obvious that it could be the member of only one phoneme. To put it another way, the facts of pronunciation—the only data relevant in classical phonemic analysis—had to point uniquely to one phoneme for each sound. [1] And, conversely, each phoneme had to be realized in terms of unique phonetic productions. This one-to-one correspondence between phonemes and allophones has been referred to as the **biuniqueness condition**.

Most languages contain some sets of words in which the divisions are not so easily made. For example, many speakers of American English pronounce the words *rating* and *raiding* identically as [réɾɪŋ]. For these speakers, most cases of intervocalic *t* or *d* before an unstressed syllable will be pronounced as the flap [ɾ], for example, *betting/bedding, letting/leading* (as in stained glass), *rated/raided, writing/riding*. These examples present an interesting predicament for the taxonomic phonemic model, as is illustrated by attempting to assign phonemic status to the forms in Exercise 2.

Exercise 2

Determine the phonemic status of the segments [d], [t], and [ɾ] in the
following corpus. Refer to the exercises in Chapter 3 for the techniques
to do this.

[dɛt]	'debt'	[dɪŋ]	'ding'
[dɛd]	'dead'	[tíŋɫ]	'tingle'
[tæb]	'tab'	[wɛ́ɾɪŋ]	'wetting, wedding'
[dæb]	'dab'	[réɾɪŋ]	'rating, raiding'
[párɾi]	'party'	[bɛ́ɾɪŋ]	'betting, bedding'
[tárɾi]	'tardy'	[hɛ́lɾɚ skɛ́lɾɚ]	'helter skelter'
[lárɾi]	'lardy'	[hárɾi]	'hearty'

   Using the criteria of contrast and complementarity discussed in Chapter 3, it is easy to conclude that there are two phonemes, one of which has
at least two allophones. Clearly, /t/ and /d/ contrast initially and finally.
The segment [ɾ] only occurs following a vowel or liquid (actually, any
[+son] segment) and before an unstressed syllable. It never occurs finally
or initially, and is in complementary distribution with both [t] and [d].
According to our procedures, then, [ɾ] should be assigned to either the
phoneme /d/ or the phoneme /t/. Let us say that because both [d] and
[ɾ] are voiced, we will assign [ɾ] to the phoneme /d/. The distribution
looks something like this:

(after a sonorant,
before unstressed
syllables)

   The difficulty with this solution becomes apparent when we examine the
resulting phonemic representations of some of the words in Exercise 2. For
example, [reɾɪŋ] under our proposed system would always be /redɪŋ/ phonemically. While such forms preserve nicely the integrity of phonemic theory,
they tend to go against our intuitions about our language. In particular,
most of us would contend that although *rating* and *raiding* are pronounced
identically by some people, they must somehow be treated differently. This
is because we know of the words *rate* and *raid*, which are related to the
corresponding forms from the corpus:

raid : *raiding*	*rate* : *rating*
[red] : [reɾɪŋ]	[ret] : [reɾɪŋ]

Our solution above would provide /red/ and /ret/ as the phonemic forms of
raid and *rate*, but only one phonemic form for both *raiding* and *rating*. Our
intuitions about English encourage us to assign the phone [ɾ] in one instance
to /t/ and in the other to /d/. If we do this, we have permitted our phonology to recognize a case of **phonemic neutralization** in which two distinct
phonemes share an identical allophone in identical contexts:

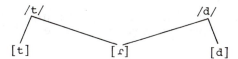

According to the assumptions presented above, this situation is not permissible because there are no surface phonetic indications in forms such as [reɾɪŋ] that tell us where to assign the flap [ɾ]. Thus, either the requirement that phonemic classifications must correspond directly to surface phonetic distinctions does not hold (the biuniqueness condition), or pairs like *rate* and *rating* are considered to come from different forms.

Apparent Phonemic Contrasts

While it may be true, as we claimed above, that some speakers of American English pronounce *raiding* and *rating* identically, many of us distinguish the words phonetically. This observation will allow us to avoid admitting phonemic neutralization, but it may lead to another, equally unsatisfying solution. For some speakers, it is quite common to pronounce *raiding* as [re:ɾɪŋ] and *rating* as [reɾɪŋ] and *bedding* as [bɛ:ɾɪŋ] and *betting* as [bɛɾɪŋ]. Given this new information, we can now use surface phonetic information to predict all instances of [ɾ] in these forms. If [ɾ] is preceded by a lengthened vowel, it is assigned to /d/, but if it follows an unlengthened vowel, it is assigned to /t/. In the cases where a native speaker would expect a /d/, there will be a lengthened vowel, e.g. [bɛ:ɾɪŋ] 'bedding', [bʌ:ɾɪŋ] 'budding'. In fact, the difference in vowel length in these examples can also be observed in the base forms of these verbs: [re:d] 'raid', [ret] 'rate', etc. So it should be possible to say that the phonemic form of *raid* is /re:d/, the form of *rate* is /ret/, and thereby preserve our original requirements that phonemic contrasts be observable in phonetic differences.

The difficulty with this solution is that using vowel length to predict the phonemic status of [ɾ] again violates our intuitions and observations about English, and forces the conclusion that English has a phonemic contrast between lengthened and unlengthened vowels. However, other than the cases we have just described, there are no clear-cut instances in English in which vowel length is the contrastive feature. If vowel length were phonemic, we would expect contrasts in identical or analogous environments in items like [ret]/[re:t] and [red]/[re:d], but they do not exist. Moreover, we may generally predict all occurrences of lengthened vowels in English. The lengthened vowels in the examples above result from a general phonological process that causes stressed vowels to be lengthened before voiced consonants. Thus, we would say that the phonemic /d/ of *raiding* is the context in which the lengthened vowel allophone of /e/ occurs. But it is a circular argument to predict both consonant voicing from vowel length, and vowel length from consonant voicing. We must choose one solution or the other. Because there are strong arguments against a contrast between lengthened and unlengthened vowels elsewhere in the phonology, we must return to the conclusion we reached above: that some basic phonological contrasts are neutralized. Notice also that the vowel lengthening phenomenon may now be used as another argument favoring the inclusion of neutralization in our grammar. It suggests that the phonemic /d/ and /t/ of *raiding* and *rating* have a deeper kind of psychological validity, for in [reɾɪŋ] 'rating', which we would like to claim contains a phonemic /t/, the vowel is not lengthened, even though it precedes a voiced consonant on the surface (namely [ɾ]).

We conclude, then, from this example and others like it that decisions about how to classify segments may not always be made solely on the basis of surface phonetic information. Considerations based on our intuitions about language (that is, native perceptions of language structure not based on deductive arguments) may provide clearer and more satisfying solutions.

Levels of Adequacy in Phonology

Examples like those just discussed were apparent for years, but linguists typically did not see them as serious problems for their basic approach to phonology. Strongly influenced by the school of behaviorism in psychology, classical phonemic analysis concerned itself primarily with the accurate recording of linguistic data and the segmentation and classification of the units of phonology by reference only to surface phonetic information. Bloch (1941: 284) expresses this view: "If we start from the actual utterances of the dialect we can never be in doubt of the class to which any particular fraction of utterance must be assigned." Accordingly, descriptions of phonology from this perspective tended to account only for what was observed. The phoneme was simply a convenient classification category for uniting and separating the phonetic facts of a language.

Chomsky (1964:63) contends that we may ask more of our analyses of language than simply to account for observations. He suggests that there are three levels of adequacy that can be achieved by grammars. Each of these levels represents a different goal for grammatical description, in the sense that the achievement of a given level of adequacy allows linguists to make certain claims about the generality and validity of their theories of grammar. Each successive level of adequacy represents a more powerful claim about our theory of language while implying that the previous level has been achieved. We should strive to achieve the highest level of adequacy possible in the construction of a theory of language.

The first level is **observational adequacy**, which is concerned, as above, with providing an accurate account of the primary data—with segmenting and classifying the directly observable units of a language. Clearly, the achievement of observational adequacy is a minimum requirement for any phonology. We have seen, however, that we may also make some rather strong claims about the "intuitions" of native speakers of a language. For example, we may claim that a particular sound (e.g. [ɾ]) is sometimes the realization of one phonemic unit and at other times the realization of another phonemic unit. We may argue convincingly that native speakers actually perceive the situation in this way. Thus, a native speaker of English will typically classify the [ɾ] of *bedding* as a *d*, and the [ɾ] of *betting* as a *t*, and we may predict that this would happen even if our speaker did not know the spellings of the words. Similarly, we argued above that what appears on the surface to be a contrast in vowel length really is not significant from the point of view of native speakers' implicit knowledge about their language.

A grammar whose goal is to account explicitly for such native intuitions attempts to achieve what Chomsky refers to as **descriptive adequacy**. What this means in practical terms is that we must discover a reasoned way, independent of particular languages, for deciding which of the many possible descriptions of a language represents the knowledge of a native speaker. Put differently, it may be necessary to alter our theory of phonology so that it reflects what we think native speakers know about their language. According to these considerations, it will increase the descriptive adequacy of our grammars if we (a) permit them to include grammatical information, thereby recognizing explicitly the relationship between such words as *permít* and *pérmit*, and (b) allow the neutralization of phonemic distinctions, as discussed above, thereby recognizing explicitly the relationship between words like *rate* and *rating*, which we feel to be part of a speaker's knowledge of English.

The ultimate level of adequacy that grammars may achieve is **explanatory adequacy**. A grammar which achieves this level must be descriptively adequate and provide a basis for explaining the universal capabilities of the human mind and speech mechanism. It answers the "why" question in terms of the underlying psychology and physiology of speech. This level is consistent with the notion that linguistic theory is ultimately a special kind of study of psychology. Capabilities built into the linguistic theory constitute claims about the language control aspects of the human mind and speech mechanism. Within phonology, the issue of explanatory adequacy has recently gained prominence within the subfield of natural phonology. The remainder of this chapter will deal with attempts to increase the descriptive adequacy of our model of phonological descriptions.

Morphology

On various occasions, we have referred to the morpheme as the smallest unit of meaning in a language. By this we mean that the morpheme cannot be broken down into any smaller parts that carry meaning by themselves. The words of a language are often composed of more than one morpheme. The word *impossibilities*, for example, contains four morphemes: the adjective *possible*, the noun marker *-ity*, the negative marker *in-*, and the plural marker *-s*. We may indicate this composition as *in#possible#ity#s* (where # indicates breaks between morphemes). At this point in our discussion, we need to outline several features of **morphology**—the way in which a language builds words from morphemes. Further consideration of phonology will sometimes require knowledge of morphology.

Returning to our example *impossibilities*, notice that only one of the four morphemes present may occur by itself: *possible*. Morphemes which can stand alone as an entire word are called **free morphemes**. Those which cannot occur alone but must attach to another morpheme are **bound morphemes**. The plural marker *-s* is an example of a bound morpheme because it cannot occur alone. Every word has a morpheme that we might consider central to its formation. In the word *impossibilities*, for example, the morpheme *possible* has this basic function. This central component of a word is referred to as the **base** or the **root** of the word. The other morphemes in a word are attached to the base, and so are called **affixes**. When an affix precedes the word base, we refer to it as a **prefix**, and when it follows the base we refer to it as a **suffix**. In our example above, the form *in-* is a prefix, and *-ity* and *-s* are suffixes.

Among the languages of the world, there are several basic strategies for combining morphemes into words. In our examination of English, we will encounter claims about three of these strategies:

(1) **Affixing**, of which we saw an example above.
(2) **Compounding**, in which roots are combined, e.g. *blackbird, Whitehouse, postman, dishwasher.*
(3) Changing vowels, consonants, or suprasegmental aspects of the base, e.g. *write/wrote, goose/geese, build/built, cóntract/contráct.*

Morphemes are often represented on the surface in several different ways. Recall that the regular plural actually takes one of three possible phonological forms according to which segment precedes it. When a morpheme has more than one realization, its alternative forms are referred to as **allomorphs** (note the parallel with allophones). Put differently, allomorphs are the **alternants** of a morpheme. We found that the regular plural morpheme has three allomorphs: /s/, /z/, and /ɪz/, and that the occurrence of each allomorph could be predicted on the basis of the phonological features of the preceding segment. Allomorphs predictable from their surrounding phonological environment are said to be **phonologically conditioned**.

Some allomorphs are not phonologically conditioned: they cannot be predicted from phonological characteristics. For example, the plural morpheme is sometimes realized as an allomorph other than one of the three described above, e.g. *child/children, ox/oxen, woman/women, mouse/mice, focus/foci, crisis/crises.* Although the processes which create these plurals from the corresponding singular nouns may have been phonologically conditioned at an earlier stage in the development of English, this conclusion is certainly not warranted for current English. The allomorph which occurs can be predicted only on the basis of its association with particular morphemes rather than a particular phonological feature. **Morphologically conditioned** allomorphs such as these are best treated in the form of lists. Such a list for plurals will associate a given noun base with its appropriate plural allomorph, for example, *ox* with *oxen*, *focus* with *foci.*

Exercise 3

Transcribe the past tense form of each of the following words. Identify those that are phonologically conditioned and those that are morphologically conditioned. For those that are phonologically conditioned, state the environments that account for the conditioning. Simply list the morphologically conditioned ones.

shop	cuff	build	rent
ruin	feel	raze	rake
come	paw	rush	hear
rub	cure	bring	beg
erase	cull	garage	move
bathe	steal	tee	go
eat	play	hatch	hum
raid	plow	judge	boo

Exercise 4

(a) On the basis of the following sentences, figure out what the suffix spelled as -*th* does in English morphology.

(b) For each underlined word determine the morphemes, and list the allomorphs of the morphemes.

1. Kids grow like weeds.
2. The growth of air pollution is breath taking.
3. How long is a yardstick?
4. A yardstick is 36 inches in length.
5. How wide is the sea, how deep is the ocean?
6. The tunnel has a width restriction.
7. The study of phonology will expand one's consciousness to an unprecedented depth.

Morphophonemics

Many of the processes we discussed in the last chapter concerned regular changes in the shape of morphemes such as regular plural suffixes, negative prefixes, and so forth. When we look at such changes, we see that they involve alternations between units which would be classified as phonemes according to the classical definition. How can such obvious regularities related to phonological and grammatical information be handled? Is it a part of the phonology, or the morphology, or both? In structural phonology, a special intermediate level was established to deal with such cases. This level was appropriately called **morphophonemics**, since it combined aspects of both morphology and phonemics. Units on this level were referred to as **morphophonemes**. These intermediate units were set up to preserve the classical phoneme as a taxonomic unit, and at the same time to recognize basic phonological alternations which account for the relationships between grammatically related forms (for example, neutralization, assimilation, and so forth). By locating predictable phonological processes on the morphophonemic level, the basic methodology for determining phonemes could be preserved. Through this extension of phonemic theory, the phoneme maintained a one-to-one correspondence to surface representations, while the morphophoneme took care of the "messier" aspects of language regularity.

Exercise 5

Given the following examples, determine the phonemic status of [s] and [k] in English. Does the [s] in *sill* seem different from the [s] in *electricity*? Remember that initial /k/ may take several different forms.

(a)
sill	kiss	kitty	ski
sis	city	kill	scoop
cut	coop	cute	scat
cool	cup	cone	skull

(b)
electric	electrical	electricity
cynic	cynical	cynicism
empiric	empirical	empiricism
elastic		elasticity
plastic	plasticate	plasticity
specific		specificity
stoic	stoical	stoicism
eclectic		eclecticism
cleric	clerical	clericism
phonemic		phonemicist
ironic	ironical	

The corpus in Exercise 5 represents a much more complex case of neutralization than we observed in our earlier examples. In the first subset of forms labelled (a), [s] is in clear contrast initially, finally, and medially with [k]. We would therefore assign [s] and the variants of [k] to different phonemes. Moreover, the phonetic variants of [k] may all be predicted from their phonetic context (they are in complementary distribution), so they should be assigned to the same phoneme. Our observations so far are represented in the following diagram (which does not include all the phonetic detail).

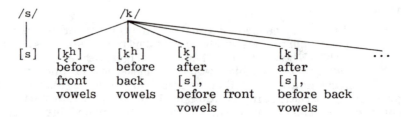

This scheme clearly maintains a direct relationship between surface phonetic information and phonemic classification. But the forms in part (b) of the exercise again introduce the need to deal with a type of neutralization. If we want our grammar to reflect the apparent relationship among forms like *cynic, cynical,* and *cynicism,* we will have to propose that somehow [s] and [k] are related at a deeper level. For example, we might propose that *electricity* is composed of the two forms /əlèktrɪk/ plus /ɪti/, and that /k/ becomes [s] in just such situations, yielding [əlèktrísɪɾi]. So we would be proposing a situation of neutralization, in which both /k/ and /s/ can be realized in the surface forms as [s].

Notice, however, that this is different from the phonetic neutralization we discussed earlier. Here, both of the variants of final /k/ in *electric* correspond to phonemes we have already established. It is only in special contexts in our corpus that [k] alternates with [s], namely before the suffixes *-ity, -ism,* and *-ist.* We might propose, then, that /k/ is realized as [s] when it occurs before [ɪ], thereby accounting for [əlèktrɪk], and for /əlèktrɪk/ + /ɪti/ becoming [əlèktrísɪɾi]. But this does not actually happen each time a /k/ occurs before [ɪɾi]. For example, consider the forms *lickety split* and *rickety,* both of which contain a /k/ before an [ɪɾi] and neither of which becomes [s]. In addition, when a word ending in /k/ occurs before another word beginning with /ɪ/ (e.g. *specific idiom*), the change to [s] does not take place. Remember also that *kill, kitty, kick,* and *kiss* all contain a [kɪ] sequence which does not change to [sɪ]. Clearly, it is significant that the [s] variant of /k/ appears only when a /k/ and /ɪ/ are in different morphemes within a word.

Somehow, the alternation between [k] and [s] is due to an interaction between the phonemes of different morphemes, a fact which led some linguists to put this sort of phenomenon into the separate, morphophonemic level of analysis. In that approach, the morphophoneme //k// (double slashes mark forms on the morphophonemic level) has two alternants, /s/ and /k/, each of which is a phoneme in its own right. The /s/ form occurs when //k// precedes a morpheme beginning with /ɪ/, such as the suffix /ɪti/. The /k/ alternant is realized in other contexts. We can represent our conclusions graphically as follows:

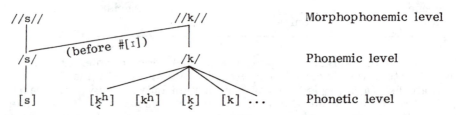

The forms *cynic, cynical,* and *cynicism* are now seen as related by a common form at the morphophonemic level: //sɪnɪk//, //sɪnɪk#əl//, //sɪnɪk#ɪzɪm//. In the context of /əl/, the allomorph /sɪnɪk/ will be chosen and the /k/ will then be realized as one of its appropriate allophones. In this context it will not be fronted because it precedes a central vowel, and typically it will not be aspirated because it is in an unstressed syllable. Thus, the phonetic form will be [sínɪkəl]. Before the suffix /ɪzɪm/, however, the allomorph /sɪnɪs/ will be chosen and the resulting phonetic form [sínɪsɪzɪm] will occur. We can represent these observations as follows:

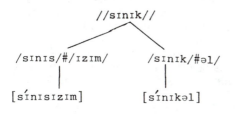

//sɪnɪk//	Morphophonemic level (morphemes represented by morphophonemes)
/sɪnɪs/#/ɪzɪm/ and /sɪnɪk/#əl/	Phonemic level (allomorphs represented by phonemes)
[sínɪsɪzɪm] and [sínɪkəl]	Phonetic level (allophones represented in phonetics)

One of the important observations about the pattern of alternation between /s/ and /k/ is its "productivity." That is, it not only applies to a set of items which might be learned by rote, it also applies automatically to all items that meet its conditions for operation. Thus, if we were to fill in some of the gaps in part (b) of Exercise 5 to form new items, we would automatically use the /k/ or /s/. Words like *phonemic* and *elastic* would probably correspond to forms like *phonemical* and *elastical*, with a /k/. If we created forms such as *ironicity* for *ironic*, we would get the /s/ variant.

Exercise 6

Consider the contrasts between /s/ and /z/ in the following minimal pairs: *zoo*/*sue*, *bus*/*buzz*, *as*/*ass*, *zip*/*sip*. Now return to Exercise 2 in Chapter 4, and propose a morphophonemic solution for dealing with the alternation in the regular English plural morpheme. Consider the /s/, /z/, and /ɪz/ variants.

To structural phonologists, the recognition of a separate, intermediary, morphophonemic level was ideal because it preserved the one-to-one phonemic-phonetic correspondence, and divorced phonemes from grammatical considerations. Aspects of neutralization relating to grammatical facts could be considered a function of allomorphic alternation. This explicitly recognized both the existence of such phenomena and the regular relationships among variants related in this way. In fact, the morphophonemic level could be used to account for many observations about language which otherwise would elude easy description.

Complex Morphophonemic Solutions

Some morphophonemic analyses of neutralization can become fairly involved. The following example is one such case, and is included simply to give an idea of the considerations that go into a particular analysis.

In addition to the regular plural in English, there are many sets of nouns which are irregular in their plural form. In one of these sets, /f/ in the singular form corresponds to /v/ in the plural.

knife/knives	wolf/wolves
sheaf/sheaves	wife/wives
leaf/leaves	scarf/scarves
thief/thieves	half/halves

This situation appears to represent a case of morphophonemic neutralization much like those described above. We know that /f/ and /v/ contrast phonemically in English (e.g. *half/have*), but in the plurals above, the /f/ is neutralized to /v/. The difference in this case is that the alternation between [f] and [v] is conditioned by both phonological and grammatical facts. In order to predict whether the neutralization takes place, we must know the specific grammatical function of the *-s* suffix. This is important in cases where a possessive *-s* suffix is added to the noun: *my wife's hat, the knife's edge*, etc. In these cases the /f/ does not neutralize for most speakers of English. We may account for this by marking the grammatical function of the *-s* suffix in the statement of distribution of the phonemes, as follows:

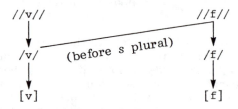

But one problem must still be accounted for. Some nouns that end with [f] in their singular form do not have [v] in their plurals: *chief/chiefs, reef/reefs, cough/coughs, rough/roughs* (in golf). In order to account for this, Harris (1951:225) has suggested that there are two kinds of *f* on the morphophonemic level: one which neutralizes to /v/ and one which does not. By this proposal, morphophonemes which neutralize should be marked differently from those that do not. Those that neutralize are marked with upper case symbols; those that do not with lower case, as in the following forms: //naᴵF// 'knife', //liF// 'leaf', //rif// 'reef', //čif// 'chief'. Forms containing an //F// will have two allomorphs: one with /f/ and one with /v/ (/naᴵf/, /naᴵvz/). Forms containing an //f// will always have a phonemic representation with /f/ (/čif/, /čifs/). We can represent this graphically as follows:

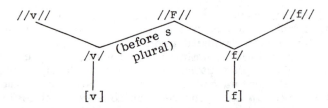

Such are the additional complexities which can enter into our formulation of morphophonemic relationships in order to capture more subtle aspects of phonological patterning.

Systematic Phonemes

As we have seen, the postulation of a morphophonemic level of analysis allows language descriptions to recognize units to which predictable variants of a form can be related. Although there have been differences in how this level was viewed, most linguists have agreed that a morphophonemic representation is a more acceptable form for describing a deeper level of regularity than phonemics. Most of the recent discussion about this level of analysis has centered on two questions:

(a) What exactly happens to a form between its representation morphophonemically and its representation phonetically?

(b) What exactly are the relationships between morphophonemic forms and surface phonetic forms?

Discussions of both of these questions have resulted in a rather drastic revision of phonology within the last two decades. This reformulation is referred to as **generative phonology**. To a large extent, this revision has taken place within the framework of transformational-generative grammar as it developed during this period. The revision goes deeper than a difference in methodology: the theoretical claims of structural phonology and generative phonology are very different. Structural phonology was content to attain observational adequacy as we described it earlier. Generative phonology, on the other hand, is concerned with descriptive adequacy, and holds explanatory adequacy as an ideal.

The relationship between morphophonemic and phonetic representations has been the subject of a considerable amount of discussion and revision in generative phonology. It has been demonstrated that the insistence upon a level of description (the classical phonemic level) between the base form the phonetic form could obscure the regularity and generality of some phonological processes. In essence, it was claimed that the classical phonemic level could and should be by-passed in going from the morphophonemic to the phonetic form.

We may describe this argument without going into the details of Russian phonology, upon which it is based (Halle, 1959). Under certain conditions, a very general process in a language (one which always occurs and which applies to a broad class of items) would have to be stated once as a morphophonemic pattern and once as a phonemic pattern if we adhered strictly to the recognition of both a morphophonemic and phonemic level.

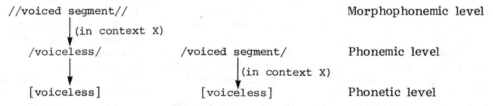

In the diagram, a voiced segment on the morphophonemic level becomes voiceless on the phonemic level. At the same time, a voiced segment on the phonemic level becomes voiceless on the phonetic level. The context for both changes is identical, so it seems unreasonable to have to state the same process twice. Doing away with the phonemic level permits such a process to be stated only once, thereby allowing processes to go directly from the morphophonemic form to the phonetic form. This allows a more general and economical statement, as represented below.

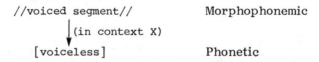

This notion of a phonology without levels between the morphophonemic and phonetic levels is consistent with the general approach to language description used by transformational-generative grammar. It proposes the existence of one underlying form, called a **systematic phonemic representation**. The **systematic phoneme** has many of the same characteristics that we outlined for the morphophoneme. Specifically, it may incorporate grammatical information, may account for neutralization, and, thus, may abstractly represent the relationships between forms. The difference in the systematic phoneme is that it is simply the beginning link in a chain of representations, the ultimate product of which is the **systematic phonetic representation**, or actual production. There are no named intermediate levels of representation. Rather, each morphophonemic alternation is represented as a **phonological rule**, the exact nature of which we will describe in Chapter 8. These rules may act upon either the original systematic phonemic representation, or on the representation which has resulted from the action of another rule. Each rule is a step toward arriving at the eventual phonetic production. If three rules apply, there is one step for each rule, and the result of applying the last rule is the systematic phonetic representation. As we examine this process in detail, we will find that rather than one separate, taxonomic level between morphophonemes and phonetics, there is a "level" for each rule that applies to a form, and that there is little justification for singling out any one level and assigning it a special status.

Derivations

The process of applying rules that we mentioned above is called a phonological **derivation**. Examining the nature of derivations will help support our observation that there may be a number of steps between the morphophonemic and phonetic levels. Earlier (in Exercise 2), we presented the phenomenon illustrated by the *raiding/rating* example. Recall that both the underlying *d* and the underlying *t* neutralize to [ɾ], but that the vowel preceding *d* is lengthened, while the vowel preceding *t* is not. In our excitement at having discovered neutralization, we evaded the fact that two processes were represented in one form: flapping and vowel lengthening. In order to understand how this could happen, we should remark, first, that our view now is that there is an underlying, abstract *t* in *rating*, and a *d* in *raiding*. By **underlying** we mean that *t* and *d* each have a psychological reality as separate units in a speaker's intuitions. The level at which the *t* and *d* exist is the beginning level of the phonological derivation: the systematic phoneme. By **abstract** we mean that the actual segments we propose for the systematic phonemic level need not be identical to the segments we observe on the surface. This systematic phonemic representation is changed by phonological rules to yield the systematic phonetic representation. So the *raiding/rating* phenomenon involves two rules. One, the Flapping Rule, revises the features of underlying /t/ and /d/ to the features of [ɾ]. The other, the Vowel Lengthening Rule, adds the length feature to a stressed vowel before a voiced consonant. These rules **derive** the systematic phonetic representation from the systematic phonemic representation. The steps in this process (sometimes called "history") make up the **derivation** of the final form. We represent derivations in the following way:

Systematic phonemic level	//red#ɪŋ//	//ret#ɪŋ//
Derivational steps { Vowel Lengthening Rule	reːd#ɪŋ	---
Flapping Rule	reːɾ#ɪŋ	reɾ#ɪŋ
Systematic phonetic level	[reːɾɪŋ]	[reɾɪŋ]

In this derivation of the forms *raiding* and *rating*, the topmost form is the systematic phonemic representation, the bottom form is the systematic phonetic representation, and each derivational step is the representation resulting from the application of a rule to the representation immediately above it. [2]

Notice that *raiding* and *rating* have different derivational histories. This is because the Vowel Lengthening Rule applies only to those representations that have a vowel followed by a voiced consonant. The dashes (---) in the derivation indicate that the rule does not apply to the preceding representation. We can observe here how various forms will have different numbers of levels of representation and no single level is more important than another. Moreover, we may demonstrate that these levels are progressive stages in the derivation. Notice that we applied the Vowel Lengthening Rule to *raiding* before we applied the Flapping Rule. That is, the Flapping Rule applied to the form that resulted from applying the Vowel Lengthening Rule. Consider what would happen if the rules were allowed to apply in the opposite order, as follows:

	//red#ɪŋ//	//ret#ɪŋ//
Flapping	reɾ#ɪŋ	reɾ#ɪŋ
Vowel Lengthening	re:ɾ#ɪŋ	re:ɾ#ɪŋ
	[re:ɾɪŋ]	*[re:ɾɪŋ]

The opposite order of application of the rules derives two identical forms, both with a lengthened vowel (because [ɾ] is a voiced consonant). Clearly, we want the Vowel Lengthening Rule to apply before the Flapping Rule so that the vowel of *rating* is not lengthened. Having demonstrated that one rule must apply to the output of another, we can claim that there is a reality to the notion of different steps in the derivation.

Exercise 7

In Exercise 6 we analyzed the regular plural in English from the perspective of morphophonemics. Assume now that //z// is the systematic phonemic representation of the regular plural morpheme. Propose two rules which will account for all three variants of the plural: [s], [z], and [ɪz]. State each rule in prose, and specify the context in which it will apply. Show the derivations of the forms: *roses*, *rats*, and *rods*. (We will explain later why we chose //z// as the underlying form of the regular plural.)

The analysis of the problem in Exercise 7 should differ in an important way from that in Exercise 6. This difference illustrates the essential distinction between the taxonomic and systematic approaches to phonology, so it is worth examining in some detail. The morphophonemic approach employed in Exercise 6 results in an analysis which provides the phonemic representations of three distinct allomorphs of the plural morpheme. In actuality, such an approach simply lists the forms that occur and matches each with the context in which it may occur. It might be represented as shown on page 116. As we have seen, such a description allows us to predict correctly which allomorph will occur with a given noun (except for those that are irregular), and to associate the three allomorphs with one morpheme. But the facts about the distribution of the plural allomorphs are represented as properties of a specific morpheme.

Our analysis in Exercise 7 should represent our observations equally correctly, but somewhat differently. Here we chose one of the variants to be

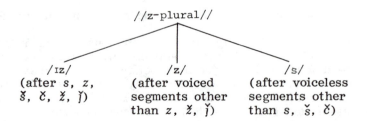

the underlying form (//z//), and we derived the other forms from it by
means of two rules. The first, an Epenthesis Rule, inserts the vowel [ɪ]
between a noun ending with s, z, š, ž, č, or ǰ and the plural suffix. The
second, the Voicing Assimilation Rule, changes the features of [z] to those
of [s] if the preceding segment is voiceless (and is not a sibilant). The
derivations for *horses, hats,* and *buds* follow:

	//hɔrs#z//	//hæt#z//	//bʌd#z//
Epenthesis Rule	hɔrs#ɪz	---	---
Voicing Assimilation Rule	---	hæt#s	---
	[hɔrsɪz]	[hæts]	[bʌdz]

There are two important differences between this analysis and the one above.
First, the variants of //z// no longer have their own status as individual
entities within the phonological system. Instead, they simply "fall out" as
derivations from a common underlying form. Secondly, they are derived by
means of rules that specify general phonological processes. The morphophonemic approach simply listed patterns where classes of allomorphs co-
occurred with classes of phonemes. Thus, our rules amount to claims about
English that we may be able to justify on the basis of broader, more general,
phonetically based principles. All we can claim about our earlier analysis is
that the plural takes three regularly distributed forms. Our explanations of
why such forms occur may make sense in terms of our knowledge about phonological processes, but the morphophonemic analysis itself does not make
those processes explicit in the same way that the generative analysis does.
According to these considerations, we may conclude that a generative approach to phonology provides us with several advantages over the approaches
we examined previously. But it also raises another problem, namely that of
the actual shape of the underlying forms.

Phonological Abstractness

When we speak of abstractness in phonology, we are referring to the relationship between basic phonological units, such as the systematic phoneme, and
surface phonetic facts. At one extreme is the position that surface phonetic
forms need not have any relation to the underlying forms. At the other is
the position that the surface forms and underlying forms are always the same.
Between these extremes are a number of positions which recognize a relationship between surface and underlying structures, while admitting that this
relationship is not always direct. According to these views, the systematic
phoneme is abstract, in that it may be removed via various derivational processes from the actual surface phonetic form. The question is, to what extent? Naturally, we would expect that less direct relationships between the
underlying and surface forms result in more abstract underlying forms.

   In a phonology designed to make claims about native speakers' intuitions,
it is important to posit underlying forms that have a high probability of

psychological validity for these speakers. In a more abstract analysis, it is possible to claim that certain items are related by regular phonological processes; however, such relationships may not reflect native speakers' intuitions. As an illustration, take the large group of words that are spelled with an initial *kn* in English, including *knock, knight, knife, knee, know,* and *knead.* Although all of these forms are now pronounced with only an initial [n], we know that several hundred years ago they were pronounced with initial [kn], and that some of them contrasted with forms with initial [n], such as *know/ no, knead/need,* and *knight/night.* At that stage in the development of the English language, the most likely phonological analysis would have been that the underlying forms of these words began with //kn//. Employing an abstract analysis, we might propose that these facts suggest an underlying form of //kn// for these words in contemporary English. Accordingly, we would identify a process which removes the underlying //k//, leaving only the [n] to appear on the surface. The derivation of *knee,* then, would look like this:

$$//kni//$$
/k/ deletion   ni
$$[ni]$$

It is fairly clear that, although //kn// is historically accurate as a form, it is unlikely to be the underlying form today. Because the //k// is never realized phonetically, there would be no way for speakers to postulate the existence of the //k// on the basis of what they hear as they are learning their language. (Remember, we are dealing with intuitions about phonology apart from spelling.) In this case //k// is too abstract. It makes claims about underlying relationships that probably do not exist in a current phonology of English. Kiparsky (1968) has labelled such processes as **absolute neutralization** because they are characterized by underlying forms that never occur on the surface. He argues that because absolutely neutralized underlying forms are unlearnable by children acquiring the language, they should be excluded from present-day phonological descriptions. Thus, one of the restrictions we may place on the degree of abstractness of underlying forms is that they will not involve absolute neutralization, even if the form may have been attested during an earlier stage in the development of the language. This claim appears to match what native speakers intuit about relationships among phonological forms. Put differently, we will insist on underlying forms that can be learned entirely on the basis of surface phonetic information available at a given point in time.

Another essential aspect of relationships between forms must be based on regular meaning correspondences. Recall that we required a common meaning for related forms in establishing the morphemes of a language. If we ignore this requirement, we may discover regular phonological patterns which unite items that really are unrelated for native speakers. In fact, without the meaning requirement, it is possible to carry our analysis to ridiculous extremes. Consider the following pairs of English words:

calf/cover	rap/rubber
laugh/lover	lap/lubber
half/hover	rat/rudder
math/mother	ant/under
bass/buzzer	hack/hugger
lamp/lumber	back/bugger

The following two phonological rules could account for these pairings:

(1) final voiceless consonants become voiced before the morpheme -er, and
(2) /æ/ reduces to /ʌ/ in the context of -er.

Exercise 8

(a) Using rules 1 and 2, above, give the derivations for the pairs *calf/
cover* and *lamp/lumber*.

(b) What is wrong with this solution? Explain why this solution does not
reflect native speaker intuitions about word and morpheme relationships.

Obviously, no one would propose a solution like this, but it does demonstrate the point that phonological analysis alone does not provide us with
criteria for deciding whether relationships among forms are realistic. Many
recent phonological analyses may be criticized for similar, though more
subtle, abstract solutions. It is clear that we need criteria for deciding
among the many analyses of a language that abstract phonology makes possible. As we discuss more reasonable underlying forms in the remainder of
this chapter, some of these criteria will become apparent.

Underlying Forms

The problem in phonology is to propose underlying forms somewhere between
the extremes of the abstract analysis presented above and the surface-bound
analyses of traditional morphophonemics, neither of which appears to describe
adequately the knowledge of native speakers. Within these limits we would
like an analysis to do at least these things:

(1) it should demonstrate the relationships among intuitively related forms;
(2) it should predict all of the variants of the forms;
(3) it should do so in the most (a) economical, (b) general, and (c) plausible way.

We will consider several examples in which these requirements are met. In
many standard varieties of American English, an underlying sequence of a
vowel, a nasal segment (particularly *n*), and a voiceless stop may be realized
phonetically as a nasalized vowel and a consonant. The words *bent* and
meant, for example, may be realized as [bẽt] and [mẽt], so that they contrast with words such as *bet* [bɛt] and *met* [mɛt] primarily on the basis of
the nasalization of the vowels. In some working class Black varieties of English, this situation may be extended to word-final nasals. In relatively unstressed contexts, words such as *bee* [bi] or *lee* [li] and *bean* [bĩ] and *lean*
[lĩ] may be distinguished on the basis of the nasalized vowel. In these same
varieties, forms like *bean* and *lean* are always realized with an *n* when a
suffix beginning with a vowel is added: *beaner* [bĩnə], *leaner* [lĩnə].
There are two ways we can account for these observations. Analysis 1
proposes that, on the basis of contrasts such as [bĩ]/[bi] and [bẽt]/[bɛt],
the underlying vowel of *bean* and *bent* is nasalized. Within this analysis, we
may account for the variant of *bean* as *beaner* and *lean* as *leaner* by inserting the nasal segment when the -er suffix is added. Thus, we would derive
bean from //bĩ// and *beaner* from //bĩ#ər// through the insertion of *n*.
Analysis 2 proposes that, as reflected in the traditional writing system,
the underlying form of *bean* is //bin//, with the nasal segment rather than
the nasalized vowel. The variants of the form are accounted for by two
rules: (1) a Vowel Nasalization Rule, which nasalizes vowels before a nasal

segment, and (2) a Nasal Deletion Rule (in this case, relating just to *n*), which removes the final *n*. In this analysis, the nasalization of the vowel is simply left as the surface contrast after the nasal segment has been deleted. Thus, [bĩ] and [bĩnə] are accounted for through the following derivations.

	//bin//	//bin#ər//
Vowel Nasalization	bĩn	bĩn#ə
Nasal Deletion	bĩ	---
	[bĩ]	[bĩnə]

How can we decide which of these proposed analyses is better? Both of them predict the proper surface form of all the words involved, and each states precisely the relationship between the variants of *bean* or *lean*, so our first two requirements are met by both analyses.

At this point, we must consider the other criteria for choosing between analyses. According to our criterion of **economy**, we would like to propose an analysis with as few systematic phonemes and as much symmetry as possible. If we adopted the solution which proposed an underlying nasal vowel contrast, we would double the number of underlying vowels, since any oral vowel may be matched with a nasal vowel in this context. We further note that the contrast between nasal and oral vowels takes place in a very restricted context. For the speaker of standard American English, the contrast is found only before voiceless stops, and for the speaker of a non-mainstream variety, it is extended to word-final, unstressed contexts. Furthermore, even in these contexts, there is alternation between a nasalized vowel without the nasal segment and one with the segment. That is, a speaker who says [θĩk] 'think', [kæ̃p] 'camp', or [sɛ̃t] 'sent' may sometimes also say [θĩŋk], [kæ̃mp], or [sɛ̃nt]. And a non-mainstream speaker who says [lĩ] or [bĩ] may also sometimes say [lĩn] and [bĩn] in word-final unstressed contexts. We see, then, that Analysis 1 proposes a whole set of contrasts between oral and nasal vowels on the basis of a very restricted context which is not even very stable. Such a solution seems to be wasting the contrastive "energy" of our basic system. Analysis 2 does not have this problem. It is economical in that it proposes only underlying oral vowels, and derives all nasalized vowels from them according to the context in which they occur.

Notice also that Analysis 2 is a more **general** analysis than Analysis 1. An analysis is considered general if a rule applies broadly across many forms, or if a rule unites several otherwise distinct processes. The choice of underlying forms in Analysis 2 maximizes the generality of rules. In Analysis 2, vowel nasalization is predicted whenever a vowel precedes a nasal consonant. In English, a vowel before a nasal consonant always carries nasalization; there are no cases of an oral vowel followed by a nasal consonant. This is a significant generalization because it applies to a broad range of items. However, Analysis 1 treats each case of a nasal vowel as a unique phonological unit, thereby ignoring the fact that nasalization can be predicted by the presence of a following nasal consonant.

At first glance, it might appear that Analysis 1 could also capture general processes by predicting that a nasal consonant will occur following a nasal vowel. But given our underlying nasal vowel, how do we determine which nasal segment is to be inserted after it? For example, if a speaker has a nasal vowel and no consonant for *bum* [bʌ̃], *bean* [bĩ], and *sing* [sɪ̃], we must be able to predict the correct nasal consonant when an *-er* suffix is added, as in *bummer, beaner,* and *singer.* At this point, the general predictability of Analysis 1 breaks down, because we would have to specify which nasal segment would be inserted according to the particular lexical item. This is not nearly as general as Analysis 2, which starts with the particular nasal consonant in the underlying form and then deletes any nasal segment in certain contexts.

We also proposed above that our analysis should be **plausible**. This means that we would like the analysis to explain the sorts of things that really happen when sounds encounter one another in our mouths. We think, for example, that the vowel nasalization rule is very plausible because the process of vowels assimilating the quality of nasal consonants is extremely common in a wide variety of the world's languages. This observation, along with the phonetic reasonableness of a vowel taking on the quality of a neighboring nasal (the velum opening during the production of a vowel in anticipation of a following nasal segment), makes for a high degree of plausibility. At this point, the plausibility argument merges with the arguments of generality and economy given above to favor Analysis 2.

In summary, then, we have decided in favor of Analysis 2 on the basis of several criteria. Such determination is not always as simple as this argument might imply, however. In many cases, the differences between competing analyses are extremely slight and often involve extended and sophisticated arguments which help to refine our understanding of the exact nature of our criteria. The following discussion is an example of a fairly easily resolved problem in the determination of underlying forms, but it leads us into a more difficult problem.

Exercise 9

(a) Transcribe the following English words in broad phonetics. Considering only these forms, determine the contrastive status of the segments [m], [n], and [ŋ].

much	con	tin
knob	sing	long
mirror	rum	nip
run	prom	sin

(b) Now transcribe these additional words. Listen for these and analogous words in actual conversations or in television commercials or talkshows. Unless you are careful, your own English competence and your knowledge of the spellings of the words will hamper your ability to record the sounds as they actually are pronounced.

intolerable	indelible	impossible
incomprehensible	indecent	imperceptible
inconvenient	imbalance	incomplete
impenetrable	inconsistent	indifferent

(c) Given that each of the forms in (b) contains a morpheme that we might gloss as 'not', propose a systematic analysis that relates all these variants to a common underlying form. Attempt to justify your choice of the 'not' morpheme and the rule(s) in terms of the criteria outlined above.

(d) How can you use the forms *inoperable, inability, inept, inequality* to support your argument?

The most plausible, economic, and general analysis of the corpus in Exercise 9 proposes a unified underlying negative prefix of the shape //ɪn//, and an assimilation rule which changes the place of articulation of the nasal consonant to that of the following segment. Thus, the negative prefix will take the form of [ɪm] before bilabial consonants, [ɪŋ] before velar consonants, and will remain as [ɪn] before alveolar consonants. The fact that the form of the negative is also [ɪn] before vowel-initial morphemes is strong evidence for an underlying //n//, because [n] would not plausibly be the result of assimilation to every vowel.

On the basis of Exercise 9, particularly part (a), it might seem reasonable to posit the existence of three classical nasal phonemes for English: /m/, /n/, and /ŋ/. However, given the types of considerations which go into the determination of systematic phonemes, the status of ŋ has become somewhat controversial. [ŋ] does not occur syllable-initially in English (there are no words like *[ŋæt]), which differentiates it from the other nasals [m] and [n]. Furthermore, [ŋ] often occurs before a velar consonant within words (*jungle, tinkle*), making its occurrence quite predictable in some contexts. Facts such as these have led some linguists to suggest that [ŋ] does not really have contrastive status on the more abstract levels of the phonology. That is, it is argued that [ŋ] is derived not from underlying //ŋ//, but from some other systematic phoneme. Several arguments have been advanced in support of this proposal, and these are illustrative of the variety of arguments used in the determination of underlying forms.

Our observations about the occurrence of [ŋ] are reminiscent of the assimilation rule we discussed in connection with the negative prefix. In this framework, we simply suggest that every occurrence of [ŋ] is derived from another nasal, say //n//. The first process operating on this //n// assimilates it to the position of a following velar consonant. The velar consonant is then deleted in certain positions if it is a //g//. This is particularly true in word-final position, where many varieties of English do not permit [ŋg] clusters to occur.[3] After the //g// is deleted, the [ŋ] is left in the surface form. So we might say that the contrastive status of [ŋ] is limited to the surface phonetics rather than the underlying systematic phonology. The following derivations result from the application of these rules.

	//rɪng//	//pɪnk//	//læŋgwɪǰ//	//rɪg//
n-Assimilation	rɪŋg	pɪŋk	læŋgwɪǰ	---
g-Deletion	rɪŋ	---	---	---
	[rɪŋ]	[pɪŋk]	[læŋgwɪǰ]	[rɪg]

A number of arguments support this analysis. One fact relates to the absence of initial [ŋ]. Recall from our constraints on word-initial clusters of consonants (Chapter 5) that initial combinations of a nasal plus a stop are prohibited in English so that there are no forms like *[ndis] or *[mbis] (or *[ŋgis]). The absence of initial [ŋ] may be explained if it always precedes underlying //g//, since *[ng] would be a prohibited initial cluster. This is partial evidence for a following //g// as a necessary conditioning segment for the occurrence of [ŋ]. If there were no following //g//, [ŋ] could behave like other nasals and occur initially.

Notice that this analysis is more symmetrical than one which proposes an underlying //ŋ//. Rather than claiming that //ŋ// does not occur initially, in contrast to //m// and //n// which do, we can make a generalization concerning all nasals. We can now say that any nasal (//m// or //n//) may occur initially as long as it is not followed by another consonant. It is also a more economical analysis, because without //ŋ// it has one phoneme fewer than the alternative. The postulation of an underlying //ng// may be supported further by the occurrence of a [g] in the surface form when certain types of suffixes are added. Thus we may get [ŋ] in word-final position in words like *long* [lɔŋ] and *strong* [strɔŋ], but [ŋg] in *longer* [lɔŋgə] and *stronger* [strɔŋgə]. Because [g] does appear on the surface in some contexts, our analysis avoids the difficulties presented by the case of absolute neutralization we examined earlier.

There are, of course, other arguments that might be advanced to support the contention that the surface form [ŋ] is most reasonably derived from an underlying //ng// rather than //ŋ// , but it is sufficient here to demonstrate the types of arguments that may be applicable to a particular analysis. The important aspect of the systematic phonemic analysis demonstrated here is its departure from strict dependence on phonetic contrasts as the basis for establishing the contrastive units in the language, and its increased dependence on considerations of generality, overall symmetry of pattern, economy of description, and plausibility of rules in terms of natural language processes.

Models of Phonology

In this chapter, we examined proposals for dealing with certain types of regularity difficult to handle within the traditional framework of structural phonology. One type of difficulty was the intersection of grammatical and phonological information, traditionally assigned to an independent level of morphophonemics. Another type was neutralization of phonemic contrasts in surface phonetic forms, where the requirement of unique phonetic variants for different phonemes in classical phonemics was violated. In trying to resolve these difficulties, we turned to the more abstract phonological unit of generative phonology, the systematic phoneme.

Although the arguments concerning the systematic phoneme versus the classical phoneme may seem somewhat ethereal to an introductory student, it must be remembered that there are important issues at stake here. One essential issue is the claim that it is the systematic phoneme rather than the classical phoneme which has legitimate psychological reality for native speakers of a language. Another issue concerns the practical description of the phonological units of a language. As we have seen, the various approaches may result in somewhat different analyses of the inventory and patterning of phonological units. Thus, these theoretical arguments have important practical ramifications for the description of language.

The dispute about valid levels of representation in phonology is not yet resolved. For example, it has been demonstrated that the systematic phonetic level within generative phonology tends to correspond almost exactly to the classical phonemic level (Schane, 1971). This appears to be an implicit recognition of some kind of psychological and practical validity for a level of contrastive forms analogous to the classical phoneme. In terms of descriptive significance, this means that there may be some psychological reality for both an underlying representation such as //ng// and a surface phonetic contrast such as /ŋ/. So while we may be justified in systematically deriving /ŋ/ from underlying //ng//, native speakers may attribute /ŋ/ contrastive status in such pairs as *sin/sing*. Of course, not all generative phonologists accept this claim, and still insist that there is no intermediate level between the systematic phoneme and surface phonetics. But there are many generative phonological analyses which seem to fit a framework recognizing the validity of both a systematic and classical phonemic level.

We conclude this chapter by comparing the classical and generative models of phonological description (diagrammed below). The generative model incorporates Schane's proposal mentioned above. Both models enable us to analyze important details of linguistic patterning, although we think that the generative phonological model can describe these patterns in a more consistent and satisfying way. The morphophonemic level of the classical model may be compared to the systematic phonemic level, and the surface phonetic contrasts of generative phonology often parallel the classical phonemic level. Although we do not want to minimize the differences between the models, there is a sense in which phonology has come full circle in the last 30 years --but a great deal has been gained in the process. In discovering that some of the earlier notions of phonology parallel more recent innovations, we have improved considerably our understanding of phonological processes and our ability to describe them in a satisfying manner.

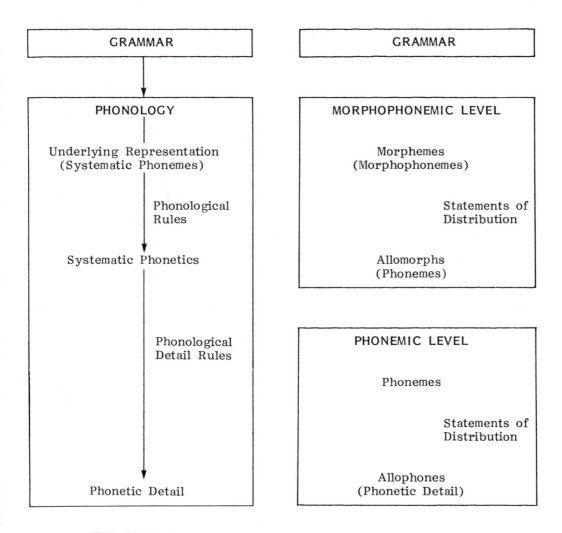

THE GENERATIVE AND CLASSICAL MODELS OF PHONOLOGY

NOTES

1. One of the classic articles on this problem within the framework of classi-
    cal phonemics is Bloch's (1941) paper entitled "Phonemic Overlapping."
    In this paper Bloch admits that partial intersection may take place in that
    two phonemes may have the same phone representing them, but the
    distribution of the sound will be unique to each phoneme. That is,
    Phone 1 may have Allophone *a* only in Context *x*, and Phone 2 may
    have Allophone *a* only in Context *y*. Thus, Bloch's claim was that
    "... the intersection is only partial and never leads to uncertainty
    or confusion" (1941:280).
2. This, of course, is a broad transcription of the vowel [e], which is
    ordinarily pronounced with an offglide [eᴵ]. For the time being, we
    are also ignoring stress.
3. We will have more to say about this context in Chapter 8 in connection
    with the discussion of boundaries. Also, notice that some varieties of
    American English do not delete the /g/, so that forms of the following
    sort occur: [sɪŋg] 'sing', [hæŋgə] 'hanger'.

SUGGESTED READING

Many of the papers which were central to the development of the theories
discussed in this chapter have been assembled by V. B. Makkai in a reader
entitled *Phonological Theory: Evolution and Current Practice* (1972). We
especially recommend the following papers to the interested student: Sapir
(1933), Swadesh (1934), Bloch (1941), Harris (1944), Pike (1947a), Halle
(1962), Householder (1965), and Chomsky and Halle (1965). Makkai's book
is also especially valuable for its extensive, topically organized bibliographies.

Two treatments of English phonology would repay examination. One, done
from a more or less classical phonemic point of view, is Francis, *The Structure
of American English* (1958). It is especially useful for locating alternations
which occur in standard American dialects. The other is Chomsky and Halle,
The Sound Pattern of English (1968), which is the primary reference work for
what is now referred to as "Standard Generative Phonological Theory." It is
fairly cumbersome reading, but will serve to fill out the sorts of arguments
about English we have introduced here. The "abstractness controversy" which
we introduced here is discussed in a number of papers, including Kiparsky,
"How Abstract is Phonology" (1968), and Hyman, "How Concrete is Phonology"
(1970).

CHAPTER 8
Making Processes Explicit: Phonological Rules

Although we have now described various types of processes and how they relate to each other in the derivation of a form, we have not yet attempted to symbolize these processes in any formal way. So far we have used only prose to describe phonological processes. But it is possible to describe these processes by using certain symbols and conventions that look like the type of formula associated with fields such as mathematics or formal logic.

Why should we bother to resort to a formal representation of phonological processes or **rules**, when we have been able to describe them in prose? The first reason is that formal representation allows us to reach a level of precision that is difficult to achieve if we simply rely on descriptive prose. It helps us become more explicit in our description, including all but only the relevant facts concerning the operation of particular processes. Such explicitness is a desired goal for any scientific description. It might certainly be possible to achieve explicitness through descriptive prose, but the use of formalism can help avoid ambiguity or vagueness that might otherwise arise.

Another advantage of using a formal system is the potential for achieving **internal consistency**. A formal, abstract symbolization may point to regularities or contradictions in a description which might not be as obvious in a system totally reliant upon descriptive prose. For example, the fact that we represent all the processes in a description by the same symbols and conventions allows us to specify formally certain relationships among different processes. (We will return to this point later in the chapter.) Here again, we are not claiming that non-formal systems of representation cannot be internally consistent, only that formalism tends to promote this characteristic.

A final reason for us to introduce certain formalisms to the description of phonological processes is largely practical. Formal rules have become a conventionalized tradition within the study of phonology, and students can expect to encounter such formalisms in current phonological descriptions. The student who wants to read and understand works in this area needs to learn certain formal conventions.

The procedures for writing rules are not particularly difficult, although some phonological rules may look rather imposing at first glance. While the procedures are not difficult, it must be admitted that formal representations of some of the more complex processes take some time to work through, even for experienced phonologists. Nevertheless, it is significant that we can write our rules in a way which formally links the underlying forms with the phonetic realization of these forms.

The Form of Rules: Preliminary Conventions

Phonological rules are formalized according to a set of fairly well-established conventions. What we present here are those most generally in current use within generative phonology, although there are certainly other conventions that might be used to capture the various processes we have discussed. Several necessary details have to be included in the formalization of a phonological rule. First, there must be an **input**, the unit which is to be affected by the process. Then, there must be a **change**, the phonological process which leads to the resultant form or **output** of the rule. And finally, there must be a relevant **linguistic environment** in which the change takes place. We have repeatedly noted the importance of linguistic environment or context as a factor in describing various changes. These facts may be captured in a simple type of convention as follows, where the arbitrary letters stand for the various units within the rule.

$$X \rightarrow Y/A \underline{\quad} B$$

In this convention, the form to the left of the arrow, X, is the input, and the form to the right of the arrow, Y, the output. The arrow indicates the change, and should be read as "becomes," or "is changed to" (or, more technically, "is rewritten as"). The diagonal / should be read as "in the context of." All information to the right of the diagonal specifies the linguistic environment in which the rule applies. That is, the process or change can only take place when the input is found in the environment specified to the right of the diagonal. The underscore, or **environmental bar**, indicates where the input X occurs within the string of items represented by the environment. The relevant environment preceding the input is placed to the left of the environmental bar (here, A____), and the relevant environment following the input is placed to the right of the bar (here, ____B). So the rule above represents the change AXB to AYB, where X is the input, Y the output, A the preceding environment, and B the following environment.

If a relevant environment is found in a position simultaneous with the input itself–such as suprasegmental stress, tone, or grammatical category of the segment–this is placed under the environmental bar:

$$X \rightarrow Y/A \underline{\quad} B \atop C$$

In this convention, if a particular environment is not relevant for the operation of the rule, it is left unspecified. Thus the specification $X \rightarrow Y/\underline{\quad} B \atop C$

means that the preceding environment is not relevant to the operation of the rule: it does not matter what is there.

As presented above, rules will operate whenever the appropriate linguistic environment for the change is present. However, this is not how all rules operate. In actuality, some rules apply every time the appropriate linguistic environment is present, whereas other rules may or may not operate when these conditions are present. The former type of rule has traditionally been called an **obligatory** rule, and the latter an **optional** rule. Optional rules are indicated by the use of parentheses ( ) around the output:

$$X \rightarrow (Y)/A \underline{\quad} B$$

If no parentheses are present, then the rule is assumed to be obligatory, operating in every instance where the appropriate linguistic environment is present. Rules discussed in previous chapters with the qualifications "sometimes" or "often" referred to the fact that the rule is considered optional rather than obligatory.[1]

Exercise 1

Convert the following prose descriptions to the formal conventions presented above. Be sure to read carefully.

1. Z becomes W when preceded by D and followed by F.
2. W is rewritten as Y preceding A.
3. R optionally becomes S when following C, preceding A and simultaneous with D.
4. *t* sometimes becomes *č* when followed by *y* and preceded by a vowel (symbolized as V).
5. *I* is rewritten as ε preceding *m*, *n*, or ŋ.
6. *t* and *d* become a flap ɾ when preceded by a stressed vowel (symbolized as V́) and followed by a vowel (symbolized as V).

Exercise 2

Give the prose descriptions which are represented in the following formulaic representations:

1. $X \rightarrow Y / D \underline{} F$
   $ C$

2. $\text{ɪ} \rightarrow \text{ε} / \underline{} n$

3. $t, d \rightarrow \text{ɾ} / \acute{V} \underline{} V$

4. $\theta \rightarrow (s) / \underline{} s$

5. $i, \text{ɪ}, u, \text{ʊ} \rightarrow \text{ə} / \begin{bmatrix} \underline{} \\ \text{-stress} \end{bmatrix}$

Feature Changing Rules

In our discussion up to this point, we have treated the conventional format as if it applied only to segmental units, such as phonemes. In reality, however, changes are indicated by altering features rather than whole segments. The use of features allows for the most explicit account of the natural classes of sounds included in the input and output. Furthermore, the use of features allows for the most explicit account of regularities in processes. Thus, the input is a set of features which minimally specifies the class of sounds affected, and the output specifies the change in the set. This can be illustrated by specifying a change ε to ɪ before nasals *m*, *n*, and ŋ, as it is found in some Southern varieties of English.

$$\begin{bmatrix} \text{+syl} \\ \text{-bk} \\ \text{-hi} \\ \text{-lo} \\ \text{-tns} \end{bmatrix} \rightarrow [\text{+hi}] \ / \ \underline{} \ [\text{+nas}]$$

 ε ɪ

The input to the left of the arrow gives the minimal feature specification of ε, the remaining feature values for ε being predictable through segmental redundancy conditions (see Chapter 4). The specifications to the right of the arrow indicate only those features which are changed by the rule. All other features in the input matrix remain unchanged in the output. The features [+syl], [-bk], [-tns], and [-lo] have the same value in the input and output, and thus are not specified in the output. The changed matrix actually specifies a new matrix:

$$\begin{bmatrix} +\text{syl} \\ -\text{bk} \\ -\text{hi} \\ -\text{lo} \\ -\text{tns} \end{bmatrix} \rightarrow \begin{bmatrix} +\text{syl} \\ -\text{bk} \\ +\text{hi} \\ -\text{lo} \\ -\text{tns} \end{bmatrix}$$

$$\varepsilon \qquad \qquad \text{I}$$

An additional step in some conventions eliminates from the input any feature that appears in the output. Thus, the feature [-hi] is eliminated from the input, since it is the feature changed in the output. The final form of the rule is thus:

$$\begin{bmatrix} +\text{syl} \\ -\text{bk} \\ -\text{lo} \\ -\text{tns} \end{bmatrix} \rightarrow [+\text{hi}] \ / \ \underline{\hspace{1cm}} \ [+\text{nas}]$$

Notice that the relevant environment, a following nasal, is simply specified as [+nas] because m, n, and η are uniquely specified by this feature. We have now incorporated into the format of the rule the conventions for feature specifications established in Chapter 4. In one form or another, the entire set of processes we discussed in Chapters 6 and 7 may be represented in rules following the conventional format we present here. For example, the simplest version of the Flapping Rule discussed in the last chapter (whereby //t// and //d// are both realized as [ɾ] between vowels) may be represented as follows:[2]

$$\text{Flapping} \quad \begin{bmatrix} +\text{cor} \\ -\text{d.r.} \end{bmatrix} \rightarrow \begin{bmatrix} +\text{vd} \\ +\text{flap} \end{bmatrix} \ / \ \begin{bmatrix} +\text{syl} \\ +\text{stress} \end{bmatrix} \underline{\hspace{1cm}} \ [+\text{syl}]$$

$$\text{t,d} \qquad \qquad ɾ \qquad \quad \acute{\text{V}} \qquad \qquad \text{V}$$

The Flapping Rule reads: a segment of the natural class t and d becomes a segment specified as voiced and flapped when immediately following a stressed vowel and immediately preceding an unstressed vowel. Some linguists counter the difficulty of reading feature bundles by including the phonetic symbols of the segments involved beneath the specification. This is simply a matter of convenience, and has nothing to do with the operation of the rule, which changes features, not segments. Linguists often use the symbol V in place of the specification [+syl], and C in place of a specification [-syl] or [+cons] (i.e. non-vowels). Thus, the environment of the Flapping Rule might be written as:

$$/ \ \begin{bmatrix} V \\ +\text{stress} \end{bmatrix} \underline{\hspace{1cm}} \ [V]$$

Again, this is only a matter of convenience, and we treat the rule as if the complete feature specifications were there.

Exercise 3

The specification of the environment for the Flapping Rule here is not complete. In addition to unstressed vowels, the following environment may include [ɾ] ([bǽɾɾ] 'batter', [sǽɾɾ] 'sadder'), and [ḷ] ([lɪ́ɾḷ] 'little', [rǽɾḷ] 'rattle'), but not [n̩] ([bʌ́ʔn̩] not *[bʌ́ɾn̩] 'button', [wʊ́dn̩] not *[wʊ́ɾn̩] 'wooden'). Revise the environmental conditions to account for this observation.

On a more substantive level, we should note that in the case of the Flapping Rule, the feature change [+vd] involves specifying a given value for a feature of unspecified value in the input. The input, which includes the natural class t and d, may either be [+vd] or [-vd]. In the output as specified here, it must be [+vd]. In our previous illustration of ε → ɪ, the feature change involved a switch from one value to another. Thus, feature changing rules can do two things: (1) switch the values of a feature specified in the input, or (2) specify the value of a feature unspecified in the input. Whether the change in a given rule is of type (1) or (2) above can only be sorted out by examining both the features in the input and in the output, and the entire inventory of segments in the language.

Exercise 4

Write the Vowel Lengthening Rule (Chapter 7) according to the conventions described above. Be sure to use only as many features as you need to specify the natural classes involved in the process. Use the feature [+long] to specify lengthened vowels. Explain in prose exactly what the rule does.

Deletion and Insertion Rules

The rules we have discussed so far involve only the changing of a few feature specifications of the input in order to derive different segments. As we noted in Chapter 7, however, there are also phonological processes which delete, insert, or permute (change) the linear order of items.

Deletion rules take the form exemplified below by the Nasal Deletion Rule we discussed earlier. Recall that in the standard varieties we discussed in Chapter 7, an underlying nasal segment is optionally deleted when it is preceded by a nasalized vowel and followed by a voiceless consonant (e.g. *bent* as [bɛ̃t]). This may be represented as follows:

$$\begin{bmatrix} C \\ +nas \end{bmatrix} \rightarrow (\emptyset) \ / \ \begin{bmatrix} V \\ +nas \end{bmatrix} \underline{\hspace{1cm}} \begin{bmatrix} C \\ -vd \end{bmatrix}$$

Here the so-called **null symbol**, ∅, indicates that the entire segment is deleted. The null symbol can be used only with reference to the entire bundle of features specifying a segment, since features cannot be added to or deleted from a segment—they can only be changed. Deletion rules are relatively common in many languages, and the mechanism for representing them is quite straightforward.

Insertion rules represent their input with the null symbol. Consider the following forms as produced in some varieties of English: *dance* [dænts], *fence* [fɛnts], and *since* [sɪnts]. Each of these forms may be realized with a final [nts] sequence. [3] Recall that there are no examples of syllable-final [ns] established for these varieties. We may assume that //ns// is the underlying form of this sequence, and that the [t] is inserted between the nasal and the fricative. The rule that inserts [t] may be written as:

$$\emptyset \rightarrow \begin{bmatrix} -d.r. \\ +cor \\ -vd \end{bmatrix} / \begin{bmatrix} +nas \\ +cor \end{bmatrix} \underline{\quad} \begin{bmatrix} +ant \\ +cor \\ -vd \\ +str \end{bmatrix} \#\#$$

$$\quad\quad\quad t \quad\quad\quad\quad n \quad\quad\quad\quad s \quad\quad \text{word finally}$$

The rule is read: a [t] is inserted between an *n* and *s* when the cluster is in word-final position.

Exercise 5

Give the formulaic representation of the following prose statements, using feature specifications where appropriate. (It is helpful to write intermediate, semi-formal descriptions when going from a prose statement to a formal rule, or vice versa.)

1. Unstressed ə may sometimes be deleted between two consonants.
2. θ becomes *s* when preceding an *s*.
3. In some styles of English, *t* and *d* may become č and ǰ respectively when followed by *y* in an unstressed syllable ([gáčyə] 'got you', [hǽǰyə] 'had you'). Represent this process.
4. In some Southern varieties of English, *l* may be deleted when it precedes a voiceless labial consonant, as in [hɛp] 'help', [wʊf] 'wolf'. Represent this process.
5. In some non-mainstream varieties of English, there is an insertion rule for *b* in the following types of items: [fǽmbli] 'family', [mɛmbri] 'memory.' Represent this rule, including the relevant environment for its operation based on the illustrative cases.
6. Formulate the rule which accounts for the epenthesis in the regular plural allomorph /ɪz/, as it was described in Chapter 7.

Exercise 6

Give the prose descriptions indicated by the following formulaic representations, indicating all but only those segments which would be affected in the English segment inventory.

$$1. \quad \begin{bmatrix} +cor \\ -d.r. \\ +vd \end{bmatrix} \rightarrow (\emptyset) / [+syl] \underline{\quad} \begin{bmatrix} +ant \\ +cor \\ +str \\ +vd \end{bmatrix}$$

Exercise 6 continued

2. $\emptyset \rightarrow \begin{bmatrix} +ant \\ -cor \\ -d.r. \\ -vd \end{bmatrix}$ / $\begin{bmatrix} +nas \\ +ant \\ -cor \end{bmatrix}$ —— $\begin{bmatrix} +cons \\ -vd \end{bmatrix}$

3. $\begin{bmatrix} +cons \\ -son \end{bmatrix} \rightarrow [-vd]$ / $\begin{bmatrix} C \\ -vd \end{bmatrix}$ ___ ##

Permutation Rules

Metathesis involves the exchange of positions of certain segments. This is a type of **permutation**, where segments change their position within a linear sequence. In the previous formalization of processes, we were limited to segments which changed their basic form but not their position in a sequence. In order to formalize permutation processes, we will have to introduce a slightly different way of representing changes. This can be demonstrated by the following hypothetical example. Suppose we found a speaker of English who pronounced words such as *ask* and *bask* as [æks] and [bæks], but who pronounced *asking* and *basking* as [æskɪŋ] and [bæskɪŋ]. We could propose that the underlying form of *ask* was //æsk//, and that this speaker had a rule which reversed the order of *sk* in word-final contexts. Such a rule would be written as follows:

$$\textit{sk}\text{-Metathesis} \quad \begin{matrix} (s) & (k) & & (k)\ (s)\ \#\# \\ \begin{bmatrix} +ant \\ +cor \\ +str \\ -vd \end{bmatrix} \begin{bmatrix} -ant \\ -d.r. \\ -vd \end{bmatrix} & \#\# \rightarrow & 2 \quad 1 \quad 3 \\ 1 \quad\quad 2 & 3 \end{matrix}$$

In this rule, the relevant string of segments (*s* and *k*) and environment (the end of the word) are represented together as the input to the rule. The segments and relevant environment are numbered, and the order of these numbers is changed appropriately to represent the output. Above, the numbers 1 and 2 represent *s* and *k*, respectively, the segments affected in the metathesis; 3 represents the relevant environment (word boundary) for the rule to operate. The use of numbers in the representation is simply a short-cut convention which saves us the trouble of writing the representations for each segment twice. This short-cut can only be used for permutation rules, since they involve a change in the position of segments, not the basic nature of the segment itself.

Exercise 7

In some varieties of English, *r* in words such as *prevent, preserve, pretend,* and *prescribe* may exchange places with the following vowel. Assume for the moment that the underlying form in each of these words is //prV// and that the rule reorders the *r* and *V*. Write the rule.

Boundaries to Phonology

Linguists have recognized for many years that compound words (those composed of two roots) are often pronounced differently than the same two items when they are not compounded. For example, the President may say, "I live in the Whítehouse," but I say, "I live in the white hoúse." Similar sorts of stress distinctions are present in *bláckbird/black bírd, Sítting Bull/sitting búll, líghthouse keeper/light hóusekeeper*. In these cases, the stress falls on the first item in the compound form, but on the second item in the non-compound forms. Such observations led structural phonologists to posit the existence of phonological elements called **junctures**. Although junctures took into account syntactic considerations, they were treated as phonological units, ultimately helping to determine such things as stress patterns. According to this view, the compound *bláckbird* contains an **internal juncture** (*bláck + bird*), while the phrase *black bírd* contains an **external juncture** (*black#bírd*).[4] It has been shown that the location of junctures may also determine other phonetic details. Recall that /t/ in English has an aspirated allophone [tʰ] initially in words, and often is realized as an unreleased allophone [t˺] in word-final position. It might be proposed that the difference in pronunciation between *white rye* [hwaɪt˺raɪ] and *why try?* [hwaɪtʰraɪ] is governed by where the external juncture occurs: /hwaɪt/#/raɪ/, /hwaɪ/#/traɪ/. Thus, juncture was used as a phonological unit which helped to account for phonetic distinctions introduced by grammatical structure. We may also appeal to the presence or absence of juncture in accounting for the type of /t/ which occurs phonetically in the examples *nitrate* [náɪtʰreɪt], /náɪtret/, and *night rate* [náɪt˺reɪt], /naɪt + ret/.

Generative phonology makes use of a similar notion to explain such phenomena. Like junctures, **phonological boundaries** are used as a basis for determining stress patterns and phonetic detail, and even enter into arguments about rule formation and underlying forms, as we will see below. Although the analysis of some languages may require more kinds of boundaries, here we will refer only to the three most commonly used boundaries. They are:

(1) the word boundary (##)
(2) the internal word boundary or base boundary (#)
(3) the "special" morpheme boundary (+).

This is not to say that word boundaries or base boundaries are not also morpheme boundaries. Our concern here, however, is the different ways in which morphemes may come together.

The boundaries are introduced directly from the syntactic level of the grammar, which is responsible for arranging words and morphemes. As the name implies, the **word boundary** (##) is the result of two words coming together in a sentence. More precisely, the divisions between the major syntactic units of a sentence are converted to boundaries as the forms become the input to the phonology. The exact way in which this conversion takes place is not important here. It is sufficient to point out that every combination of words is separated by at least two # symbols (i.e. ##).

The **internal word boundary** (#) occurs between some bases and affixes, between affixes within the same word, and between the members of a compound. Thus, the word *impossibilities*, which we referred to earlier, has the following boundaries: *##in#possible#ity#s##*, and occurrences of inflectional affixes such as Plural, Past, or the third person singular (3PS) will be separated from their bases by an internal word boundary: *##boy#Plural##* 'boys', *##walk#Past##* 'walked', *##see#3PS##* 'sees'. (The special morpheme boundary (+) is dealt with below.)

Clearly, the presence of boundaries in a word or phrase helps to determine how they are pronounced, so it is necessary to include information about boundaries in phonological rules. For example, in the forms ##white#rye## and ##why##try##, the difference between the *t*'s may be specified by adding boundaries to our rules. [5]

(a) $\begin{bmatrix} +\text{cor} \\ -\text{d.r.} \\ -\text{vd} \end{bmatrix}$ → [+asp] / ##___

 t   t^h

(b) $\begin{bmatrix} +\text{cor} \\ -\text{d.r.} \\ -\text{vd} \end{bmatrix}$ → [-released] / ___##

 t   t$^\daleth$

Rule (a) will apply only if the input *t* is immediately preceded by a word boundary, and Rule (b) will apply only if the input *t* is followed by a word boundary.

   If a rule has ___# as a context, the rule will apply only if the input precedes either a # or a ## in the string. That is, any rule that applies in a # context will also apply in a ## context (but not vice versa), because the word boundary (##) includes the weaker internal boundary (#). Recall our argument in Chapter 7 that //ng// underlies every occurrence of [ŋ], which is derived by two rules: the Nasal Assimilation Rule and the *g*-Deletion Rule. Notice in the examples below that in most standard varieties of English, the *g*-Deletion Rule does not apply to forms like those in column B.

	A		B	
sing/singer	[sɪŋɚ]	finger	[fɪŋgɚ]
ring/ringer	[rɪŋɚ]	jungle	[ǰʌŋgl̩]
bring/bringer	[brɪŋɚ]	hunger	[hʌŋgɚ]

Specifically, the *g* is not deleted in *finger, jungle,* and *hunger.* The *g*'s in these words differ from those in the other forms in that they are not followed by any phonological boundary, while the *g* in *singer* is followed by # (##sɪng#ər##), and that in *sing* is followed by ## (##sɪng##). Our *g*-Deletion Rule will now include the boundary specification # in its context, and the rule will therefore only apply before either # or ##.

g-Deletion $\begin{bmatrix} -\text{ant} \\ -\text{d.r.} \\ +\text{vd} \end{bmatrix}$ → Ø / [+nas] ___#

           g

The following derivations show that this version of the *g*-Deletion Rule permits both those forms with and those without the [g] on the surface.

	//##sɪng##//	//##sɪng#ər## //	//##fɪngər##//
n-Assimilation	##sɪŋg##	##sɪŋg#ər##	##fɪŋgər##
g-Deletion	##sɪŋ##	##sɪŋ#ər##	---
	[sɪŋ]	[sɪŋɚ]	[fɪŋgɚ]

Recall also that the *n*-Assimilation Rule applies in several situations: (a) when there is no boundary—*sing, finger*; (b) when there is an internal word boundary (#)—*in#consistent*; (c) when there is a word boundary (##)—*pancakes* [pǽŋkeɪks], *handgrenades* [hǽŋgrəneɪdz].[6] When a rule may apply in the context of any boundary or no boundary, we simply do not indicate a boundary in the rule's context:

$$n\text{-Assimilation} \quad [+\text{nas}] \rightarrow \begin{bmatrix} -\text{ant} \\ -\text{cor} \end{bmatrix} / \underline{\quad} \begin{bmatrix} -\text{ant} \\ -\text{d.r.} \end{bmatrix}$$

$$n \qquad \qquad ŋ \qquad \qquad g,k$$

There is one remaining problem with our analysis of [ŋ]. We claimed above that if there were a boundary present after an *ng* sequence, the *g* would be deleted. There are several forms, however, that do not work this way in most varieties of English: *younger, stronger, longer*. Clearly, the *g* in these forms is followed by a boundary, for the [ə] in each word is the regular morpheme for the comparative form of adjectives: *redder, hotter, finer*. But when this morpheme is present, the phonetic form of bases ending in //ng// is different, in that the [g] remains on the surface. For such cases we employ the **special morpheme boundary** (+). This is a different kind of boundary, and rules with # or ## in their environment will not apply before +. So *stronger* has the underlying form //##strɔng+ər##//, and does not meet the conditions for the application of *g*-deletion.

As an example of one way in which the presence of boundaries in phonological rules may enter into other types of phonological arguments, let us return to our discussion of the regular English plural in Chapter 7. There we introduced //z// as the underlying form of the regular plural, without explaining why we chose it over the other allomorphs. Although there are arguments against an underlying form //ɪz// or //ɪs//, we will not outline them here. Instead, we will restrict our discussion to the choice between //s// and //z//, because it involves the location of the internal word boundary # in plural nouns. Recall that we proposed two ordered rules to derive the three regular plural allomorphs from //z//:

(1) an Epenthesis Rule which inserted [ɪ] between an alveolar or palatal sibilant and the plural.

([ɪ] corresponds to the pronunciation of many speakers, but the range of the inserted vowel may actually vary considerably.)

$$\text{Epenthesis} \quad \emptyset \rightarrow \begin{bmatrix} +\text{syl} \\ -\text{bk} \\ +\text{hi} \\ -\text{tns} \end{bmatrix} / \begin{bmatrix} +\text{str} \\ +\text{cor} \end{bmatrix} \# \underline{\quad} \begin{bmatrix} +\text{ant} \\ +\text{cor} \\ +\text{str} \\ +\text{vd} \end{bmatrix}$$

$$\text{PLURAL}$$

$$\text{ɪ} \qquad \text{s,z,š,ž,č,ǰ} \quad \text{before Plural z}$$

(2) a Voicing Assimilation Rule which changes //z// to [s] when the plural occurs after a noun ending in a voiceless segment.

$$\text{Voicing Assimilation} \quad \begin{bmatrix} +\text{ant} \\ +\text{cor} \\ +\text{str} \end{bmatrix} \rightarrow [-\text{vd}] / [-\text{vd}] \quad \# \quad \underline{\quad}$$

$$\text{PLURAL}$$

$$\text{z} \qquad \qquad \text{s} \qquad \text{voiceless}$$

The addition of the boundary and grammatical information makes the operation very specific to the plural. We will want to relax some of these restrictions later to allow the rule to apply to other //z// morphemes, for example, possessive and third person singular. The derivations of three representative segment sequences are:

	//s#z//	//t#z//	//d#z//
Epenthesis	s#ɪz	---	---
Voicing Assimilation	---	t#s	---
	[sɪz]	[ts]	[dz]
	buses	*rats*	*buds*

Now consider an alternative proposal. It assumes that //s// rather than //z// is the underlying form of the regular plural. This alternative would require a Voicing Assimilation Rule which would change //s// to [z] (the opposite effect of the above Assimilation Rule), and we would still need an Epenthesis Rule. Also recall that voicing assimilation must follow epenthesis (Chapter 7). In the following derivations the Epenthesis Rule is the same as that above.

		//s#s//	//t#s//	//d#s//
Epenthesis	$\emptyset \rightarrow ɪ$ / $\begin{bmatrix} +str \\ +cor \end{bmatrix}$ # ___ PLURAL	s#ɪs	---	---
Voicing Assimilation	//s// $\rightarrow$ [z] / [+vd] # $\underline{\qquad}$ PLURAL	---	---	d#z
		*[sɪs]	[ts]	[dz]

The presence of the epenthetic vowel should cause the //s// to become voiced, but there is no boundary between them, so the assimilation rule cannot apply to the derivation of //s#s//. One way around this is to rewrite the Epenthesis Rule so that it inserts the vowel before the boundary as in the following derivation.

	//s#s//
$\emptyset \rightarrow ɪ$ / $\begin{bmatrix} +str \\ +cor \end{bmatrix}$ ___ # PLURAL	sɪ#s
//s// $\rightarrow$ [z] / [+vd] # $\underline{\qquad}$ PLURAL	sɪ#z
	[sɪz]

Although this solution derives the proper phonetic form, it may be criticized on the grounds of descriptive adequacy. Our goal in proposing any phonological rule is to represent the native intuitions of the speakers of the language as closely as possible. Although this analysis allows us to derive correct representations, most of us would agree that the epenthetic vowel of the plural should be represented as part of the plural suffix and not as part of the noun base. This second solution is counter to these intuitions. These observations suggest that our original choice of //z// as the underlying form of the regular plural is preferable, and demonstrate one way in which phonological boundaries may play a role in discussions about phonological analysis.

Exercise 8

Using the discussion above as a model, construct an argument about the underlying form of the past tense marker (e.g. as in *looked*, *tagged*, *treated*).

Assimilation Rules and Alpha Variables

Technically speaking, assimilation rules are a specialized variety of feature changing rules. As we saw in our discussion of phonological processes, assimilation involves changing one or more features of a segment to match the phonological environment of that segment. The Vowel Nasalization Rule we discussed in Chapter 7 demonstrates this clearly. Recall that this rule nasalizes a vowel when it precedes a nasal consonant.

$$\text{Vowel Nasalization} \quad V \rightarrow [\text{+nas}] \ / \ \underline{\quad} \ [\text{+nas}]$$

The Nasal Assimilation Rule (also discussed in Chapter 7) is another example of how assimilation rules are represented formally.

Exercise 9

Write the two rules that assimilate //n// to the place of articulation of the following consonant in the forms in Exercise 9(b) in Chapter 7. In one rule //n// will change to [ŋ], and in the other //n// will change to [m].

The results of Exercise 9 indicate that in each of the two rules, the output of the rule matches the specifications for [anterior] and [coronal] indicated in the rule environment. Below, we add the third context (that of alveolars), which was unnecessary above because //n// is already specified as an alveolar.

Input	Output		Context	
$\begin{bmatrix} C \\ \text{+nas} \end{bmatrix}$	$\begin{bmatrix} \text{+ant} \\ \text{+cor} \end{bmatrix}$ (n)		$\begin{bmatrix} \text{+ant} \\ \text{+cor} \end{bmatrix}$ (t,d, etc.)	
	$\begin{bmatrix} \text{+ant} \\ \text{-cor} \end{bmatrix}$ (m)		$\begin{bmatrix} \text{+ant} \\ \text{-cor} \end{bmatrix}$ (p,b, etc.)	
	$\begin{bmatrix} \text{-ant} \\ \text{-cor} \end{bmatrix}$ (ŋ)		$\begin{bmatrix} \text{-ant} \\ \text{-cor} \end{bmatrix}$ (k,g, etc.)	

It is apparent that the processes represented by these three separate rules are all part of the same process of assimilation. Therefore, we would like our rules to represent the fact that they involve a unified, general process. Rather than specifying separately that *n* becomes *m* before labials, *n* becomes ŋ before velars, and *n* remains *n* before alveolars, we should be able to show the process as a unified phenomenon and say simply that //n// assimilates in place of articulation to a following obstruent or nasal.

Such generalizations may be incorporated into a rule through the use of alpha-variables. Instead of a plus or minus before certain features in a rule, we use a Greek letter (alpha α, beta β, gamma γ, delta δ). This letter indicates that the feature may be either plus or minus, but each time that the Greek letter is specified as a plus at one point in a particular rule, it must be plus where that Greek letter appears elsewhere in the rule. If it is specified as minus, it must be minus where it appears elsewhere. A rule employing this convention must therefore have at least two occurrences of a particular Greek letter. For example, a rule that reads:

$$V \rightarrow [\alpha hi] / \underline{\hspace{1cm}} \begin{bmatrix} V \\ \alpha hi \\ +bk \end{bmatrix}$$

will indicate that a vowel assimilates in height to the height of a following back vowel. Here, if the height of the back vowel in the context is [+hi], then the output will be [+hi], because the values of alpha must match. If the value of the back vowel is [-hi], then the output will be [-hi].

Of course, this convention may also be employed in assimilation rules to specify a matching of certain features of consonants. In the Nasal Assimilation Rule, if we use Greek letters in the context of the rule, the same Greek letters in the output will cause the segments to match.

$$\text{Nasal Assimilation} \quad \begin{bmatrix} C \\ +nas \end{bmatrix} \rightarrow \begin{bmatrix} \alpha ant \\ \beta cor \end{bmatrix} / \underline{\hspace{1cm}} \begin{bmatrix} -son \\ \alpha ant \\ \beta cor \end{bmatrix}$$

This rule now changes the specifications for [anterior] and [coronal] in an underlying //n// to those of the following obstruent in the following way. If the specification for [anterior] in the context is +, then that of the output will be +. If [anterior] in the context is -, the output will be -. Similarly, if [coronal] is + in the context, it will be + in the output, and likewise for -. Notice that the values for α and β are independent of each other; [coronal] may have either the same or the opposite value of [anterior]. The rule derives the following forms.

Variables	Specifications	Derived nasal	Context
$\alpha = +$ $\beta = +$	+ant +cor	n	alveolars
$\alpha = +$ $\beta = -$	+ant -cor	m	labials
$\alpha = -$ $\beta = +$	-ant +cor	ñ	palatals [7]
$\alpha = -$ $\beta = -$	-ant -cor	ŋ	velars

The combination of these rules into one assimilation rule represents a significant generalization about the phonology of English. The use of alpha variables in rules permits us to incorporate explicitly such generalizations into our representations of phonological processes.

Our use of alpha variables in the assimilation rules so far functioned to combine several aspects of a single process into one rule. Specifically, the use of alpha variables in assimilation rules specifies an agreement between the output of a rule and some part of the rule's environment. This is one common use for alpha variables, but they may also be used for specifying details other than assimilation. In some cases they can indicate agreement between

---

Exercise 10

In casual English speech styles, we observe that word-final *d* may become a *g* when followed by a *g*-initial word (e.g. *good grief* [gʊggrif], *good game* [gʊggeᴵm]), and word final *d* becomes a *b* when followed by a word beginning with *b* (e.g. *good boy* [gʊbbɔᴵ], *good bye* [gʊbbaᴵ]). Use alpha variables to represent the assimilation process.

---

a feature value in the input and in the context, as in the following hypothetical example.

$$\begin{bmatrix} C \\ \alpha vd \end{bmatrix} \rightarrow \emptyset \; / \; \underline{\hspace{1cm}} \begin{bmatrix} C \\ \alpha vd \end{bmatrix}$$

Here, the alpha variable indicates that the deletion occurs only when that consonant agrees in voicing with the following consonant; that is, the input consonant and following consonant are always both [+vd] or both [-vd]. There are also cases in which a change takes place only when two parts of the context agree in some specification. In the following hypothetical rule, a vowel is inserted between two consonants that match in their specification for [coronal] and in their specification for [anterior].

$$\emptyset \rightarrow \text{ə} \; / \begin{bmatrix} C \\ \alpha ant \\ \beta cor \end{bmatrix} \underline{\hspace{1cm}} \begin{bmatrix} C \\ \alpha ant \\ \beta cor \end{bmatrix}$$

Exercise 11

Consider some more data concerning the assimilation of alveolar stops to velar and bilabial stops shown in Exercise 10. The assimilation may also operate for word-final *t* (*right key* [raᴵk ki], *right kind* [raᴵk kaᴵnd], *right piece* [raᴵp pis], *right place* [raᴵp pleᴵs]). However, in order for this process to work, the voicing of the final *t* or *d* must agree with that of the word-initial bilabial or velar stop. Items like *good kind, good place, right girl, right boy* do not show this assimilation process. Use the alpha convention to represent the voicing agreement. Now rewrite the rule to capture all of the observations made here.

Exercise 12

(a) In some varieties of working-class Black English, certain word-final consonant clusters are simplified by deleting the final consonant. Which clusters may be simplified is governed by certain phonological features of the cluster itself. What are the conditions which determine whether or not the final member of the cluster will be deleted? State these conditions in prose. Hint: look at the type of final segment involved and the voicing of each member of the cluster.

Exercise 12 continued

[tɛs]	'test'	[bɛlt]	'belt'	[ɛkspɛk]	'expect'
[was]	'wasp'	[fɪnɪš]	'finished'	[kol]	'cold'
[dɛs]	'desk'	[rez]	'raised'	[ol]	'old'
[sɔf]	'soft'	[læf]	'laughed'	[man]	'mind'
[fan]	'find'	[sɪks]	'six'	[lɛf]	'left'
[wal]	'wild'	[gʌlp]	'gulp'	[mæs]	'mask'
[æk]	'act'	[kræŋk]	'crank'	[græs]	'grasp'
[ǰʌmp]	'jump'	[læps]	'lapse'	[lɪs]	'list'
[rægz]	'rags'	[sɛns]	'sense'	[baks]	'box'

(b) Using alpha variables, write the formal rule that deletes the final member of the cluster.

Although we shall not discuss it in detail here, alpha variables can also be used to indicate when features must have opposite values rather than the same value. If we have a variable pair such as [αX] and [-αY] somewhere within a rule, it should be read as follows: X may have a plus or minus value, but whatever value it has, Y will have the opposite value. That is, if X is +, then Y is -; but if X is -, then Y is +. This is a logical extension of the alpha convention discussed above.

Combining Rules: Abbreviatory Conventions

The alpha convention allows us to combine different aspects of a general process within a single phonological rule representation. Without this convention, we might have to treat as separate rules the different dimensions of a general, unitary process. There are several other abbreviatory conventions that also allow us to combine potentially different rules. These conventions can best be presented by looking at several situations in which different rules seem to be unified by a more general process.

First, let us return to the rules which account for alternations of the English plural. We have already mentioned that many morphemes alternate in an identical way to the plural //z//, and others alternate analogously. The following examples indicate a way in which such alternations occur in English:

	Voiceless	Voiced	Epenthetic
Plural //z//	rat/rats	road/roads	horse/horses
3PS //z//	eat/eats	read/reads	wash/washes
Possessive //z//	cat/cat's	town/town's	thrush/thrush's
Reduced is	The cat's eating	The man's going	
Reduced has	The cat's eaten	The man's gone	
Past //d//	walk/walked	jog/jogged	pet/petted
Participle //d//	has walked	has jogged	has petted

These examples indicate that there are two general processes in English phonology whereby (a) all //z// and //d// suffixes assimilate the voicing of the final segment of the base, and (b) an epenthetic vowel is inserted if the preceding segment matches the consonant of the suffix in certain features. In the case of //z//, as we indicated above, the epenthetic vowel is inserted after the strident, coronal segments s, z, š, ž, ǰ, č. In the case of //d//, however, the epenthetic vowel is found after the coronal stops d and t.

Exercise 13

Using the Plural Epenthesis Rule as a model, write the Epenthesis Rule for the //d// past tense.

Notice that the ways in which we represent the contexts of the epenthesis rules for //d// and //z// are very similar. They are repeated here with some redundant feature specifications in parentheses.

Plural Epenthesis

$$\emptyset \rightarrow \text{I} \ / \ \begin{bmatrix} +\text{cor} \\ +\text{str} \\ (-\text{son}) \\ (+\text{d.r.}) \end{bmatrix} \# \ \underline{\quad} \ \begin{bmatrix} +\text{cor} \\ +\text{str} \\ +\text{ant} \\ +\text{vd} \\ (-\text{son}) \\ (+\text{d.r.}) \end{bmatrix} \#$$

$$s,z,\check{s},\check{z},\check{c},\check{j} \qquad\qquad z$$

Past Epenthesis

$$\emptyset \rightarrow \text{I} \ / \ \begin{bmatrix} +\text{cor} \\ -\text{d.r.} \\ (-\text{son}) \\ (-\text{str}) \end{bmatrix} \# \ \underline{\quad} \ \begin{bmatrix} +\text{cor} \\ -\text{d.r.} \\ +\text{vd} \\ (+\text{ant}) \\ (-\text{son}) \\ -\text{str} \end{bmatrix}$$

$$d,t \qquad\qquad d$$

In fact, these two contexts represent a general process in which two similar segments must be separated by a vowel. We may capture this generalization by collapsing these contexts through the use of alpha variables. Examining the feature specifications above, we see that the final segment of the base must be [-son, +cor] and either [+str, +d.r.] or [-str, -d.r.]. Similarly, the final segment of the suffix must be [-son, +cor, +ant, +vd] and must match its values for *str* and *d.r.* with those of the preceding segment. This is expressed as follows.

Epenthesis

$$\emptyset \rightarrow \text{I} \ / \ \begin{bmatrix} -\text{son} \\ +\text{cor} \\ \alpha\text{str} \\ \alpha\text{d.r.} \end{bmatrix} \# \ \underline{\quad} \ \begin{bmatrix} -\text{son} \\ +\text{cor} \\ +\text{ant} \\ +\text{vd} \\ \alpha\text{str} \\ \alpha\text{d.r.} \end{bmatrix} \#$$

So the use of the alpha variable convention allows us to collapse related rules in order to express general phonological processes more clearly. Similarly, the Voicing Assimilation Rules by which //z// becomes [s] and //d// becomes [t] in the examples above are structurally related and may be combined to express a generalization. The two rules are repeated below for comparison. Notice that in both the Epenthesis Rule and the Voicing Assimilation Rule, we now use boundaries to specify the context rather than grammatical categories, such as PLURAL.

//z// Devoicing $\begin{bmatrix} -\text{son} \\ +\text{ant} \\ +\text{cor} \\ +\text{str} \end{bmatrix} \rightarrow [-\text{vd}] \; / \; [-\text{vd}] \; \# \; \underline{\quad} \; \#$

        z   s

//d// Devoicing $\begin{bmatrix} +\text{cor} \\ -\text{d.r.} \end{bmatrix} \rightarrow [-\text{vd}] \; / \; [-\text{vd}] \; \# \; \underline{\quad} \; \#$

        d   t

In these rules, everything to the right of the arrow is identical, suggesting that the two segments are subject to the same phonological process. We would like to express this process by collapsing the two rules into a single rule, but a different abbreviatory convention is required. In this case, the distinctive definitions of z and d share all feature specifications except [d.r.] and [str]. We may combine the feature bundles of both in one feature matrix by using the **brace notation**. Braces indicate "either/or" conditions. When feature specifications appear within braces, one is applied and the other is ignored for purposes of that application of the rule. The use of braces in this way allows us to specify groups of segments that are not natural classes according to our system of phonological features, but which nevertheless are subject to identical processes. The rule describing this process will then apply to the entire class of segments. Say, for example, that a certain process pertains to nasals and obstruents but not to liquids, semivowels, or vowels. Referring to the phonological feature chart in Chapter 4, we see that we may define this class of segments as either [+nas] or [-son]. That is, all obstruents are [-son] and all nasals are [+nas]. Furthermore, liquids, semivowels, and vowels are neither of these. This class is characterized using braces as:

$$\begin{Bmatrix} [+\text{nas}] \\ [-\text{son}] \end{Bmatrix}$$

Returning to the Voicing Assimilation Rules above, we may employ braces to unite the two rules. The configuration

$$\begin{bmatrix} -\text{son} \\ +\text{ant} \\ +\text{cor} \\ +\text{vd} \\ \begin{Bmatrix} -\text{d.r.} \\ +\text{str} \end{Bmatrix} \end{bmatrix}$$

specifies those segments which are [-son, +ant, +cor, +vd] and either [+str] (z) or [-d.r.] (d). Notice that z and d cannot be combined uniquely as a natural class on the basis of our discussion of natural classes in Chapter 4. The combined rule is:

Devoicing $\begin{bmatrix} -\text{son} \\ +\text{ant} \\ +\text{cor} \\ +\text{vd} \\ \begin{Bmatrix} -\text{d.r.} \\ +\text{str} \end{Bmatrix} \end{bmatrix} \rightarrow [-\text{vd}] \; / \; [-\text{vd}] \; \# \; \underline{\quad} \; \#$

Rule Collapsing and Rule Ordering

The decision to collapse phonological rules cannot be made without considering certain consequences for rules. One of the issues that arises concerns rule ordering. In Chapter 7 we discussed the importance of ordering relations among rules. The critical question is what happens to ordering relationships when we collapse two or more processes into one rule.

When two or more rules are collapsed, we want to be able to retain the ordering relations that held between them in their independent forms. When we collapsed the Nasal Assimilation Rule from separate rules, the issue of ordering did not come up because there is no case in which the output of one of these rules is the input for another. If one rule applies, the others will not. For example, if we have an *n* preceding a *k*, only that rule changing *n* before velars will apply; the others will not apply because their environments do not match the specifications of the velar segment. Another way of saying this is that the four rules do not apply sequentially. Only such non-sequential rules may be collapsed through the application of the alpha convention. Thus, the alpha convention always implies non-sequential rule order.

The brace convention is unlike the alpha convention in that a particular order of application is implied. This order is indicated within the rule by the top-to-bottom order of the material within the braces. The subrule choosing the topmost material in the braces will apply first, then the subrule using the next expansion may apply, and so forth. This relationship is called conjunctive rule order.

We may demonstrate conjunctive ordering by examining the Devoicing Rules in our discussion of braces above. First, we must determine if the independent devoicing rules for //d// and //z// are sequentially ordered. Does the output of one become the input to the other, and does their order of application make a difference in the output? Obviously, if they are not ordered in this way, it will not matter which rule is ordered first in the collapsed version of the rule. When the //d// suffix (the participle) occurs together in a word with a //z// suffix (either the plural or the possessive), //d// precedes //z//. Consider the underlined words in the following passage.

> Rapidly replacing the category of the Young Marrieds in the city
> is that of the growing army of young divorced people. Where
> formerly their social life might have centered on children, homes,
> and gardens, the Young Divorceds now find themselves immersed
> in the world of singles....

Specifically, the Devoicing Rule operates twice in the form *divorceds* [dɪvɔ́rsts]. Clearly, the rule //d// → [t] must apply before //z// → [s], because the voiceless *t* must be present as the conditioning context for devoicing //z//. Thus, in the following derivations, order A derives the proper output, while order B does not.

	A		*B*
	//dɪvɔrs#d#z//		//dɪvɔrs#d#z//
d → t	dɪvɔ́rs#t#z	z → s	---
z → s	dɪvɔ́rs#t#s	d → t	dɪvɔ́rs#t#z
	[dɪvɔ́rsts]		*[dɪvɔ́rstz]

This ordering relation is incorporated into the combined Devoicing Rule above by indicating the feature which specifies d [-d.r.] above that which specifies z [+str] (i.e. $\left\{ {-d.r. \atop +str} \right\}$). Such an ordering relationship will always be implied by rules employing the brace notation. [8]

In the preceding sections, we have looked at some of the formal conventions for writing rules in generative phonology. There are certainly other conventions, and alternative ways of representing some of the conventions we have introduced here. The particular notation used in our rules is simply established by convention, and other notational systems might have been used. On another level, however, the choice of what to include in our rules, and the types of relationships indicated in our formalization, are a direct reflection of a particular theory of phonology. In this sense, rules must be seen as a formalization of our theory, and thus represent claims that we make about the organization of phonological systems.

NOTES

1. In reality, the simple distinction between "obligatory" and "optional" rules is not sufficiently precise. Careful examination of so-called optional rules indicates that some subsets of the appropriate environment regularly favor the operation of the rule over other subsets, and that this must be included as an essential part of a formal representation of what speakers know about their language. For a discussion of such constraints on rules, see Wolfram and Fasold (1974), Chapter 5.
2. The feature *flap* here is an *ad hoc* feature that we have introduced to eliminate the difficulty of representing [ɾ] in the features we discussed in Chapter 4.
3. It is, of course, possible to get a nasalized vowel replacing the *n*, as we discussed above. In such a case it appears that the Nasal Deletion Rule is ordered following the *t* insertion. This results in forms like [æ̃ts] 'ants', [fɛ̃ts] 'fence', and [sɪ̃ts] 'sense'.
4. The symbols # and + indicate juncture in structural phonology. They should not be confused with the boundaries used in generative phonology, which we discuss below.
5. There are, of course, other phonological dimensions that are important in accounting for aspirated and unaspirated realizations of /t/ (see Chapter 3), but we will ignore these for our discussion of boundaries.
6. The *handgrenade* example requires application of one rule that deletes the *d* of *hand* before the *n* can assimilate.
7. We did not deal with the palatal nasal earlier. Francis (1958) discusses its distribution.
8. Another abbreviatory convention we used in Chapter 5 is parentheses ( ), which indicate optional material. In actuality, ( ) combines rules that are disjunctively ordered. That is, no two rules collapsed by ( ) may apply to the same form.

SUGGESTED READING

Most introductions to generative phonology cover the basic conventions for writing rules, although some are much more specific in their presentation than others. One of the earlier attempts to present the conventions for rule writing is Chapter 4 in Harms' *Introduction to Phonological Theory* (1968). Schane (1973), Sloat, Taylor, and Hoard (1978), and Hyman (1975) all present some of the same conventions covered in our treatment, although on a rather more selective basis. Naturally, these books are heavily dependent on the set of conventions originally set forth in Chomsky and Halle's classic work (1968), although some of these have now been modified. Anderson (1974, Chapter 6) gives more extensive treatment to rule combining and the relationship of simplicity to formalism. His discussions, however, are more appropriate for advanced than beginning students. During the last twenty years, the journal *Language* has contained many articles on phonology employing some of the conventions presented here, and a number of articles directly concerned with the finer details of formalism in phonology.

CHAPTER 9
Variation, Change, and Naturalness in Phonology

Language Variation and Phonological Change

In our many references to examples from English, we have often had to qualify our statements by referring to "certain varieties of American English." This qualification was necessary in indicating important phonetic details and in showing how certain phonological processes work. However, such differences in pronunciation are not only of interest to phoneticians and the curious traveller. In many instances, they have become the supporting evidence in the development of a number of new theoretical advances in phonology. An understanding of the features, sources, and processes involved in language variation is crucial to understanding the most recent developments in phonological theory.

The impression we may have sometimes given that English is an unchanging, regular system has been largely for the convenience of explaining how phonological systems in general are put together. In fact, the label "English" applies to language systems as varied as the English spoken by the inhabitants of former British colonies in Africa, to that of the Oxford-educated literature professor, to that of a network newscaster, to that of a resident of rural Mississippi. In fact, any person studying the phonology of English must account for social, geographic, and individual variations from the idealized model often presented in our analyses.

Virtually every variety of English has traditionally been assigned some degree of positive or negative evaluation by the group using it, by groups using other varieties, and by society's institutions. However, such variation must be seen as perfectly ordinary. The differences between varieties of English—including those between "standard English" and "non-standard English" (or, as we often refer to these varieties, nonmainstream)—must be viewed as just that: differences. All varieties of English, whether evaluated positively or negatively, are highly organized and systematic. In addition, there are systematic patterns to the differences between varieties. The evaluations assigned to any variety are given for social reasons, and do not reflect intellectual or linguistic inadequacies in any way. Such differences result from principles of organization and change that are shared to some extent by all human languages, and that appear to make sense in terms of the physiological and cognitive linguistic capacities of all humans.

Dialects: Sources of Linguistic Variation

One of the most easily noticeable differences among varieties of English is lexical variation. An Oregonian visiting Boston, for example, is likely to be disappointed in what passes for a *milkshake*, just as an American in Britain may have difficulty in finding the *boot* on a car. Similarly, a *rap* may be a considerably different sort of event among young Black men than among a group of suburban, White college students. Although such differences are interesting, they are relatively insignificant from the perspective of phonological variation.

The important point in phonological variation is that each of the diverse lexical items will be produced according to the rules of the speaker's own grammar. Thus, aside from the differences in meaning, the word *boot* might be pronounced slightly differently by a Britisher and by an American. Such differences in pronunciation of words result from differences in the phonological systems of the speakers. In order to understand systematic differences of this sort, it will be helpful to examine some of the factors accounting for variation in American English.

At the finest level of analysis, every person talks differently from every other person. Personal language varieties, called **idiolects**, result from the fact that all people in a sense create their own language system on the basis of observations of their surroundings while they are learning the language. It is also true, however, that given individuals share many more details of their system with some people than with others. Thus, differences between idiolects may be slight or great. We may, in fact, specify identifying features for the systems of fairly large groups of speakers at various levels of fineness. The term **language**, when applied to English, incorporates a number of quite diverse varieties, but may be identified on the basis of many shared systematic details that make all varieties of English different from, say, French or Nahuatl. It is also possible to identify certain systematic features that distinguish among the varieties themselves. Although the boundaries around the varieties, and the terms to be applied to them, are sometimes difficult to pinpoint, the term **dialect** is often used to refer to distinguishable varieties of English. We prefer to use **variety** in order to avoid the pejorative meaning often associated with "dialect" in its popular uses.

The most important points about varieties of English are (1) that the varieties are best identified by differences in the system of rules that underlie and account for actual speech productions, and (2) that these systematic differences tend to correspond to specific social groupings. Such social groupings may be constituted around any of a number of different socially diagnostic attributes, such as geographic region, age, socio-economic class, or ethnicity. Such factors influence a person's pattern of contact and identification with other people. Children, of course, learn language through contact with other people, so such socially diagnostic attributes may be seen as both the conditioning and identifying factors in language variation.

Geographical region is one of the more apparent attributes for identifying language varieties in America. We have all had the experience of visiting another region and noticing that the people there pronounce words differently. More surprisingly, in such situations we are often told that we talk "funny," when in fact we think we talk "right." Regional differences may correspond to rather large geographic regions. For example, many people from the South pronounce the words *pin* and *pen* identically as [pɪn], whereas most Northern and Western Americans distinguish the words as [pɪn] and [pɛn]. The Southern version of such words is not to be seen as a "mispronunciation." Nor can it be said that Southerners make no distinction between //ɪ// and //ɛ//. If we subject a number of forms to a phonological analysis, we will find that the neutralization of [ɪ] and [ɛ] is quite regular in certain contexts, but that the distinction is maintained in others. Consider the following forms from a Southern speaker.

[pɪn]	'pin'	[pɪk]	'pick'
[pɪn]	'pen'	[pɛk]	'peck'
[sɪnd]	'send'	[pɪt]	'pit'
[sɪn]	'sin'	[pɛt]	'pet'
[hɪn]	'hen'	[blɪs]	'bliss'
[bɪn]	'bin'	[blɛs]	'bless'
[bɪn]	'Ben'		

The forms in the first column all show the neutralization of //ɪ// and //ɛ// in words that contrast phonetically in Northern speech. The forms in the other column, however, demonstrate that the contrast is retained in many other minimal pairs, so we argue that this Southern variety of English has the expected underlying phonemic contrast between //ɪ// and //ɛ//. Because the neutralization takes place only when //ɛ// occurs before *n*, we may say that the speakers of this dialect have a phonological rule that changes //ɛ// to [ɪ] before *n* (the context is actually more general for most varieties of Southern English and may include all nasals, rather than just *n*).

$$\varepsilon \rightarrow \text{ɪ} / \underline{\quad} \text{n}$$

So one difference between these two regional language varieties may be accounted for by a rule that applies in many Southern dialects but not in Northern and Western dialects. There are numerous other differences between Southern and Northern varieties of English, each of which may be accounted for by some sort of difference in rules between the two regional varieties.

Exercise 1

In certain parts of New England, people use what has come to be called an "*r*-less" dialect. Below are some forms from New England speech, compared with forms from the Midwest United States. Does the New England dialect have an underlying //r//: (a) in any forms, (b) in forms like *car*? Write the rule which accounts for the absence of [r].

	New England	*Midwest U.S.*	
1.	[ka]	[kar]	'car'
2.	[ban]	[barn]	'barn'
3.	[mɛri]	[mɛri]	'merry'
4.	[pak]	[park]	'park'
5.	[paɾi]	[parɾi]	'party'
6.	[raɪd]	[raɪd]	'ride'
7.	[gəraž]	[gəraž]	'garage'
8.	[ǰa]	[ǰar]	'jar'
9.	[ǰarɪŋ]	[ǰarɪŋ]	'jarring'
10.	[sari]	[sari]	'sorry'
11.	[baro]	[baro]	'borrow'
12.	[karɪnðəgəraž]	[karɪnðəgəraž]	'car in the garage'
13.	[ǰarəvǰæm]	[ǰarəvǰæm]	'jar of jam'
14.	[kabaɪðəgəraž]	[karbaɪðəgəraž]	'car by the garage'
15.	[ǰafɔǰæm]	[ǰarfɔrǰæm]	'jar for jam'

Even within a given geographic region, not all people talk alike. In every region there are important systematic phonological differences that correlate with differences in **socio-economic status**. Although socio-economic status is quite difficult to determine objectively, sociolinguists have developed a number of techniques in recent years for identifying socially diagnostic linguistic structures. They have found that a number of phonological differences tend to correlate with what social class a speaker belongs to. A well-known example of phonological variation based on socio-economic status is the pronunciation of *-ing* as [ɪn] in unstressed syllables. Studies of this variation in several different places have indicated that a change from //ɪŋ// to [ɪn] in items such as *playing* [pleyɪn] or *laughing* [læfɪn] is much more frequent among working class populations than their middle class counterparts. Observe again that the difference in pronunciation here is due to the application of a phonological rule changing the place of articulation, and is not "careless" speech.

The devoicing of final voiced stops (Chapter 6, Exercise 4) is likewise conditioned by social status. In some varieties of working class Black speech, the forms *salad, good, lid* are pronounced as [sælɪt], [gʊt], and [lɪt],[1] whereas speakers of standard varieties of English pronounce these forms with a final [d]. This difference is explainable by the presence of a devoicing rule in these varieties that is not present in standard varieties:

$$\begin{bmatrix} +\text{cor} \\ -\text{d.r.} \end{bmatrix} \rightarrow [-\text{vd}] \; / \; \_\_\_ \; \#\#$$

In some communities, certain differences associated with geographic region may also function to differentiate socio-economic class. The degree of *r*-lessness in the speech of New York City residents to a large extent reflects socio-economic class. In speech recorded in interviews, it was found that upper-middle class New Yorkers were *r*-less about 70% of the time—that is, in 70% of all cases where the *r*-Deletion Rule could have operated, it did operate. Lower middle class speakers were *r*-less about 80% of the time, working class speakers between 85 and 90%, and lower class speakers above 95%. Thus, it appears that the application of the *r*-Deletion Rule in some way marks the class identity of English speakers in New York. But it should be noticed that this variable does not sharply distinguish between classes. Rather, it is gradient in its application. None of the groups apply the *r*-Deletion Rule all of the time, but lower class speakers apply the rule more often than the middle classes.

The rule which neutralizes the contrast between //θ// and //f// in certain Black varieties is also correlated with different socio-economic classes within the community. This rule changes //θ// to [f] in morpheme-final and morpheme-medial positions, as in [tuf] 'tooth', [mæf] 'math', and [æflɛɹɪks] 'athletics'. Middle class Black speakers generally apply this rule infrequently (less than 10% of the time), whereas working class speakers may apply the rule in over 50% of the cases where it might be applied. Rules that are associated with low-status groups are usually referred to as **stigmatized** rules; those associated with high-status groups are referred to as **prestige** rules. In American English phonology, there appear to be many more stigmatized rules than prestige rules.

Phonological variables are also subject to change in different social contexts. Most people talk differently in formal situations, such as school or church, than they do in casual situations, such as conversations with family or friends. Such differences are regular enough for us to identify certain speech styles which influence rule choices appropriate for particular situations. An important factor in speech style seems to be how much conscious attention is paid by an individual to his or her speech. Sociolinguists typically identify a number of speech styles, each elicited by a different kind of interview procedure or social situation. The most casual styles of speech will emerge when a person is talking comfortably with a friend or peer. Interviews with an outside investigator using a tape recorder will generally produce careful speech styles. A more formal reading style may result from an individual reading a written passage aloud, while a very formal style will generally be used to read a list of words. All classes tend to shift the percentage of application of rules in different kinds of situations.

The Interdental Fricative Stopping rule changes initial //θ// (*think, through*) to a corresponding affricate [tθ] or stop [t]. The graph below (from Labov, 1972b:113) shows the percentages of application of this rule in four different styles by five socio-economic class groupings in New York City. Each line represents the responses of a different class. The higher values are higher percentages of [t] or [tθ]. As the speech style of a speaker becomes more formal, the percentage of applications of the rule decreases (from left to right across the graph).

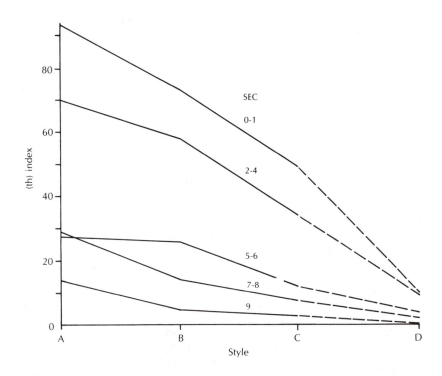

Class stratification of a linguistic variable with stable social significance: (th) *in* thing, through, *etc. Socioeconomic class scale: 0-1, lower class; 2-4, working class; 5-6, 7-8, lower middle class; 9, upper middle class. A, casual speech; B, careful speech; C, reading style; D, word lists.*

(Reprinted with permission of the University of Pennsylvania Press from Sociolinguistic Patterns *by William Labov, 1972.)*

Some important linguistic differences relate to a speaker's **age**. As we will see, many differences among varieties result from innovations in rules. Younger generations of speakers may use forms resulting from rules added fairly recently—rules that older speakers may not use. Thus, by examining different generational groups we may see specific language varieties in the process of change. In the varieties of English spoken in the Appalachian Mountains, the older pronunciations of *ain't* and *it* as [hent] and [hɪt] occur frequently among older speakers, but only rarely among younger speakers. The original pronunciations of these words in Middle English had initial [h]. At some point in the history of English, a rule deleting this *h* was introduced, so that most contemporary English varieties say [ent] and [ɪt]. The *h*-Deletion Rule has been added only recently in Appalachian English, so that older speakers apply it in a limited way, while younger speakers apply it more broadly. We will examine this phenomenon in more detail later in this chapter.

There are other factors that may determine differences among language varieties. For example, women and men may exhibit phonological differences, as may individuals from different ethnic groups. It is the combination of all such factors that creates the vast array of varieties of English. The differences relate ultimately to differences in the structure of the phonologies involved. These structural differences result largely from language change.

Language Change

All languages are constantly in the process of change. But while change in languages is constant, the exact nature of the changes that take place is not always predictable. Even though language changes normally make sense from the perspective of phonetic or organizational principles, exactly which changes will take place and how sweeping they will be is not entirely determinable. As we said earlier, phonological change often takes the form of innovations in the rules or changes in the underlying forms of adult language users. No matter how extensive or minute the change, children acquiring a language will end up with grammars different from those of speakers two or three generations older. As long as members of a community of speakers remain in regular contact, such changes over time will remain fairly constantly distributed across the community. Although some generational differences may be noticeable in such a community, most speakers of each generation would share the innovations. However, if for any reason the speech community is divided, either physically or socially, so that the members of some segment of the community communicate among themselves more than with the members of another segment, two varieties will eventually emerge. Even though certain processes of change may be in motion before a speech community is divided, the ultimate details of the changes are relatively unpredictable, and separated communities will often incorporate them in different ways.

Generally, the longer the two communities remain separated, the more different their language varieties will become. In fact, if they remain isolated for a long period of time, the varieties they speak may become mutually unintelligible and on the surface appear quite different. But even after thousands of years of separation, two varieties will retain many traces of their common heritage. In the phonological component, one such remnant from the past can be found in the inventory of sounds. We may compare certain words of different modern languages and find regular **sound correspondences** that indicate a mutual common source:

Sanskrit	pitar	pad	(matsyah)
Greek	pater	podos	psari
Latin	pater	pes	piscis
French	pere	pied	poisson
Spanish	padre	pie	pescado
German	fater	fuss	fisch
Norwegian	far	fot	fisk
English	father	foot	fish
Arabic	ʔabb	qadam	samak
Japanese	chichi	ashi	sakana

Correspondences such as those between initial *p* and *f* suggest that all the modern languages in the above list, except Arabic and Japanese, are **related**. This means that they all stem from a mutual common "ancestor" language. In terms of the processes of division and change we have been discussing, we may propose that at one time there was a common language, now dead, from which all these modern languages developed independently. This old form of the language, generally called Proto Indo-European, was not the only original language in the world. The languages related to Arabic share a different mutual common ancestor, and those related to Japanese share yet another. It is possible to posit proto languages for numerous clusters of modern languages —the Semitic languages, groups of different African languages, groups of American Indian languages, and so on.

It is also possible to demonstrate differing degrees of relationship within any such major language grouping. There are clusters of increasingly closely related language varieties, and we can trace lines of relationship among them. Returning to the comparisons above, we see that English, German, and Norwegian share certain sound correspondences (e.g. initial *f*) that the other Indo-European languages do not. This suggests that these languages stem from a mutual ancestor more recent than Proto Indo-European. Such degrees of relationship are often traced by means of a "family tree." For English, the line usually is represented as follows (with examples of distantly related languages in parentheses).

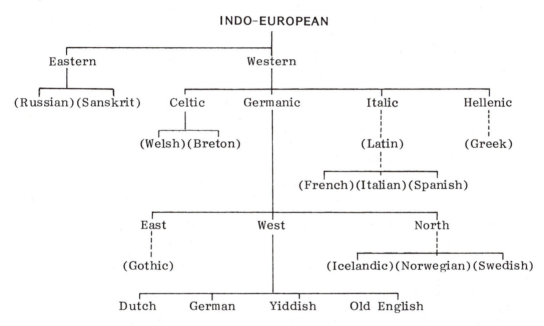

Within English itself, it is possible to trace similar historical relationships. It appears, for example, that during the Anglo-Saxon period in England about 1,300 years ago, there were at least three major dialect areas. These and other regional and social differences were maintained during the Old English (approximately 500-1100 A.D.), Middle English (1100-1500 A.D.), and Modern English (1500-Present) periods. At the time North America was colonized, there were important dialect differences in different regions of Great Britain. Particular regions of North America were settled by people who tended to come from the same area of Britain. Thus, certain regional differences in American English are still traceable to dialect differences in Britain during the 17th and 18th centuries. Although many local changes have taken place since, we are reasonably certain that the East Midlanders and Southeasterners from Britain, who settled Eastern New England and the Virginia Tidewater Region, brought with them an *r*-less variety of English. The Ulster Scotch-Irish settlers of

Western New England, Upper New York, and the Great Lakes regions brought a variety of English that retained post-vocalic *r*. Numerous regional differences in American English stem from original settlement patterns, and from subsequent patterns of movement across the continent. These patterns, combined with indigenous changes resulting from geographic, socio-economic, and ethnic group differentiation, have produced a mosaic of varieties in American English.

Describing Phonological Change

So far in our discussion of language variation, we have simply observed that phonological differences between language varieties may be traced to differences in rules. That is, the phonological variables that help us to identify different dialects are traceable to the fact that people speaking one dialect use one rule, whereas speakers of another dialect use another rule (or perhaps none at all). Because closely related dialects share a fairly recent mutual common ancestor, we can usually trace the differences between them to some sort of change in the rules of one or both dialects. Each of the varieties is the end product of a series of changes from a mutual common ancestor. It is not sensible to assume that any one of the existing varieties is the basis for any of the other varieties. Each variety, as we see it now, is the result of a series of changes. The connection among the varieties is a common language that existed at some time in the past. Thus, "standard English" cannot be viewed as the foundation of other varieties, nor the other varieties as "deviations" from Standard English. In some cases, what we view as Standard English has undergone certain changes which other varieties have not undergone, but by the same token, other varieties may have changed in ways that Standard English has not. With this in mind, let us examine four major kinds of phonological rule change: **rule addition**, **rule simplification**, **rule reordering**, and **restructuring and rule loss**.

Rule Addition. Often, a given phonological difference between two varieties can be described by the presence of a rule in one variety and its absence in the other. One dialect has often added a rule, while the other has not. Although there could be any of a number of reasons for adding a rule, we will see later that it usually relates in some way to making either the phonological system or the phonetic forms conform more closely to the ways in which we expect human languages to operate. Most of our previous examples of dialect differences resulted from the addition of a rule in one dialect. We accounted for "*r*-lessness" in certain New England varieties of English by the presence of an *r*-Deletion Rule not present in "*r*-ful" American dialects. Historical evidence suggests that the *r*-Deletion Rule was added to the dialects spoken in middle eastern and southeastern Britain, and subsequently brought to New England (and the Virginia Tidewater region) by settlers from those areas. Similarly, the rule that devoices final stops in words like *salad* [sælɪt] has been added to certain nonmainstream dialects but probably not to Standard dialects.

Exercise 2

We have already discussed the rule that changes //ɛ// to [ɪ] before *n* in some Southern dialects. What are some arguments for suggesting that this should be regarded as a rule addition?

Exercise 3

The historically older forms of the words *which, what, why, whether,* and *when* began with [hw]. Many Americans still pronounce the words in this way, thereby distinguishing them phonetically from *witch, wye* (the letter), *weather,* and *wen.* Many other Americans, however, pronounce the so-called *wh*-words with an initial phonetic [w], so that they become phonetically indistinguishable from their counterparts with //w//. Which dialect added a rule, and what is the form of that rule? Is it important or not that the contrast between the *wh*-words and the *w*-words has been lost? Why?

Rule Simplification. Another source of differentiation among dialects results not from the presence of a rule in one dialect and its absence in another, but from slightly different forms of the same rule in both dialects. From a historical perspective, we may often explain differences by showing that the rule has been simplified by one dialect and not by the other. The resulting differences in the rules account for phonological differences between the dialects. In practical terms, rule simplification means that the rule is changed so that it applies to a broader variety of forms than previously. For example, a rule may be extended to apply within a more general range of phonological contexts. A series of dialects may progressively remove restrictions from the context of a rule. Consider the following example concerning our //ɛ// to [ɪ] rule. We stated previously that the rule applies only before *n,* but let us presume that there are three different dialects that have added the rule. The following data represent the pronunciations of several items in each dialect.

	Standard dialect	Dialect 1	Dialect 2	Dialect 3
'ten'	[tɛn]	[tɪn]	[tɪn]	[tɪn]
'Engles'	[ɛ́ŋgɬz]	[ɛ́ŋgɬz]	[ɪ́ŋgɬz]	[ɪ́ŋgɬz]
'hem'	[hɛm]	[hɛm]	[hɛm]	[hɪm]

The standard dialect has not added the rule. Dialect 1 has added the rule, but it applies only before [n]. Thus, the context of the rule must be specified formally as [+nas, +cor]. Dialect 2 has altered the specification of the context so that the rule applies before both [n] and [ŋ]. This class is specified as:

$$\begin{bmatrix} +\text{nas} \\ \left\{ \begin{matrix} +\text{cor} \\ -\text{ant} \end{matrix} \right\} \end{bmatrix}$$

(which permits a more general application). Dialect 3 has generalized the rule so that it applies before all nasals, specified simply as [+nas]. This progression may be seen as a kind of rule simplification, in that it permits the rule to operate on more forms as the context is generalized. Clearly, the simplest or most general rules would operate on all forms in the language, thereby entirely eliminating the specification of a context. We will discuss the implications of such a rule below.

There are many cases in which certain phonological differences between American English dialects may be traced to more or less restrictive applications of a rule. This process of progressive generalization of rule context is sometimes observable in the phonological differences exhibited by different generations of speakers of a given dialect. One such case is the *h*-Deletion Rule mentioned above, by which *hain't* becomes *ain't* and *hit* becomes *it*. Most varieties of English have added a rule deleting the initial *h*. If we examine application of the rule in three different age groups among Appalachian speakers, we find an orderly progression of less-restrictive contexts of application. First, in the dialects of some older speakers we would find that the *h*-Deletion Rule applies only when the words in question are unstressed, and then only sometimes. In the sentences *I like it* and *I ain't gonna go*, we might find *it* and *ain't* pronounced sometimes with, and sometimes without, an [h]. Other occurrences of *it* and *ain't* (in relatively stressed contexts) will always be pronounced with the [h]: *Hít's over there, That's good, háin't it?* For this generation of speakers, the rule applies optionally in restricted contexts.

In the speech of some middle-aged speakers, the context of application is somewhat more general. These speakers apply the *h*-Deletion Rule optionally, but have extended it to apply in both unstressed and stressed contexts. The example sentences above would sometimes have an [h], and sometimes not. For the younger generation of speakers, the rule always applies in the unstressed contexts (the *it* of *I like it* would never be pronounced with [h]), and sometimes applies in other contexts (the tag question *ain't it* might sometimes have an [h] and sometimes not). Thus, we see several age-related varieties in one community, each generation applying a rule more widely than the last. If the trend continues, a future generation will apply it always in all contexts, which will ultimately have an important impact on the underlying forms.

Exercise 4

There is a rule in some American English dialects that reduces final consonant clusters ending in a stop in certain contexts (Exercise 12, Chapter 8). One such final cluster is *st*, which is reduced to [s]. The following is a comparison of the pronunciation of the word *test* in several contexts by the speakers of two varieties. Dialect A is that of middle class Northern White speakers. Dialect B represents that of some working class Northern Black speakers.

		Dialect A	*Dialect B*
Context 1:	*testing*	[tɛstɪŋ]	[tɛstɪŋ]
Context 2:	*test example*	[tɛst ɛgzæmpl̩]	[tɛs ɛgzæmpl̩]
Context 3:	*test case*	[tɛs kes]	[tɛs kes]

What are the contexts that determine when the Consonant Cluster Reduction Rule applies in each dialect? Which is the more general application of the rule?

Rule Reordering. In Chapter 7 we discussed the relative ordering of the Flapping Rule, which changes //t// and //d// to [ɾ], and the Vowel Lengthening Rule, which lengthens vowels before voiced consonants. We suggested there that the Lengthening Rule applied first in order to preserve differences between forms such as *latter* and *ladder*. The following four derivations illustrate the rules applied in this order.

Underlying Form	//lætər//	//lædər//	//bæd//	//bæt//
1. Lengthening Rule	---	læːdɚ	bæːd	---
2. Flapping Rule	læɾɚ	læːɾɚ	---	---
Phonetic Form	[læɾɚ]	[læːɾɚ]	[bæːd]	[bæt]

A classic case of rule reordering would involve one dialect that applied these rules in the order specified above, and another that used the opposite order. This would result in important phonological differences between the dialects. Reordering the rules would neutralize the difference between *ladder* and *latter*, as follows:

Underlying Form	//lætər//	//lædər//	//bæd//	//bæt//
1. Flapping Rule	læɾɚ	læɾɚ	---	---
2. Lengthening Rule	læːɾɚ	læːɾɚ	bæːd	---
Phonetic Form	[læːɾɚ]	[læːɾɚ]	[bæːd]	[bæt]

Exercise 5

We have previously discussed rules relating to nasal segments within words. The first was a Nasal Deletion Rule which removes the nasal segment from a final cluster of Nasal + Voiceless Consonant. Recall that this rule applies after the Vowel Nasalization Rule, to produce such forms as [bɛ̃t] 'bent' and [tɛ̃t] 'tent'. The other rule is the one that changes //ɛ// to [ɪ] before an *n*, which also applies after the Nasalization Rule to produce forms like [tɪ̃n] 'ten' and [bɪ̃n] 'Ben.' Consider the following forms from two different English dialects.

	Dialect A	Dialect B
'tint'	[tɪ̃t]	[tɪ̃t]
'tent'	[tɪ̃t]	[tɛ̃t]
'tin'	[tɪ̃n]	[tɪ̃n]
'ten'	[tɪ̃n]	[tɪ̃n]

From the forms for *ten* and *tin*, we can determine that the rule changing //ɛ// to [ɪ] before *n* operates in both dialects, but in one it applies before the Deletion Rule and in the other it applies after it. In which order do the rules apply in Dialect A? And in Dialect B? Give derivations that demonstrate the ordering.

Restructuring and Rule Loss. The reordering of rules is often a move toward more expectable phonetic forms. Often the different types of changes operate together (or progressively) in a given dialect. A given dialect might add a rule, then later change it to apply more generally, and then reorder it with respect to other rules that apply to the same forms. Certain changes may proceed to a point where they ultimately do away with the need for a rule. This is usually accomplished by **restructuring** the underlying forms to which the rule applies, so that the context of application no longer exists and therefore there is no need for the rule. Most examples of rule loss in English appear to have occurred in response to restructuring of the underlying forms.

There are a number of ways in which underlying forms of lexical items can be restructured. Practically, all of them involve the way in which successive generations of speakers learn their language. It sometimes happens that rules of the sort described above cause certain underlying forms in the language of the parents' generation to be unlearnable by the children's generation. That is, some rule changes cause such sweeping adjustments in pronunciation that there are no surface traces of the original underlying form for children from the next generation to learn. As a result, they learn the surface form as an underlying form.

Consider, for example, the differences in pronunciation of *wh*-words, discussed as a rule addition in Exercise 3. This is the simplest form of restructuring. A rule is added, and once a generation of speakers use it regularly, the next generation cannot learn the underlying form. There are three stages to consider.

		Dialect A	Dialect B
Stage I	*Underlying form*	//hw//	//hw//
	Phonetic form	[hw]	[hw]
Stage II	*Underlying form*	//hw//	//hw//
	Phonetic form	[hw]	[w]
Stage III	*Underlying form*	//hw//	//w//
	Phonetic form	[hw]	[w]

Stage I occurs before the rule is added. Both Dialect A and Dialect B have underlying //hw// forms (*what* [hwʌt]). In Stage II, the speakers of Dialect B have added the rule changing //hw// to [w]. Dialect A speakers have not added the rule, so they continue to pronounce [hw].

Now consider the language acquisition task of the next generation of speakers of Dialect B. Suppose the Stage II rule applies to all occurrences of //hw//. The next generation of speakers will never hear the pronunciation [hw], but always hear [w]. Thus, there is no possible way for them to learn //hw// as an underlying form. The Stage III underlying form for words like *what* and *which* will contain an initial //w//, and because there are no cases of underlying //hw//, there is no reason for speakers of this generation to learn the rule that deletes [h]. Dialect B has restructured the underlying forms and has lost the rule deleting [h].

Such a progression of changes rarely occurs within three consecutive generations. It is usually a gradual process working its way into a dialect bit by bit in progressive generations, much like *h*-deletion in *ain't* in the Appalachian dialect described above. In that situation we saw that several generations of speakers each generalized the contexts in which the rule could apply. The youngest present-day generation now applies the rule in almost every context. It is likely that some future generation will remove the context of the rule entirely, thereby setting the stage for restructuring of the underlying form and loss of the *h*-Deletion Rule. This has already occurred in Standard English, a fact that no doubt is contributing to the pressures toward generalization and the ultimate loss of the rule in this Appalachian dialect.

The Appalachian example also underscores our earlier observation that phonological change often progresses from rule addition, through simplification, to restructuring and rule loss. In the long run, this relates to an interesting ebb and flow in the phonologies of languages. As we will see below, rules are often added to increase the incidence of more natural phonetic segments or sequences. The rules are then simplified or reordered to create progressively increasing occurrences of the favored segments or sequences. Ultimately, these are built into the underlying forms of lexical items, and the phonology is simplified by the loss of a rule. We observe such a progression of changes in the rule that devoices the final stop in words like *salad* and *lid*. Below are comparisons of phonetic forms for these words in four American dialects.

		salad	*lid*	*salads*
A.	Standard English	[sǽlɪd]	[lɪd]	[sǽlɪdz]
B.	Working Class White	[sǽlɪt]	[lɪd]	[sǽlɪdz]
C.	Some Working Class Black	[sǽlɪt]	[lɪt]	[sǽlɪdz]
D.	Other Working Class Black	[sǽlɪt]	[lɪt]	[sǽlɪts]

In the Standard variety (A), there is no Devoicing Rule, so that each form is pronounced with a [d]. Some working class White varieties (B), however, have added the Devoicing Rule, permitting it to apply in unstressed syllables but not when the plural morpheme is added. The underlying form of //a// is still preserved on the surface. Some working class Black varieties (C) have generalized the rule, now permitting it to apply in both stressed (*lid*) and unstressed syllables (*salad*), but still not across the plural boundary. The underlying //d// is preserved in the surface representation of *salads* as [sǽlɪdz]. Other Black dialects (D), however, have restructured the underlying form to //t//, as demonstrated by the occurrence of the /s/ allomorph of the plural morpheme in *salads* [sǽlɪts]. Thus, it might be argued that the Devoicing Rule has been lost in some instances because there is no longer an underlying form to which it may apply.

Exercise 6

Look at your conclusions to Exercise 4, above. Now consider a rural Southern Black variety in which the following forms occur: [tɛs kes] 'test case', [tɛs ɛgzæmpl̩] 'test example', [tɛsɪŋ] 'testing.' Explain why we may say that this is a case of restructuring.

Explaining Phonological Change

In our discussion, we have described how phonological change may be accounted for by changes in the rules or underlying forms. We have only hinted at the reasons for such changes. Recent approaches to explaining phonological changes have focused on a notion called "naturalness." More traditional approaches have focused on other causes, among which are language contact, the balance of phonological inventories, and ease of articulation. In fact, most changes probably result from a complex of causes, which is one reason that changes are so difficult to predict.

Clearly, **language contact** has been one of the most important sources of lexical items for English, and in some cases the borrowing of many words from another language has resulted in structural changes in the phonological system. In Old English, for example, the difference between voiced and voiceless fricatives was not contrastive because voiced fricatives occurred only between sonorants, and voiceless fricatives never did. French, however, maintained a voicing contrast in the fricative inventory. After the Norman invasion of 1066, the extensive borrowing of French words into English led to the occurrence of numerous voiced and voiceless fricatives in the "wrong" contexts. It might have been possible to reinterpret and adapt the French words to the extant English phonological inventory. However, the extensive borrowing, in combination with the presence of a French-speaking ruling class, caused a revision of the entire fricative inventory to incorporate a contrast between voiced and voiceless fricatives.

A related mechanism of phonological change concerns the filling of "holes" in the pattern of contrast of phonological inventories. More commonly called **structural balance** or maintenance of symmetry, the pattern of balance in a phonological inventory may encourage changes to fill holes, or may retard other changes that might destroy symmetry. Accordingly, English readily accepts foreign words with [ž] because it nicely fills the hole in the fricative system:

$$
\begin{array}{cccc}
f & \theta & s & š \\
v & ð & z &
\end{array}
$$

Even though [ž] is relatively rare in English, it seems to maintain its integrity as a phoneme because of its role in balancing the phonological inventory.

Another often-cited reason for the occurrence of phonological changes is the **ease of articulation** of sequences of sounds, especially in rapid, casual speech styles. We previously noted that rapid English speech may involve considerably more assimilation, reduction, and deletion than corresponding sentences in a more formal or less rapid style of speaking (Exercise 18, Chapter 2). It has long been recognized that certain phonological processes may begin as rules that apply to some forms in rapid speech, then are extended to many forms in rapid speech and some forms in other styles, and so on, until the process is common to all forms in most styles. Thus, the introduction of some changes may initially be based on phonetic plausibility—the ease with which the tongue is able to shift rapidly between the various positions it must take in producing common words. Many cases of assimilation discussed in Chapter 6 can be explained in this way.

Although we may feel that many processes are clearly motivated by ease of articulation, such claims are somewhat difficult to justify in physiological terms. We really have little knowledge of what vocal gestures are physiologically easier than others. Considerations of naturalness such as those we discuss below may ultimately help to clarify such questions.

Naturalness in Phonology

Much of our discussion above has been related to changes that in some sense (either physiological or systematic) make certain aspects of the phonological system more **natural**, that is, more sensible or more expectable from the perspective of how people talk, or of how the systems they use work. Advances in the analysis and description of phonological systems during the past several decades have increased dramatically our understanding of how these systems work. From these more recent perspectives, it has become possible to begin to **explain** the structure of phonological systems and phonological change rather than simply to **describe** it. But with these advantages has come the realization that some models for description may be so "powerful" they might account for almost anything, without reference to what makes sense to the people who use a language. Our earlier discussion of the abstractness of underlying forms indicated such a concern. There is now a general feeling that models for phonological description, such as generative phonology, must be limited in their power, so that they take into account what it is natural to expect in human language.

We will approach naturalness from three perspectives, although there are a number of others that we might also have included. First, we may make claims about the naturalness or expectability of the composition of phonological inventories, particularly what sorts of inventories can be expected in all languages. Secondly, we can argue that certain phonological processes within a language system are more natural than others. And, thirdly, in conjunction with these two notions of naturalness, we are better able to understand certain aspects of how and why phonological systems change as they do.

When we speak of **linguistic universals** we may be referring to any of the three dimensions mentioned above. All of these perspectives share the notion that there are certain things held in common by all human languages. Such phenomena probably derive from how language is organized in the human mind, and from the physiological capabilities of the speech producing mechanism. Of course, we are far from understanding the exact nature of the organization of the mind. However, certain discoveries made in the search for linguistic universals now suggest that in any language, specific patterns, processes, and changes are more expectable or plausible than others. Linguists now appear to have agreed upon the term **naturalness** to refer to notions of plausibility and expectability.

Universals of Content

The most clear-cut claims for naturalness can probably be made about what to expect in the inventory of sound segments in a language. Such claims are based primarily on two kinds of observation. First, extensive studies have now been undertaken to compare the phonemic inventories of hundreds of the world's languages. These comparisons have led to numerous claims, based on frequency of occurrence and patterns of occurrence, about the relative naturalness of sound segments. For example, it is clear that some vowels are more expectable than others. It appears that all languages have at least three vowels, namely /i/, /a/, and /u/, as a part of their phonemic inventory. Furthermore, the most common vowel systems are those which contrast five basic vowel qualities. Individual vowels can also be predicted on the basis of particular cooccurrence patterns. Thus, languages with four or more vowels have /ɛ/ or /ɨ/, and languages with six or more vowels have /ɔ/. There are a number of cooccurrence restrictions of this type which lead to predictions about the expectability of particular vowels in language inventories.

Exercise 7

Glossolalia, or "speaking in tongues," is a type of phonological activity associated with particular religious groups, such as the various Pentecostal denominations. In this activity, a person utters a stream of phonological segments that do not have apparent meaning in the native language of the speaker. A common claim made about these utterances is that they represent another natural language not known by the speaker or hearers. In light of this claim, consider a vowel inventory of a glossolalia sample that reveals only the vowels /i/, /ɛ/, and /a/. What can the study of phonological universals say about the possibility that these utterances represent a natural language system?

Similar findings have been made for consonants. Voiceless obstruents are more expectable than voiced obstruents, stops and fricatives are more

expectable than affricates, and alveolar stops are more expectable than alveopalatal stops.

The second argument for claims of relative naturalness among different
sound segments derives from recent studies of child language acquisition.
Such studies indicate that sounds which emerge early are in some sense more
natural than those that emerge later. Because we will discuss this in more
detail in Chapter 10, it is sufficient to say here that, for the most part, these
observations conform to the findings mentioned above.

Although universals of content are reflected in the phonological inventory
of all languages, many universals are not absolute constraints. Rather, they
are tendencies that may be realized in different ways. All languages will
have systems that are basically natural, but naturalness will take different
forms. Languages are not prohibited from using less natural segments. For
example, English makes use of affricates even though they are less natural
than stops and fricatives. Because less natural segments somehow go against
the grain of the ways in which our minds and bodies want to work, using
them should "cost" the system more than natural segments. The degree of
naturalness with which segments are incorporated into the inventory should
be reflected in our theoretical framework. This is in part what we were dealing with in our discussion of natural classes in Chapter 4. There, we pointed
out that certain classes of segments were more simply described by features
than others, and that the more simply described classes were in some sense
more natural. For the most part, however, our feature system does not directly reflect the universal notions of naturalness we are discussing now.
For example, the discussion of natural vowel systems above claims that a language using only three vowels is more likely to use *i*, *a*, and *u* than *i*, *æ*,
and *o*. If the natural classes proposal is correct, we would expect our features to distinguish *i*, *a*, and *u* from one another more simply than they could
distinguish *i*, *æ*, and *o*. Applying feature specifications for these two systems
demonstrates that they are each distinguished by four nonredundant specifications (redundant features are indicated by parentheses):

	i	*a*	*u*
Hi	(+)	-	+
Bk	-	(+)	+

(a)

	i	*æ*	*o*
Hi	+	-	(-)
Bk	(-)	-	+

(b)

Thus, although matrix (b) is less natural than (a), it requires the same number of nonredundant feature specifications and therefore does not overtly indicate that (b) is a less natural class than (a). Chomsky and Halle (1968)
have attempted to build into the feature system a recognition of the relative
naturalness of sound segments. Their approach employs a set of **universal
marking conventions**, through which certain feature specifications are **unmarked**
(meaning that they are more expected), and others are **marked** (meaning that
they are less expected). Thus, because voiced vowels are more natural than
voiceless vowels, the specification [+vd] for vowels is unmarked for all languages. On the other hand, a language using voiceless vowels is using the
marked specification [-vd], which must be specified and counted. In the
following matrix, which again presents the vowels discussed above, those features specified with +, -, or *m* are marked; those with *u* are unmarked.

(a')		i	a	u
Hi		u	u	u
Bk		–	u	+

(b')		i	æ	o
Hi		u	u	m
Bk		–	m	+

The actual details of the universal marking conventions are somewhat more complex than our discussion here permits, and there are numerous problems yet to be ironed out. They do, however, show matrix (a') as more natural than matrix (b') because (a') contains only two marked specifications (+ and -), whereas (b') contains four (+,-, and *m*).

There is another way in which the theoretical framework we have so far described is inadequate from the perspective of naturalness. In Chapter 4 we suggested that natural classes were natural partly because the members of a class tend to be involved as a group in some phonological process. This is true of some natural classes; voiceless stops in English all tend to aspirate syllable initially, and deaspirate following *s*. This class may be specified very simply with two features:

$$\begin{bmatrix} -vd \\ -d.r. \end{bmatrix}$$

Of course, there are many cases where such natural classes function together in phonological systems, but it is not true that the most easily specified classes are those that typically function together. The "natural" classes [+vd] and [-nas] are specified by single features, but very few languages employ phonological rules that operate on these simple classes. While it appears that natural classes capture something important about related sounds, they do not directly reflect the fact that certain groups of sounds are more likely to participate together in phonological rules than are others. Just counting features does not help us understand why certain classes of sounds consistently participate in phonological processes.

Similarly, certain kinds of phonological processes are more plausible than others. Many languages employ a Nasal Assimilation Rule similar to that presented for the English negative morpheme //m//:

$$\begin{bmatrix} C \\ +nas \end{bmatrix} \rightarrow \begin{bmatrix} \alpha ant \\ \beta cor \end{bmatrix} / \underline{\quad} \# \begin{bmatrix} -son \\ \alpha ant \\ \beta cor \end{bmatrix}$$

Because a rule of this type occurs so frequently in languages, it is considered to be very "plausible." But a similar rule, assimilating all [+cont] segments to the place of articulation of a following consonant occurs rarely, although it involves the same number of features. More importantly, it is commonly recognized that many assimilation rules involving only a few features will probably never occur. Rule (a) below, for example, although extremely simple, rarely occurs, while Rule (b) is very common.

$$\text{(a) } C \rightarrow [-nas] / \underline{\quad} \begin{bmatrix} V \\ -nas \end{bmatrix}$$

$$\text{(b) } V \rightarrow [+nas] / \underline{\quad} \begin{bmatrix} C \\ +nas \end{bmatrix}$$

Thus, our system of features and the notion of natural classes, for all their help in descriptions, do not go far enough in explaining the relative naturalness of phonological processes. We must also take into account considerations aside from the structure of rules themselves.

Natural Processes

One promising approach to the development of a more satisfying incorporation of naturalness in phonology is suggested by Stampe (1973). Stampe proposes that there is one universal set of natural phonological processes that accounts for the kinds of naturalness we have discussed above. These processes are a part of the human capability to use language, and, as such, are an integral part of a child's innate language learning ability, present before any actual language is learned. The combined application of all the natural processes would reduce virtually every utterance to a neutral but ultimately natural syllable, perhaps [pa]. According to Stampe, children at the earliest stages of language learning apply all the natural processes with which their first phonological component is innately fitted. This explains why the child's first syllables are limited to the most neutral ones. Among the natural processes operating are: deletion of final consonants (favoring the more natural CV pattern), changing of fricatives to stops, and devoicing of final obstruents. As a child acquires adult pronunciations of the words of the language, this innate phonological component must be altered in the ways discussed below.

First, certain natural processes might be **suppressed**, that is, they may cease to apply. For example, children tend to apply consonant harmony, whereby the initial consonant of a CVC syllable assimilates in place of articulation to a final segment ([gɔg] 'dog'). Because it does not apply in adult forms, consonant harmony must be suppressed in order to produce adult English words. Second, some natural processes may be **restricted** in their application by limiting the contexts in which they apply. The natural process that causes children to devoice all final stops must be suppressed for a speaker of Standard English (where final voiced and voiceless stops contrast), but it is only restricted in its application for those varieties that neutralize *t* and *d* in some final contexts.

Another kind of change in the phonological system is the addition of **language-specific** rules that may not be highly plausible. These may produce morphophonemic alternations that appear to be unnatural. The English Velar Softening Rule, which changes final //k// to [s] in forms like *electricity* and *cynicism*, is a good example of such a learned rule. While there may not appear to be a good articulatory reason for this change to take place currently, we can trace the rule through a plausible historical development. To a child learning English without access to this history, it must simply be learned as an alternation that occurs in the context of certain suffixes, rather than as a plausible phonological process. We have already seen that the process applies to nonsense words or to other words not ordinarily attached to the *-ity* or *-ism* suffixes (*rubric/rubricity*), so it is a productive rule for adult speakers of English.

Stampe's proposals help to explain why all languages make use of similar natural processes but at the same time may employ very implausible rules. These considerations raise an interesting question: how is it that different languages make use of natural processes in different ways? We cannot really answer this question now, but we can help shed some light on it.

Naturalness and Language Change

The simultaneous presence of highly natural and less natural processes in language is best understood by examining naturalness in the light of language change. From the standpoint of naturalness, rules enter a language for a number of reasons, including:

(1) to make segments in a sequence phonetically more compatible with each other,
(2) to increase the number of unmarked segments in surface productions, or
(3) to make the structure of syllables more natural.

In our many references to assimilation rules, we have hinted at how they reduce the articulatory effort applied in producing an utterance. By the same token we have seen that other rules are not phonetically plausible, even though they can be formulated as phonological rules. So, other things being equal, phonetic plausibility should lead to a steady increase in the naturalness of a language.

A second motivation for natural processes is to increase the incidence of unmarked segments in utterances. The common natural process whereby voiced obstruents become unvoiced in final position is an example of this. Voiceless obstruents are more expected and more natural than voiced obstruents, and therefore are considered to be unmarked. Thus, the incorporation of the Final Devoicing Rule into some varieties of English represents a language change yielding more natural segments. It is interesting that many such natural processes create neutralizations, whereby an underlying contrast does not appear on the surface in certain utterances. This phenomenon was troublesome for classical phonemics, but it seems to be well motivated by considerations of naturalness. Vowel reduction may be an example of this kind of naturally motivated neutralization. At a number of places, we have noted that vowels in unstressed syllables in English tend to reduce to a schwa-like vowel. In effect, such vowel reduction neutralizes the differences between vowels in unstressed syllables, but also accounts for an increased incidence of the more natural vowel in these contexts.

A third motivation is the tendency to introduce rules that make the structure of syllables simpler or more natural. The universal and most natural syllable is CV. Many processes enter a phonological system to cause other underlying syllable types to approach more closely the unmarked CV pattern. Epenthesis rules, whereby a vowel is inserted between two consonants, and rules that delete one member of a consonant cluster, shift utterances toward a CV pattern.

These three motivations for processes may be at work at once in a language. Interestingly, the natural by-product of a particular process may be some unnatural syllables or sequences. The natural process of vowel reduction, carried to its extreme, might result in removing the vowel altogether, which, in turn, might have the effect of bringing two consonants together. For example, the loss of a vowel in the unstressed syllables of *police* and *baloney* might be naturally motivated, but would also result in an initial consonant cluster ([plis], [bloni]). This introduces a less natural sequence, and the need for another process to begin to bring the sequence back toward the ideal CV pattern. This sort of adjustment and readjustment, in combination with the effects of language contact, must certainly be a part of the reason for constant change in all phonological systems.

NOTES

1. This final [t] may actually be an unreleased [t˺] or a glottal stop [ʔ],
   or a glottal stop *and* unreleased [ʔt˺]. This rule actually devoices a
   wide range of obstruents in this context. Our version is simplified to
   apply only to //d//.

SUGGESTED READING

Language variation, language change, and language naturalness have become
prominent topics in American linguistics in recent years. However, as is the
case with any relatively new subdiscipline, there are few real textbooks on
the topics discussed in this chapter. For the most part, the interested reader
will have to dig relevant discussions out of journals like *Language* and *Language in Society*, or wait patiently for the publication of basic texts.

Wolfram and Fasold's *The Study of Social Dialects in American English*
(1974) provides an introduction to the methodology and theory of language
variation, with a focus on American English. Materials on specific language
varieties may be found in works by Labov, especially *Sociolinguistic Patterns*
(1972b) and *Language in the Inner City* (1972a), and in Wolfram and Christian,
Appalachian Speech (1976).

Almost any introductory linguistics text will contain a chapter on Comparative and Historical Linguistics, but Bloomfield's "Language History" section of
Language (1933) is still one of the most cogent presentations of the traditional
view of language change. More current approaches may be found in King,
Historical Linguistics and Generative Grammar (1969), and in Stockwell and
Macaulay (1972). Useful summaries and criticisms of recent debates in this
area appear in Hyman (1975) and Sommerstein (1977).

Various approaches to naturalness and related theoretical concerns in
phonology have surfaced in recent years. Dinnsen (1979) provides a representative collection of papers summarizing most of the current major approaches.
Again, Hyman and Sommerstein present the most readable condensations of the
field. The Stanford Language Universals Project, under the direction of J.
Greenberg (1978), has now published several volumes on universals of content.

CHAPTER 10
The Acquisition of Phonology

The Application of Phonological Analysis

In the previous chapters, we have focused on analysis and description in phonology. While such an interest is often seen as an end in itself, the study of phonology does have application beyond this descriptive orientation. As we stated at the outset, phonological analysis is useful and, in some cases, indispensable in a number of educational fields. The understanding of certain types of patterned phonological behavior can provide a vital perspective for the educator who must deal with some aspect of the organization of sound systems. In the remaining chapters, we shall consider several of these applications.

Applications of phonological analysis may involve knowledge ranging from the most surface phonetic details to the most abstract, underlying phonological units. We will see examples using these different levels in the following chapters. In fields such as speech pathology and foreign language teaching, a person cannot go very far without an adequate working knowledge of phonetics. Such knowledge certainly must go beyond the ability to transcribe reliably the broad phonetics of English words in a careful citation style. Important insights into "speech disorders" or "foreign accents" are often dependent on the fine phonetic details of natural speech. At the other end of the organization of a phonological system, an understanding of more abstract levels is necessary to comprehend the nature of the English spelling system. When certain underlying relationships are understood, the patterning of English spelling may take on new significance. This type of information can be crucial for the reading and language arts specialist who is attempting to teach basic skills in decoding (for reading) and encoding (for spelling) English orthography.

Between the extremes of abstract representation and surface phonetics, an understanding of essential phonological contrasts and patterning is also helpful at many points in educational diagnosis and teaching. Foreign language teachers, speech pathologists, reading teachers, and language arts specialists all can profit from such a perspective. Of the various aspects of phonology discussed in the preceding chapters, the formal representation of a phonological description has the least immediate application. This knowledge may be important for understanding linguists' analyses, but the principles of phonological organization can be captured without using these formal conventions. So students in other fields need not avoid the application of phonological analysis simply because some formal conventions look rather imposing. The observation of systematic patterning in phonological behavior is the important thing, not the formal conventions that represent such patterning.

Phonological Development

Several areas in which phonological analysis is applied to educational concerns depend upon understanding the acquisition of phonology. Ultimately, the study of phonological development combines important theoretical and applied dimensions, but in this chapter we will focus on its application.

First, knowledge of how phonology is acquired is important in order to define "normal" phonological development and various phonological disorders. Such information is crucial in fields such as speech and language pathology or special education. It is also essential for educational tasks which presume the attainment of particular levels of language development. Certain kinds of decoding skills in reading, and particular definitions of "reading readiness," may be dependent on such knowledge. Even more practically, parents may use such knowledge in understanding the emerging language world of their children. Although we will concentrate here on the acquisition of English as a first language, some important principles also emerge when we look at the acquisition of phonology in second language learning.

As we would expect, the acquisition of a phonological system cannot be isolated from the development of other skills. On one level, phonological acquisition must simply be viewed as one manifestation of physical and cognitive development. From our perspective, this is a very important process, but it is only one aspect of human growth and development. Other dimensions of behavior are developing at the same time, ranging from simple physical maturation to the progression of cognitive capabilities. Ingram (1976:11) shows how the various stages in a child's phonological development parallel other linguistic stages as well as the cognitive levels of development set forth by the influential psychologist-educator Jean Piaget. The table on page 167 illustrates these parallels with approximate corresponding age levels. For our purposes, the important dimension in this table is the correlation of phonological development with other developing aspects of human capabilities. A more extensive table might have connected this with more finely detailed aspects of sensori-motor development, but we are concerned simply with establishing that phonological development does not take place independent of other types of development. In the following sections, we briefly describe the five essential stages of phonological development classified by Ingram. Some stages are obviously more relevant than others to particular fields, but a complete picture of phonological acquisition only emerges from considering each stage.

Preverbal Vocalization

The sounds of language do not simply burst forth when a one-year-old child utters its "first word." As any parent can attest, there is ample phonetic activity long before the first discernible word. This activity involves considerably more than the cries of the child to express certain basic biological needs. Not only do babies produce a range of sounds during this stage, they also can make certain discriminations among the sounds that surround them. Originally, it was thought that children could discriminate only gross features such as intonational contours and intensity in the earliest stages, but recent research indicates that some of the differences received during the first few months of life may be considerably finer in detail.

Some linguists have considered that the vocalization activities during this first stage play little or no role in the later formation of the phonological system, but recent research has established essential relationships. Preverbal vocalization is a preliminary activity upon which later phonological development will build. Certainly, the phonetic inventories of children during this stage extend well beyond the limits of the system they later acquire, but they do not use all the possible sounds the speech mechanism can produce. It seems the types of sound sequences produced are already constrained by certain principles of naturalness. Unfortunately, the reliability of phonetic data collected for this stage has sometimes been suspect. Some studies prominent in forming accepted views of preverbal vocal activity have used a broad transcription system based on adult English phonology. Thus, many

PIAGET'S STAGES	LINGUISTIC STAGES	PHONOLOGICAL STAGES
Sensori-motor period (0;0-1;6) Development of systems of movements and perception. Child achieves notion of object permanence.	1 Prelinguistic communication through gestures and crying.	1 Prelinguistic vocalization and perception (birth to 1;0)
	2 Holophrastic stage. Use of one-word utterances.	2 Phonology of the first 50 words (1;0-1;6)
Period of concrete operations (1;6-12;0) Preconcept subperiod (1;6-4;0) The onset of symbolic representation. Child can now refer to past and future, although most activity is in the here and now. Predominance of symbolic play.	3 Telegraphic stage. Child begins to use words in combinations. These increase to point between 3 and 4 when most sentences become close to well-formed, simple sentences.	3 Phonology of single morphemes. Child begins to expand inventory of speech sounds. Phonological processes that result in incorrect productions predominate until around age 4 when most words of single morphological structure are correctly spoken.
Intuitional subperiod (4;0-7;0) Child relies on immediate perception to solve various tasks. Begins to develop the concept of reversibility. Child begins to be involved in social games.	4 Early complex sentences. Child begins to use complements on verbs and some relative clauses. These early complex structures, however, appear to be the result of juxtaposition.	4 Completion of the phonetic inventory. The child acquires production of troublesome sounds by age 7. Good production of simple words. Beginning of use of longer words.
Concrete operations subperiod (7;0-12;0) Child learns the notion of reversibility. Can solve tasks dealing with conservation of mass, weight, and volume.	5 Complex sentences. Child acquires the transformational rules that embed one sentence into another. Coordination of sentences decreases, v. the increase in complex sentences.	5 Morphophonemic development. Child learns more elaborate derivational structure of the language; acquires morphophonemic rules of language.
Period of formal operations (12;0-16;0) Child learns the ability to use abstract thought. Can solve problems through reflection.	6 Linguistic intuitions. Child can now reflect upon grammaticality of his speech and arrive at linguistic intuitions.	6 Spelling. Child masters ability to spell.

(Reprinted with permission of Edward Arnold Publishers Ltd. from Phonological Disability in Children by David Ingram, 1976.)

crucial details of the children's vocalizations could not be noted. Other studies have attempted to adopt a transcription system appropriate for such vocalizations, but we still do not have an accurate and exhaustive inventory of sounds produced during this period.

Preverbal vocalizations are sometimes referred to as cooing or babbling. Cooing usually refers to the sounds made during the first four months. It is characterized phonetically by the production of vocalic sounds and an abundance of velar or palatal consonantal sounds, such as [x], [ɠ], [k], [g]. Functionally, cooing appears to be associated with the expression of pleasure. Babbling, which takes place during the later months of the first year, reveals a shift toward more labial sounds ([p], [b], [ɓ], [w]), and the more precise production of syllable combinations. Babbling is associated with play for its own sake, as opposed to expressions related to physical comfort *per se*. During the latter phases of babbling, the child begins to imitate some of the words used by adults if they contain sounds similar to the ones the child has been producing spontaneously. This is apparently a preparatory activity for the eventual acquisition of adult words, which begins near the end of the first year and during the first months of the second year. Babbling does not cease when direct imitation begins, but can continue well into the next stages of phonological development. The evidence, then, points to an essential role for babbling as the first step in the eventual imitation of adult models. At this point, much more data and analysis are needed on this stage of preverbal vocalizations, as well as a more precise description of how such vocalizations prepare the way for later phonological acquisition.

Exercise 1

Try recording a sample of infant vocalization and have several different students transcribe it independently. Now do the same thing with some adult speech. In what areas is there agreement and disagreement over the transcription? Do transcribers disagree more about the infant or adult forms? Why?

The Phonology of the First 50 Words

The child's acquisition of a limited set of lexical items is a gradual process, occurring between the approximate ages of a year and a year-and-a-half. While this stage might be seen simply as a transition between babbling and rapid phonological development, certain characteristics set it apart from its surrounding stages. As babbling continues, certain items emerge which become identified as "words."

Several different criteria, combining phonetic and social and semantic considerations, are useful in defining the emergence of a word. Phonetically, there is a clarity of vowel and consonant production, indicating basic distinctions of vowels from consonants as they are programmed into syllables. There is also a shift toward a more consistent approximation of vowel targets, instead of the fluctuating ranges for vowels found in the babbling stage. And the emergence of a word is typified by the use of a single expression followed by silence rather than the continuous flow observed in babbling. From a social-semantic standpoint, these utterances are used in conversation with other people, and correlate with specifiable recurring conditions (objects, activities, contexts, and so forth). We will focus on the phonological characteristics of the words that occur during this initial period of language acquisition.

Although some studies have concluded that there is a universal sequence of developing phonological contrasts during this stage, such a conclusion seems premature. In reality, the comparison of different children
during this period shows considerable flexibility in the particular phonetic
segments and sequences which are found. Nonetheless, there are some
general characteristics. The inventory of consonants in the first words is
most likely to contain labials, less likely to contain alveolars, and least likely
to include velars. We cannot, however, make a blanket statement to this
effect, since some children show a preference for velars, and the prominence
of a sound may be highly sensitive to its position in the syllable. Stop
consonants and the nasal *m* occur, but other sounds may also be present.
Some children also have [f] or [s] during this stage.

The vowel system varies from speaker to speaker, but it appears to
favor vowels which represent the basic vowel triangle of [i], [a], and [u].
Individual children may include other vowels as well. During this stage, the
preferred syllable structure is *CV*, with some incidence of *VC*. Speakers
may also use *CVC* syllables, but it is usually not a preferred type. Some
children show a considerable amount of syllable reduplication in *CVCV* forms
(e.g. [dada]), while others use it hardly at all. Once again, we are confronted with considerable variation among different speakers within a framework of general tendencies.

Recent research on this stage of development shows that the contrast
of particular sounds must be considered in terms of the words in which they
occur. The relevant conditioning environment in this stage appears to be
the word itself rather than phonological environment *per se*. Several observations support this conclusion. In the first place, children show considerable variation in sounds that are used with particular words. For example,
a child may use [b], [w], and [p] for the initial sound in *baby*, [b] and
[ɓ] for *bye-bye*, and only [b] for *ball*. Some words are more stable than
others in the occurrence of a given sound. This suggests that two or more
sounds may have contrastive status in one word, but may fluctuate in a non-
contrastive way in another.

A second characteristic showing the importance of particular lexical items
is the existence of **progressive phonological idioms**. This refers to forms that
appear initially in what might be considered a more advanced phonological
form, so that an item like *pretty* might first occur something like [prɪti],
even though the child does not generally use the [pr] cluster or contrast
[t] with [d]. In time, the item may be modified so that it is produced something like [bɪdi], which is more reflective of the child's overall phonological
patterns. Other items, however, may show basic modification from the onset, so that an item like *pretzel* might be produced as [bɪdi] from the start.
Such cases again stress the importance of considering particular lexical items.
During this stage, children may also show a preference for words containing
particular sounds. Words with initial [b] may be chosen over words with [k],
even though both kinds of words occur frequently in the child's environment.

One final characteristic of this period has been described as the "growth
and decay" pattern of the phonetic system (Labov and Labov, 1978). Minute,
daily observation has indicated that, after a steady increment in the complexity of the system during the first half of this stage, there is a period of
dramatic decline. Words appear and then disappear. Phonetic elements are
integrated into words and then apparently abandoned again. There are gains
and losses in the phonetic distinctiveness of words. While we can only specu-
late on the reasons, it has been suggested that such a pattern indicates
shifts in focus as the child learns skills for the period of rapid phonological
acquisition. Thus, a child might first focus on a basic vowel target, such
as [u], then turn to intensive experimentation with consonantal obstruents

such as [f] and [s]. Subsequently, the child may return to experimenting with vowels. In the meantime, other sounds and words fall into disuse, only to be reinstated later.

The 50-word stage of development shows contrast more in the phonetics of particular lexical items than the individual sound segments or phonological environments. This level of differentiation is a necessary precursor to the next stage, when more precise contrast between distinct phonological segments takes definite shape.

Exercise 2

Examine the phonological status of *m* and *n* in the following items, which were all produced by a 15-month-old child in one conversational setting. If just *mother* and *no* were considered, what might be concluded about the contrastive status of *m* and *n*? What if just *banana* and *mine* were considered? How does this demonstrate the importance of the lexical items during the 50-word stage?

1.	[manə]	'banana'	7.	[ma]	'mother'
2.	[no]	'no'	8.	[na]	'mine'
3.	[ma]	'mine'	9.	[nanə]	'banana'
4.	[mam]	'mother'	10.	[mam]	'mother'
5.	[no]	'no'	11.	[no]	'no'
6.	[nan]	'banana'	12.	[ma]	'mine'

Phonology of the Simple Morpheme

Following the stage in which a limited number of vocabulary items are learned with a first approximation of a phonological system, there is a period of rapid linguistic development. Between approximately 18 months and four years of age, there are major developments in a number of essential language areas. The syntax of the child shows increasing complexity, the vocabulary expands dramatically, and the perceptual and productive capabilities are refined into a system of phonologically contrastive units. The child enters this period with a limited inventory of productive sounds and a restricted phonotactic structure, and emerges with a substantive phonological system.

Phonological data on this stage have been collected in quite different ways, depending on the interests of the researcher. In linguistic research, case studies of particular children (often the researcher's) have provided the basis for analysis. In most instances, the spontaneous utterances of the child have simply been recorded and analyzed. Other fields, however, have approached phonological acquisition by obtaining elicited responses from large numbers of children in a testing situation. In many cases, the purpose of this approach was to establish norms for the acquisition of the particular sounds of the language. These studies usually resulted in a list of phonemes arranged in chronological sequence and correlated with an approximate age level. The table on page 171 (reproduced from Ingram, 1976:28) presents a typical sequence for consonants.

While studies of the acquisition of individual sounds provide certain types of useful information, they also suffer from some theoretical and methodological shortcomings. We have seen repeatedly that the organizational principles underlying the system of phonology are patterned in terms of classes, not individual sounds. Limiting the study to individual sounds may overlook important patterns of acquisition. In the table on page 171, where

AVERAGE AGE ESTIMATES FOR THE ACQUISITION OF ENGLISH SOUNDS

Sounds	Median Age of Customary Usage	Age of 90% of Subjects
p,m,h,n,w	1;6	3;0
b	1;6	4;0
k,g,d	2;0	4;0
t,ŋ	2;0	6;0
f,y	2;6	4;0
r,l	3;0	6;0
s	3;0	8;0
č,š	3;6	7;0
z	4;0	7;0
ǰ	4;0	7;0
v	4;0	8;0
θ	4;6	7;0
đ	5;0	8;0
ž	6;0	8;6

(Reprinted with permission of Edward Arnold Publishers Ltd. from Phonological Disability in Children *by David Ingram, 1976.)*

consonants are treated as independent items, we see that stops as a class of contrasts appear relatively early, while fricative contrasts tend to appear considerably later. Fricative and affricate contrasts, in fact, are not usually completely acquired until the next stage. The important point is that the sounds are not simply learned as independent, arbitrary units, but are acquired in terms of a systematic set of contrasts. For the most part, the major inventory of contrastive units is complete enough by the end of this stage for children to converse with strangers without serious intelligibility problems.

During this stage, phonotactic structure also increases in its complexity, so that syllable-final consonants now appear regularly. Some consonant clusters are acquired, but this is not as complete as the inventory of single consonant units. Following is a summary of some of the English clusters typically acquired by the age of four.

Acquired Clusters

Syllable-Initial

s + nasal	*snow, smell*
s + stop	*spot, stop*
stop + liquid	*black, brown*
stop + glide	*quick, twin*

Syllable-Final

nasal + voiceless stop	*jump, thank*
liquid + voiceless stop	*help, belt*
stop + fricative	*box, rips*

Clusters Not Yet Present

s + stop + liquid	*scream, street*
s + stop + glide	*squirrel, squeeze*
fricative + liquid	*fresh, three*
fricative + glide	*swim, few*

s + stop	*desk, wasp*
liquid + stop	*Barb, bulb*
liquid + fricative	*health, elf*
nasal + voiced stop	*hand, find*
stop + stop	*act*

The position of the cluster in a syllable, and the segments that comprise it, are often important in accounting for different phonetic productions. Even though these distributions are open to individual variation, they may be quite regular. In some cases, the initial member of the cluster is typically absent ([krim] 'scream'), while in other cases the final member may be absent ([hæn] 'hand'). Still others may have a regular correspondence, such as a glide for the adult liquid ([f̫wɛš] 'fresh').

The child phonological system shows regular correspondences with the adult system that serves as its model. One way of describing its relation to the adult system is to identify various types of processes by which the child modifies that system. From this perspective, the adult system serving as the model is modified by the application of natural phonological processes ("natural" in the sense we discussed in Chapter 9). In a sense, the acquisition of phonology may be viewed as the gradual elimination or restriction of an innate, universal set of natural processes. Following are some of the processes which have been observed to operate.

Syllable Structure Processes

Deletion of Final Consonants
    [bo]   'boat'   [kɪ]   'kid'
Reduction of Consonant Clusters
    [tap] 'stop'   [bu]   'blue'
Unstressed Syllable Deletion
    [næn] 'banana'   [tedo] 'potato'

Neutralization of Phonetic Contrast (Partial or complete)

Stopping of Fricatives (or Sonorants)
    [bæn] 'van'   [ti]   'see'   [dɪp] 'lip'
Fronting of Palatals, Velars
    [ti]   'key'   [sɪp]   'ship'
Gliding of Liquids
    [wʌn] 'run'   [kæwət] 'carrot'   [yæp] 'lap'
Vocalization of Liquids
    [bæwə] 'barrel'   [wiəd] 'wierd'
Final Devoicing
    [dɔk] 'dog'   [bɪp]   'bib'

Assimilation

Velar Consonant Harmony
    [gɪŋ] 'ding'   [gɔg]   'dog'
Labial Consonant Harmony
    [pap] 'top'   [pɪp]   'sip'
Prevocalic Voicing
    [do]   'toe'   [bap]   'pop'
Nasalization
    [dʌ̃]   'done'   [bã]   'bomb'

There are many more processes, and many qualifications on the phonological contexts in which they may take place. More than one process can operate on a single item. An item like [tɪp] for *ship* might indicate both palatal fronting and stopping. [pɪ̃] for *pin* might reveal both nasal assimilation and final consonant deletion in an ordered relation. Although the appeal to certain natural phonological processes may not explain all the differences,

it certainly shows many of the regular correspondences between the child
and adult systems.

Exercise 3

What types of processes can account for the following child forms? Remember
that more than one process may operate on a form in some cases. In some
cases, you may have to refer to Chapter 6 in order to identify the process
(e.g. [twæs] 'trash': gliding and fronting).

1.	[bo]	'blow'		6.	[wɪdə]	'little'
2.	[bip]	'peep'		7.	[bʌt]	'brush'
3.	[tawi]	'sorry'		8.	[kɪk]	'stick'
4.	[du]	'juice'		9.	[lʌp]	'love'
5.	[fwɛ̃]	'friend'		10.	[yɪp]	'slip'

Exercise 4

Predict the child's pronunciation of the following items based on the application of the particular processes specified for each item. That is, after the
designated process applies, what does the form look like?

1. [šɪp] fronting ([sɪp])
2. [ǰʌǰ] fronting, stopping
3. [strit] cluster reduction, liquid gliding
4. [trɪk] cluster reduction, velar assimilation
5. [tap] labial assimilation, prevocalic voicing
6. [hænd] cluster reduction, nasalization, final consonant deletion
7. [stov] cluster reduction, stopping, final devoicing
8. [zɪpɚ] stopping, labial assimilation, vocalization
9. [šʌv] fronting, stopping, final devoicing
10. [væləntàɪn] stopping, unstressed syllable deletion, liquid vocalization,
   nasalization, final consonant deletion.

Completion of the Phonetic Inventory

Although major gains in phonological development have now taken place, a
number of aspects of the child's phonological system still remain to be developed or refined. During the next stage, roughly between the ages of 4
and 7, the major contrasts in surface phonetic segments are completed. For
example, the contrast between the different fricatives and affricates is stabilized, and the acquisition of various consonant cluster combinations is completed. By the end of this period, the child can typically produce all of the
English sounds, so that phonetic production comes in line with the adult norm.
   Although all the basic phonetic contrasts are usually evidenced during
this period, there may remain particular contexts in which selected contrasts
are not maintained consistently. For example, polysyllabic words still may not
match adult pronunciations: *vegetable, thermometer, valentine,* or *pneumonia*
may still differ from the adult forms. In these cases, processes similar to
those discussed above may be observed. *Valentine* or *vegetable* might show
stopping with the initial fricative ([bæləntáɪn]). Cluster reduction may affect
syllable sequencing in *vegetable* ([vɛǰəbl̩]). An item like *pneumonia* might

reveal metathesis ([mənonyə]), or a reduction of the initial segment so that the item is homophonous with *ammonia* ([əmonyə]).

Exercise 5

Compile a list of multisyllabic items which children may produce differently from adults even after they have mastered the basic phonetic contrasts in monosyllabic items. This list should extend the list of items given here. What types of processes can account for the differences between the child and the adult forms? Are there any patterns that can be predicted?

In this stage of development, initial steps take place in the acquisition of the morphophonemic system of the language. That is, the alternant phonological forms of particular morpheme combinations (i.e. the allomorphs) are being put to productive use. Children are starting to show their knowledge of certain rules governing these different forms rather than a simple list of memorized forms. In a classic study of the acquisition of English suffixes (Berko, 1958), children in this age range were given a list of nonsense items and asked to add various suffixes such as plurals, possessives, and third person singular. Given a list of items such as *wug, rick, gutch,* and *niz*, it could be determined if alternant forms like /z/, /s/, and /ɪz/ were being used productively. The results indicated that the children were using the /z/ and /s/ forms, but had still not mastered consistently use of the /ɪz/ forms for appropriate items, even though they might have used forms with /ɪz/ suffixes in their spontaneous speech. Some, but certainly not all, of the productive aspects of morphophonemic alternation were learned by this time.

Morphophonemic Development

The final stage in the acquisition of the phonological system is the development of a system of rules governing the combinations of morphemes in their various forms. As we saw above, the use of a particular form does not ensure that a child has acquired the general rule governing its morphophonemic alternations. The fact that a child uses the form *electric* with a final [k] and *electricity* with [s] does not necessarily mean that the child has productive use of the rule changing //k// to [s] before *-ity*. Such abilities start emerging in the earlier years of the morphophonemic stage and continue to develop well into adolescence. It is, in fact, difficult to determine the cut-off point for the complete acquisition of such morphophonemic processes, because learning details of such rules may extend up to and beyond the age of 12.

There is also evidence suggesting that some of the more detailed aspects of morphophonemic development may be related to the acquisition of other skills, such as spelling. For example, several patterns of vowel alternation such as /aɪ/ and /ɪ/ (*divine/divinity, collide/collision*), /e/ and /æ/ (*profane/ profanity, explain/explanatory*), and /i/ and /ɛ/ (*serene/serenity, obscene/ obscenity*) are productively used only by older children, and then in apparent conjunction with the learning of spelling and reading. In fact, even many adults may not have productive knowledge of this set of vowel shift rules. Most productive morphophonemic alternation rules are, however, acquired before puberty.

During this final stage, the relationship between grammatical category and phonological alternation is acquired, as indicated by a child's ability to distinguish stress in noun compounds versus noun phrases (*Whitehouse/white hoúse, bláckboard/black boárd*). The use of stress to distinguish noun and verb forms such as *récord/recórd, présent/presént,* or *cóntract/contráct* is also acquired.

Exercise 6

Give the following list of uncommon or nonsense words to several different native English speakers representing different age levels. Include an adult, a child about 10-12, and one about 7-9. In presenting the items to these individuals, you might want to introduce it something like the following:

> There is a group of words that can add something like *-ity* to the end of the word. For example, if you have a word like *intense* or *sterile*, you can get *intensity* or *sterility*. Or, if you have a word like *electric*, you can add the *-ity* and get *electricity*. Add the *-ity* to the words I give you to say. Some of them aren't really words, but just add the *-ity* as if they were words.

confirm	*pretense*	*loopile*
elastic	*rapic*	*fastic*
fistic	*rubric*	*stupid*

What conclusions might be drawn about the productive use of the //k// → [s] alternation as indicated by the different speakers?

In the preceding discussion, we have attempted a brief overview of the various stages in the development of a phonological system. As we have learned more about the various stages of phonological acquisition and the relationships between them, our insight into the workings of the phonological system has increased greatly.

SUGGESTED READING

A well-organized discussion (whose lines we have followed here) of the different stages of phonological development in children is found in Ingram's *Phonological Disability in Children* (1976). A comprehensive case study of phonological acquisition from the perspective of generative phonology is Smith, *The Acquisition of Phonology* (1973). Recent research on child phonology can be found in collections such as *Papers and Reports on Child Language Development* (published by the Linguistics Department at Stanford University), and two volumes on *Child Phonology* edited by Yeni-Komshian, Kavanagh, and Ferguson. One of these volumes (1980) deals with production, and the other (1981) with perception. Articles on child phonology sometimes occur in the *Journal of Child Language, Journal of Speech and Hearing Research,* and *Language.*

CHAPTER 11
Phonological Disorders

The usefulness of phonological analysis and description is not limited to normal language development and organization. It also offers insight into the nature of systems that deviate from the typical language patterns of a given community. So-called articulation problems or speech disorders may be subjected to some of the same kinds of phonological analysis we have discussed in the preceding chapters.

Our central interest in phonological disorders is the patterned nature of deviant production or perception. These disorders do not consist simply of random lists of "error" sounds, but are systematically organized. So, when we speak of a phonological disorder, we do not mean a system without order, but a system whose order is not in line with the normative one. Although such systems are certainly different, their organizing principles are typically the same as those which govern the more normal system.

Disordered phonological systems show patterning on two different levels. First, they may be seen as systems in their own right, with their own patterns of contrast and distribution. The patterning is not identical to normal adult systems, but the sounds that are used are organized in some way. In other words, if we look at these systems in isolation, we can describe their patterns of contrast and distribution. This is similar to the situation in child phonology, where we may describe a system of contrast and distribution for certain stages of development by employing the basic principles of phonological analysis. The system is different from the adult one, but it is a system nonetheless.

A disordered system is also patterned in how it relates to the normal adult system. Its differences show certain principles of organization by comparison with the model. Systematic patterns govern its deviation and particular rules can be cited to account for the ways in which it departs from the normal adult model. Information on the patterned nature of the deviation can be crucial in arriving at an accurate diagnosis, which in turn serves as the basis for effective remediation. Phonological analysis, then, seems indispensible for speech pathologists and other professionals concerned with the diagnosis and treatment of speech disorders.

Discussion in speech pathology has sometimes focused on the phonological characteristics of disorders associated with particular organic conditions, such as a hearing impairment, cleft palate, mental retardation, and so forth. However, the most effective approach highlights a general model of analysis and description. This is not to deny that particular phonological characteristics may be associated with various organically based conditions, but we must keep in mind that our primary concern is to describe the patterned nature of phonological disorder. Virtually every study undertaken from a linguistic perspective reveals a **system of disorder**, so our focus is on the system. Our principles of analysis can be applied to a disability regardless of the organic or functional condition which may have brought it about.

An adequate approach to phonological disorders may involve knowledge on all levels of organization within the phonological system, ranging from aspects of fine phonetic detail to the more abstract relations between sounds. Traditional cover terms for articulation disorders such as "substitution," "omission," and "distortion" hardly do justice to the systematic ways in which the system is patterned in itself; nor do they adequately cover the ways in which the system departs from the adult normal system. Below, we explore some of the ways in which our approach to phonology is relevant to the understanding of phonological disorders.

The Phonetic Base

In our chapter on phonetics, we said that in a real sense a phonological analysis cannot go beyond the accuracy of the phonetic material with which it has to work. This is particularly true with respect to phonological disorders. Without accurate phonetic material, it is impossible to go very far in the systematic study of phonological disorders. It is important to point out that we are talking about greater phonetic detail than that indicated in the broad transcription of English. We cannot be sure that a disorder will include only those sounds traditionally found in the normal adult English system, nor that the phonetic detail will be organized in the way the normal adult system is. Phonetic detail must be examined in terms of how it is used within the disordered system.

The traditional label "phonetic distortion" is not adequate as a classification term for a disorder. It is phonetically imprecise and may obscure important information about an individual's phonological system. Practically, this term has been applied to those sounds not readily covered by the broad transcription of English. So, if the production of an s sound is different from any known English sound, it might be described as an "s-distortion." The basic phonetic material in disordered phonology must go beyond this level. Our framework for phonetic description must allow us to describe the actual sounds in a precise way, whether they are conventional English sounds or not. The need for detailed phonetic accuracy here is justified by several observations. In the first place, the range of phonetic detail in a disorder may extend considerably beyond the normal sound production of English. In our experience with phonological disorders, we have heard many productions of sounds not typical in normal adult English. This is certainly evidenced by the list of phonetic productions we have heard in place of the normal adult English s sound (in syllable-initial position only).

Symbol	*Description*
ḷ̥	voiceless alveolar lateral
ḷ̥ɫ	voiceless fricativized lateral (similar to the voiceless alveolar lateral but with more friction at the point of articulation)
x	voiceless velar fricative
x̜	voiceless palatal (or fronted velar) fricative
š̜	voiceless fronted alveopalatal fricative (produced in between the position of [s] and [š])
s̶	ungrooved alveolar fricative (produced as fricative at same position as s but no tongue grooving)
s̜	grooved fronted (or dental) alveolar fricative
θ	voiceless interdental fricative
θ̜	voiceless interdental fricative with extensive tongue protrusion through the teeth

Symbol	Description
$t^=$	unaspirated alveolar stop[1]
t^h	aspirated alveolar stop
$k^=$	unaspirated velar stop
k^h	aspirated velar stop
$k^=_<$	unaspirated palatal (or fronted velar) stop

Such a list is not all-inclusive. Even so, a number of these productions would have to be included among the more common productions for an "s-problem." Many of these have been traditionally hidden behind the vague label of "phonetic distortion." Productions as different as the ungrooved alveolar fricative [s], the fronted alveolar [s̪], fronted alveopalatal [š̪], and the velar [x] and palatal [x̟] fricatives have all been subsumed under this label. Analysts concerned with accurate diagnosis must be prepared to deal with the full range of actual phonetic production.

Fine phonetic detail may also be essential in understanding the basis for contrast within a disordered phonological system. Consider a situation in which the ungrooved alveolar fricative [s] occurs where [s] is normally found. An analyst who erroneously assumes that the ungrooved alveolar fricative is simply the same as the interdental fricative [θ] might conclude that there is no contrast between θ and s in the disordered system. In such a situation, however, s and θ do contrast, but the contrast is based in phonetic detail different from the normal adult model. That is, //s// is produced as [s] and //θ// as [θ].

Phonetic detail may take on further significance for the more abstract relations of phonological units. Consider the significance of an unaspirated voiceless stop in the production of the word *stop* as [t⁼ap]. Now, if the *t* of an item such as *top* [tʰap] is aspirated, this preserves a surface phonetic basis for contrast between *top* [tʰap] and *stop* [t⁼ap]. The unaspirated *t* might indicate the speaker's awareness of an underlying conceptual unit *s* in *stop* even though it is not produced. (Recall that *t* would normally be un-aspirated following *s* in English.) On the other hand, if both *stop* and *top* were produced as [tʰap] with an aspirated *t*, it might indicate that the speaker has no underlying conceptual *s* preceding the *t* in *stop*.

Finally, accurate phonetic detail is essential in the design of remediation strategies with speakers who reveal disorder. Knowledge of the precise production of sounds must serve as a basis for planning what types of corrections are relevant for achieving the normal adult production of sounds. Consider again the case of the ungrooved alveolar fricative production [s] for the adult *s*. If this is identified erroneously as [θ], it might be assumed that the correction strategy will involve manipulating both the place and the manner of the fricative, with the emphasis in most cases on the place of production. But if the production is [s], the basic problem may be the tongue grooving, and remediation procedures should concentrate on achieving this detail of production. That is, the focus will be the contrast of [s] and [s]. Matters of accurate phonetic detail, then, are relevant to all aspects of phonological disorders, from the initial diagnosis to remediation strategies devised to overcome a disability.

Exercise 1

Following are some of the more common phonetic details that have proven relevant in the transcription of phonological disorders. For each of these categories, think up some words that might be affected in a disorder, transcribing their deviant production.

1. aspiration/unaspiration   e.g. [p^h] versus [p$^=$]
2. grooving/ungrooving of fricatives   e.g. [s] versus [s̪]
3. fronting/non-fronting of sounds   e.g. [š] versus [š̬]
4. backing/non-backing of sounds   e.g. [s] versus [s̬]
5. glottal stop/consonant   e.g. [ʔ] versus [g̊]

Phonological Contrast and Disorders

A disordered phonological system can be viewed both as a system of contrast in its own right and as a system in which contrast differs systematically from the normal adult model. Traditionally, the latter viewpoint has occupied those working directly with speech disorders, because of the practical concern for their remediation. Actually, both perspectives come into play in considering the disordered phonological system.

Several different possibilities exist for the units of contrast within a disordered system. We have already seen that it is possible for a basic contrast in the adult system to be maintained, but to be manifested in different phonetic detail. If we simply have a different phonetic production of *s* which does not interfere with this sound's contrast with other sounds in the system, basic phonological contrast has not been disrupted. In a strict sense, we can refer to this as an "articulation disorder," since the basic phonological system is not disrupted, only the productive phonetic detail. On the other hand, many disorders may affect the system of contrasts in important ways. Different patterns of contrast may exist. By comparison with the adult system, many contrasts are **neutralized**—typically referred to by the traditional label **sound substitution**. If we have an item such as *vacuum*, which is produced with the same *b* used in *bat*, we may say that a neutralization of *b* and *v* has taken place. In traditional terms, *b* substitutes for *v*.

There are several important questions that need to be asked about the status of a contrast, or lack of a contrast. When neutralization takes place, we need to know how complete it is. Neutralization may be limited to particular phonological environments, or it may be absolute (occurring in all environments). A contrast may be neutralized only in syllable-final or syllable-initial position, or it may be eliminated completely. Phonological environment is just as important here as it is in describing a normal phonological system. Position in a word or syllable, surrounding sounds, and suprasegmental factors such as stress must all be considered in giving an adequate description of a disorder. Within the tradition of speech pathology, the typical designation of sound substitutions in terms of word-initial, medial, and final position indicates the relevance of phonological environment in examining contrast. Unfortunately, these broad-based environments are not always adequate to account for the actual influence of phonological context. More specific phonological contexts, including position in syllables and particular classes of surrounding sounds, must be identified in order to give an adequate account of a disorder. For example, we may find that *y* corresponds to normal adult *l* when followed by a front vowel ([yɪp] 'lip', [yæp] 'lap'), but *w* is used with back vowels ([wʊk] 'look', [wo] 'low'). Or, we may find that *d* is deleted word medially when following another consonant ([wɪno] 'window'), but retained when

intervocalic ([læðə] 'ladder'). A serious treatment of phonological environment in disordered phonology must consider all the dimensions of environment
we have used in examining normal phonological systems.

Another important question to be asked about contrast in a disorder is
the consistency of neutralization. First, we want to know if the contrast (or
lack of contrast) in a given phonological context is **categorical or variable**.
Does the substitution always take place or just sometimes? Does *b* in syllable-
initial position **always** correspond to *v* ([bækyum] for *vacuum*), or does it
occur only **sometimes?** We may get [bækyum] for *vacuum* one time and [vækyum]
another time. Or, we may have a client who uses [bækyum] categorically, but
v and *b* fluctuate in other items beginning with *v* in the adult model. We cannot simply assume that the neutralization of contrast will take place with only
one other sound, for example, with *b* always being used for *v* in syllable-
initial position. We might get both *b* and *d* corresponding to *v*, either in
different items or even in the same item. So, it is possible to get [bækyum],
[dækyum], and [vækyum] from the same person. The range of correspondences
and the consistency of a neutralization may, of course, intersect with each
other, with the following possibilities for the *v* example.

	Single Correspondence	*Multiple Correspondence*
Inconsistent neutralization	b~v/v	b~d~v/v
Absolute neutralization	b/v	b~d/v

Descriptive information about the range and consistency of contrast in
each relevant environment provides essential insight for diagnosing the nature
of a disorder, with important implications for devising a set of remediation
procedures. For example, it appears that the most severe problem with phonological contrast is when a multiple correspondence occurs with absolute
neutralization. The least severe is inconsistent neutralization of a single
correspondence. This kind of diagnostic information may be important in deciding what to work on and how. Working to reduce the range of correspondences, and admitting inconsistent neutralization as an intermediate stage
of progress, may be important steps in devising an effective program of
therapy.

Exercise 2

Describe the pattern of the phonological disorder involving the *s* of the
normal adult English system based on the following items. Consider the status
of *s* in terms of phonological environments—including, but not limited to, initial
and final position. Be sure to describe the consistency of the neutralizations
in terms of our discussion above. Is the neutralization absolute or inconsistent
for a particular environment, and are there single or multiple correspondences?

1.	[xɪk]	'sick'	8.	[xɪʔ]	'sit'
2.	[ɓak]	'box'	9.	[s̬ɪk]	'six'
3.	[bʌʔ]	'bus'	10.	[bak]	'box'
4.	[sɪʔ]	'sit'	11.	[sʌb]	'sub'
5.	[t⁼ʌb]	'sub'	12.	[t⁼æk]	'sack'
6.	[sæk]	'sack'	13.	[sɪk]	'sick'
7.	[kɪʔ]	'kiss'	14.	[fɪk]	'fix'

Classes of Disorders

At the outset of our discussion, we said that disorders of phonology did not consist simply of random lists of problem sounds. Instead, there are unifying principles of phonology that combine sounds into classes of disorder. One way of unifying sounds in groups is on the basis of natural classes, as we discussed this concept in Chapter 4. We expect disorders of phonology to affect natural classes of sounds rather than individual sounds. Distinctive features allow us to see how a restricted set of properties of sounds may account for a whole series of affected contrasts. "Substitutions" between English sounds such as *p* for *b*, *k* for *g*, *f* for *v*, *s* for *z*, and so forth are seen in terms of one feature difference: voicing.

Distinctive features may also give us insight into the degree of difference between the normal and disordered systems. For example, the disorder mentioned in the preceding paragraph involved only one feature—voicing. Other kinds of substitution patterns may involve more dimensions. If we have a pattern of disorder in which both [t] and [g] occur where we expect ŋ, the features [vd], [ant], [cor], and [nas] are all involved. While we do not want to say that a disorder involving fewer distinctive features is necessarily less severe than one involving more features, knowledge of distinctive features can give us a measure of precision that is not obtainable by simply comparing sounds. We would now have a basis for saying that [g] for [ŋ] approximates the adult model more closely than the production of [t] for [ŋ]

Information about distinctive features also has implications for therapeutic procedures. A program designed to work on problem sounds grouped on the basis of natural classes should be preferable to one which treats sounds without regard to their relation to the total phonological structure. Precise knowledge of properties of sounds may also be used to guide a person's gradual progression toward the target sound. For example, procedures for correcting [t] for [ŋ] may focus initially on attaining accurate velar placement ([-ant], [-cor] as in [k]) and proceed from that point to [ŋ] and its voicing and nasal properties. Entire programs of diagnosis and therapy have been designed around the analysis of phonological disorders in terms of distinctive features. While we caution against the unqualified acceptance of such programs, there is little doubt that the appeal to distinctive features provides descriptive and practical insight not found in the traditional concern with isolated, individual sounds.

Exercise 3

In the following disordered productions, describe the distinctive feature contrasts which have been neutralized. Cite only those features that are not redundant.

1.	[tæt]	'cat'	8.	[pɪb]	'fib'
2.	[pæt]	'fat'	9.	[dot]	'goat'
3.	[paɪb]	'five'	10.	[dʌd]	'judge'
4.	[tɪt]	'sit'	11.	[tip]	'keep'
5.	[du]	'zoo'	12.	[tip]	'sheep'
6.	[dɪb]	'give'	13.	[wɪt]	'wish'
7.	[tip]	'cheap'	14.	[bot]	'vote'

Phonological Processes in Disorders

When we compared the developing phonological system of a child with the adult norm, we observed that many of the differences in the child's system could be described by appealing to a set of natural phonological processes. This set of universal processes accounted for the predictable ways in which the adult norm was modified by children in the process of phonological development. Processes such as the stopping of fricatives, the gliding of liquids, and the reduction of consonant clusters reflected natural tendencies toward language modification. These processes had to be overcome or suppressed in the eventual acquisition of the complete adult system. Many general patterns in phonological disorders can also be captured by appealing to processes. We cannot be certain that all of the processes which emerge from the comparison of normal and disordered phonological systems can be called natural in the sense we described it in Chapter 9, but many of these processes do operate. Consider, for example, a list of some of the most commonly observed processes revealed in various samples of phonological disorders.

Cluster Reduction

    [tap] 'stop'   [bɛd] 'bread'

Stopping

    [ti] 'see'   [gɪb] 'give'

Fronting

    [sɪp] 'ship'   [do] 'go'

Deaspiration

    [t=o] 'toe'   [p=i] 'pea'

Gliding

    [wʌn] 'run'   [bwɛd] 'bread'

Final Consonant Deletion

    [dɔ] 'dog'   [faᴵ] 'five'

Voicing/Devoicing

    [tup] 'tube'   [di] 'tea'

Nasalization

    [bĩ] 'bean'   [sĩ] 'sing'

Lateralization

    [l̥i] 'see'   [l̥ɪp] 'sip'

Many of these processes, such as cluster reduction, stopping, and gliding, are similar or identical to those found in language acquisition. Certain types of phonological disorders, then, may be viewed simply as the persistence of natural phonological processes beyond the age when they are suppressed or restricted in normal language development. When an eight-year-old child persists in using glides for [r] and [l], it becomes noticeable because most children overcome the process by this time. Or, when stopping for [s] and [š] still occurs beyond the age of five or six, a child's phonological acquisition is not progressing at a normal rate.

Although most processes found in disorders are similar to those in normal developmental stages, there may be instances where they differ. A particular process revealed in a disorder may not be found in normal development, or it may be found only to a very limited extent. For example, the use of a voiceless lateral fricative [ɬ] for adult [s] is not a widespread process in normal language development[+] (although it occurs normally for *sl* clusters in some children). Yet it is not uncommon as one of the manifestations of an "s-problem." There appears, then, to be a restricted set of disorders which differ from processes of normal acquisition. In a technical sense, these processes may be considered **deviant**, as opposed to those natural processes which indicate a **delay** or persistence of the natural phonological processes found in any developing phonological system.

The appeal to processes in phonological disorders adds another dimension to accurately identifying the system as it stands in relation to the normal adult system. This is an important perspective for any person charged with the responsibility of diagnosing and treating disordered systems. It provides another organizational principle for therapy which focuses on the general nature of the disorder rather than isolated sounds in the system. For example, it seems consistent to work on the group of sounds affected by the process of deaspiration, rather than working on sounds which have no obvious linguistic relation to each other.

Exercise 4

Identify the phonological processes found in the following items. In cases where more than one process applies, be sure to identify all of them.

1.	[wʌp]	'rub'		6.	[tɪ]	'stick'
2.	[lɪ]	'sit'		7.	[tsip]	'cheap'
	ɬ̯			8.	[yæp]	'lap'
3.	[p⁼ɛk]	'Peg'		9.	[tʰa]	'cot'
4.	[p⁼aɪp]	'five'		10.	[t⁼op]	'stove'
5.	[gɔg]	'dog'		11.	[t⁼ãʊ]	'count'
				12.	[t⁼u]	'shoe'

Compare the kinds of processes identified in these items with those in Exercises 3 and 4, Chapter 10. How similar or different are the kinds of processes identified in these exercises?

Phonotactic Patterns

Phonological systems also show patterning in the sequencing of units, and this dimension must be considered in the analysis of phonological disorders. Traditional treatments have considered the role of sound sequencing in two ways. First, the possible effect of phonological environment on "error" sounds has been recognized. We considered this dimension when we discussed phonological contrast in disorders. Contrast or lack of contrast always has to be considered in terms of phonological environment, including surrounding sounds and syllable and word position. The second aspect of sound sequences crucial for the study of phonological disorders is the phonotactic patterns as we discussed them in Chapter 5. It is possible for a disorder in phonology to be manifested either in the basic inventory of sounds or in the particular combinations of sound sequences. In fact, a speaker may reveal a phonotactic disorder without revealing a disorder in sound contrasts. A person may not reveal problems with s in simple consonant + vowel sequences ([si] 'see'), but have difficulty with initial clusters such as sp ([pat] for spot), st ([tap] for stop), or sk ([krim] for scream).

In the traditional framework of speech pathology, these kinds of phonotactic disorders are referred to as "blend" problems. Here again, the traditional viewpoint has pointed to a legitimate area of disorder, but a more detailed phonological analysis can add insight into its precise nature. For example, it is necessary to differentiate different kinds of sequences by position within a syllable and the syllable types revealed (CV, VC, etc.). It is also important to consider the various phonological properties of the clusters or "blends" affected in a disorder. Speakers may have difficulty producing stop + liquid clusters ([bwek] for break, [kwɪp] for clip), but not sibilant + consonant clusters (stop or snow). It is impossible to capture the exact basis for phonotactic disorders without knowledge of the precise properties or features of various sounds in combination. Phonotactic disorders, then, may intersect with other aspects of sound inventory disorders, or they may function as a particular kind of disorder in themselves.

Exercise 5

Examine the following speaker's patterning of English clusters. What kinds of clusters are affected, and what forms do they take? What are the properties of the clusters affected and the syllable position in which they are found? What do the data in items 6, 10, and 15 indicate about the role of syllable boundaries in defining the clusters?

1.	[gwo]	'grow'	9.	[bwɛd]	'bread'
2.	[tap]	'stop'	10.	[rɪski]	'risky'
3.	[ket]	'skate'	11.	[pwiz]	'please'
4.	[rɛs]	'rest'	12.	[kwaᵁn]	'clown'
5.	[dɛs]	'desk'	13.	[sno]	'snow'
6.	[postɚ]	'poster'	14.	[bwo]	'blow'
7.	[slɪp]	'slip'	15.	[wɪspɚ]	'whisper'
8.	[was]	'wasp'	16.	[kwik]	'creek'

Phonological Analysis and Therapeutic Procedure

In the preceding sections, we have shown how phonological disorders are patterned on several levels of the phonological system. In most instances, the insights from phonological analysis provide for a more adequate diagnosis of a disorder. It is essential to understand that effective remediation is based on accurate diagnosis. Insight into the patterned nature of a disorder ultimately forms a basis for organizing the steps of therapy. A speech pathologist who approaches a disorder from this perspective is certainly at an advantage over one who considers no organizational principles of language in remediating disorders. A program of therapy which focuses on one process at a time (e.g. deaspiration or stopping) seems more in line with how systems are organized than one which treats each misarticulated sound as an individual entity.

Furthermore, "transfer" (the generalization of learning from one item to others) can be checked by examining items united on the basis of some linguistic principle. For example, therapy on the aspiration of syllable-initial voiceless stops might start with one sound such as p, but the mastery of the property of aspiration would not be considered complete until it could be produced spontaneously for t and k as well. The extent to which this kind of generalization to t and k can be expected to take place without direct training is currently in debate. However, it is quite clear that the items p, t, and k constitute the class which must be examined in order to evaluate the ultimate control of aspiration.

Principles of phonology may also assist in setting up appropriate therapeutic steps in acquiring target adult forms. As in language acquisition, people may be expected to go through various stages in the eventual acquisition of certain classes of items. For example, children who have used only open syllables do not suddenly start using all the appropriate syllable-final consonants. They may start with a glottal stop, then acquire other stops, and from there move to other manners of articulation (nasals, fricatives, and liquids), and finally to syllable-final consonant clusters. Knowledge that these stages follow natural classes and apply various phonological processes may be helpful in sequencing materials. Also, linguistic principles may give a formal basis for determining how the different approximations of a target sound may come progressively closer to the adult target sound classes. We might expect and encourage a glottal stop as the first approximation of a final consonant, and then other oral stops, before moving on to the other consonant classes such as fricatives and liquids. It is crucial for anyone engaged in remediation programs to have a basis for unifying classes of sounds, and sequencing therapy progressively in the direction of the adult target sound classes.

There are important dimensions to therapy which go beyond a consideration of linguistic principles of organization, and these must also be given consideration in setting up an effective program. Linguistic organization is only one dimension of therapy. However, since disorders are organized on important principles of phonology, it seems only reasonable that these principles should be given their due consideration. It is difficult to conceive of an effective therapy program that does not at least implicitly integrate this knowledge into its procedural strategies.

NOTE

1. We use the symbol $=$ here to mark explicitly the absence of aspiration. This is somewhat different from how we indicate unaspirated sounds

elsewhere in the book, where it is unmarked. We mark it in this section to avoid confusion with the broad transcription of English, where aspirated and unaspirated stops are typically not indicated.

SUGGESTED READING

Ingram's *Phonological Disability in Children* (1976) is the most thorough discussion of phonological disorders from the standpoint of phonological analysis. This text gives particular emphasis to the identification of phonological processes in disorders. More recently, detailed assessment strategies for phonological processes have been offered by Weiner (*Phonological Process Analysis*, 1979), Hodson (*The Assessment of Phonological Processes*, 1980), and Ingram (*Procedures for the Phonological Analysis of Children's Language*, 1981). *Phonology and Speech Remediation: A Book of Readings* (Walsh, 1979) contains many of the important articles on the phonological analysis of speech disorders which have appeared in the last decade. More recent textbooks on articulation disorders indicate the trend toward phonological analysis in speech pathology (for example, Bernthal and Bankson's *Articulation Disorders* (1981)), but it still has not been granted an adequate role within traditional treatments. Articles on the application of phonological analysis to speech disorders are appearing with increasing frequency in the *Journal of Speech and Hearing Disorders* and the *Journal of Speech and Hearing Research*, both published by the American Speech, Language and Hearing Association.

CHAPTER 12
Phonology and Second Language Learning

Learning to speak a foreign language involves learning another phonological system. While this acquisition may be likened in some respects to learning phonology in the native language, there are some obvious and important differences. In the acquisition of the native language phonological system, certain natural phonological processes have to be overcome or suppressed in learning the specific phonological patterns of the language. In the acquisition of another language, it is the phonological patterns of the native language which have to be suppressed in learning the new system. Failure to overcome the patterns of phonology in the native language (abbreviated as L_1) in speaking the **target language** (L_2) results in "foreign accent." Technically, this is called **interference** or **language transfer**, referring to the fact that L_1 patterns are imposed on the L_2 system.

The range of interference manifested by a given speaker may vary, but in all cases we can expect L_1 and L_2 to interact systematically. Speakers of a given native language background often make the same kinds of "errors" when learning a particular foreign language. The productions of a Japanese speaker learning English differ systematically from those of a Spanish speaker, and these differences can be traced in most cases to the internalized system of phonology that they bring to the new language. A Japanese speaker may confuse the *l* and *r* of English, since the L_1 system does not have a contrast between these sounds comparable to that found in English. A Spanish speaker, however, may distinguish *r* and *l* in English, but use a different phonetic production for both sounds. The systematic differences in the L_1 and L_2 phonological systems are the basis for applying phonological analysis in foreign language learning.

Contrastive Phonology

The comparison of language systems related to foreign language learning has become a specialized field in its own right, often referred to as **contrastive linguistics**. Traditionally, contrastive analysis has compared "equivalent" structures in the L_1 and L_2 in order to predict and explain foreign language learning difficulties. During the 1970's, some of the traditional tenets which guided earlier contrastive studies met with strong opposition. Two aspects of traditional contrastive analysis are particularly troublesome. First is the notion of equivalence between the items of two languages. How do we formally determine when the units of L_1 are equivalent to L_2, so that we can say that sound X in L_1 is equivalent to sound Y in L_2? How do we determine the equivalent of English θ and ð in German, which has no comparable units in its phonological inventory? A number of different criteria have been used to establish this correspondence, including similarity of phonetic description, perceptual similarity, phonological relationships, historical relationships, and similarity in spelling. This matter is not necessarily resolved even by looking at the observed data of interference. One speaker of German may use [t] for English //θ// and another may use [s]. Or both [t] and [s] may be used, depending on the phonological environment. Furthermore, experimental studies show that production may differ from perception. Establishing equivalence is not always as apparent as it was assumed in some of the earlier contrastive studies.

The second problem is the notion of predictability. It was often claimed that a comparison of the structures of L_1 and L_2 would naturally lead to predictions about the specific kinds of interference to be found in L_2. Thus, we might predict that the German speaker will produce English //θ// as [s]. Empirical studies, however, showed that this was not always the case. For a variety of reasons, the interference predicted by contrastive analysis does not always match the observed interference. Notwithstanding the problems of traditional contrastive studies, much insight can still be derived for the foreign language teacher or learner who systematically compares the phonological systems of L_1 and L_2.

Phonemic Contrast and Language Learning

Within the tradition of contrastive phonology, the majority of attention has been devoted to comparing phonological units on the surface level. That is, the phonemes of L_1, as realized in their various allophones, are compared with the phonemes of L_2 in their realizations as a basis for explaining interference. This emphasis can be traced partly to the historical development of contrastive analysis, which flourished during a period when structural phonology was still prominent. But this concern may be justified by the apparent interaction of systems on the more concrete levels of phonology—the surface phonetic contrasts. These are, after all, the data that speakers of L_1 have access to initially as they relate to the new system.

A typical traditional study might compare the phonemes of one language with another, making note of different contrastive units and different phonetic realizations. Based on a comparison of the inventories of phonemes and their allophones, several different types of interaction and resultant interference can be isolated. In a classic summary of language interference, Weinreich (1953) distinguished four kinds of interaction and interference from a phonemic point of view. These categories remain useful regardless of how we view the classical phoneme.

1. Underdifferentiation. This takes place when two or more contrastive sounds of L_2 are treated as noncontrastive, because no phonological contrast exists for these sounds in L_1. For example, Spanish does not contrast s and z; [z] is an allophone of /s/. English, on the other hand, contrasts these sounds in items such as *sip* [sɪp] and *zip* [zɪp]. Thus, in learning English, a speaker of Spanish may not differentiate between the s and z contrast, possibly confusing items such as *sip* and *zip*, or *peace* and *peas*. Because underdifferentiation of this type can obviously lead to confusion among lexical items, it is considered one of the more serious types of phonological interference. A similar problem of underdifferentiation might be faced by the English speaker learning an Asian language such as Hindi. In Hindi, the difference between aspirated and unaspirated stops is contrastive. English speakers who treat [p] and [pʰ], or [k] and [kʰ], as if they were part of the same contrastive unit (as they are in English), underdifferentiate the contrastive units of Hindi.

2. Overdifferentiation. In overdifferentiation, contrasts from L_1 are applied to the sounds of L_2, even though they are not required by the L_2 phonological system. For example, an English speaker learning Spanish might consider s and z to be contrastive items in Spanish because they are contrastive in English. But as we noted, [s] and [z] are not contrastive sounds in Spanish, so that their conceptual differentiation is not necessary. Similarly, a Hindi speaker learning English might treat [p] and [pʰ] as if they were different contrastive units. Cases of overdifferentiation may not affect production in any significant way, but the learner's conception of contrastive units will differ from that of the native speaker. Understandably, overdifferentiation does not lead to the confusion among lexical items that underdifferentiation might. It is therefore not usually considered a problem in foreign language learning. Nonetheless, it must be recognized as one type of interaction between phonological systems that affects the ways in which the units of L_1 and L_2 are conceptualized.

Exercise 1

A speaker learning English as a second language produces the following items. What type of contrasts might not be found in the speaker's native language system? Examine both consonants and vowels.

1.	[sɪn]	'thing'	6.	[šɪp]	'cheap'
2.	[sɪn]	'then'	7.	[šɪp]	'jeep'
3.	[fɪt]	'fit'	8.	[lɪn]	'ring'
4.	[fen]	'vain'	9.	[lɪp]	'leap'
5.	[sɪp]	'zip'	10.	[let]	'rate'

Exercise 2

In Mandarin Chinese, aspiration is used to differentiate sets of stops from each other. In other words, units such as /pʰ/, /tʰ/, and /kʰ/ are differentiated from /p/, /t/, and /k/. The aspirated stops are always voiceless; however, the unaspirated stops may be voiced or voiceless. In other words, /pʰ/ is always produced as [pʰ] whereas /p/ may be produced as [p] or [b]. Specify the kinds of contexts in which you might expect a speaker from this background to have difficulty distinguishing English /b/ from /p/, /t/ from /d/, and /k/ from /g/. (Hint: consider where English speakers aspirate and do not aspirate their voiceless stops.) Why would you expect difficulties in these environments? How could you classify the various productions in terms of the categories of "underdifferentiation" and "overdifferentiation?"

---

3. Reinterpretation of Distinctions. In the reinterpretation of distinctions, the contrast of units in the target language is maintained, but on a basis different from that found in L_1. Thus, phonetic features that are redundant in L_2 may be used as the basis for maintaining contrast by the L_1 speaker. Consider how a speaker of German learning English may utilize vowel length contrastively in a context where an English speaker would use vowel length redundantly. In both instances, the end result is the differentiation of items, but on a different basis. German uses phonetic differences in vowel length to distinguish items. The difference between [štat] 'city' and [štaːt] 'state', and [kan] 'can' and [kaːn] 'boat', is indicated by the length of the vowel. In English, however, length is typically much more predictable on the basis of the following environment. As we noted in earlier chapters, vowels are lengthened before voiced segments ([bɪːd] 'bid'), and unlengthened before voiceless segments ([bɪt] 'bit').

Another difference between German and English phonology relates to the voicing of obstruents in word-final position. In German, only voiceless obstruents are produced in this position, whereas in English both voiced and voiceless obstruents are found. Using the German word-final devoicing pattern, German speakers will often devoice the final voiced obstruents in English items such as *bead, pig,* and *buzz*. Despite the devoicing of the final obstruents, however, contrast may be maintained for German speakers confronted with these English items. The German speaker who devoices final obstruents may use the length of the preceding vowel rather than the voicing contrast to distinguish items, producing *bead* [biːt] and *beat* [bit], *pig* [pɪːk] and *pick* [pɪk], *buzz* [bʌːs] and *bus* [bʌs]. In an informal experiment conducted by one of the authors, it was clearly indicated that native German speakers were cueing on the vowel length rather than final voicing to distinguish these items. Thus, we see that English redundant features may take on distinctive status for speakers from a different language background.

Exercise 3

Recall our discussion in Chapter 7, where we observed that vowel length in English might be the only surface phonetic distinction retained between *latter* [lǽɾɚ] and *ladder* [lǽːɾɚ]. Now consider the fact that English speakers learning German often have difficulty learning vowel length differences in German words, while German speakers do not have any difficulty perceiving vowel length differences in English. How would you account for these differences? What are the possible implications in terms of differing levels of phonology as we discussed in Chapter 7?

---

4. *Actual Phone Substitution.* In phone substitution, the contrastive units of L_1 and L_2 are comparable in terms of their contrastive status, but their phonetic production differs. For example, the German and French lateral *l* may be considered to be equivalent to English *l*, but the phonetic production may be different. German and French employ only the alveolar [l], whereas English often produces an alveovelar lateral [ɫ]. The difference in phonetic production may not lead to any particular confusion in terms of contrastive units, but the use of the English [ɫ] in speaking French or German will sound somewhat accented. Similarly, the exclusive use of [l] by French or German speakers using English will sound slightly accented in certain environments where English uses [ɫ].

Distinctive Features

The identification of interference categories given above is probably most readily understood from the viewpoint of distinctive features. In describing an independent sound system, the appeal to distinctive features allows us to capture certain regularities and generalizations that would not be accessible otherwise. Similarly, an appeal to this ultimate contrastive unit allows us to observe regularities in the patterns of interference revealed by language learners. Many instances of interference relate to natural classes of sounds rather than isolated sound units, and these natural classes are formed on the basis of their shared features.

Problems in language learning which result in "underdifferentiation" or "overdifferentiation" obviously concern the different use of features contrastively across L_1 and L_2. However, the distinctive and redundant features of a system may interact in different ways in the interference. A feature may, for example, be used distinctively in one system, but redundantly in the other system. Thus, flapping may be used distinctively in Spanish, whereas it is always redundant in English. Similarly, aspiration in Hindi is a distinctive feature, while it is redundant in English. It is also possible for a feature to be used distinctively in both L₁ and L₂, but to be applied to different natural classes. For example, Spanish uses voicing distinctively for stops, distinguishing p, t, and k from b, d, and g. However, it does not apply voicing contrastively to fricatives, so f and v, and s and z, are not differentiated. So languages may differ not only in terms of the absence or presence of particular distinctive features, but also in the application of these features to classes of sounds. In the case of reinterpretation, we saw a redundant feature of L₂ used to compensate for the absence of a contrast in a particular context in L₁. Thus, the distinctive use of vowel length from German was applied to English to compensate for the absence of a word-final voicing distinction for obstruents in German.

Exercise 4

The Spanish vowel system consists of contrasts between the following vowels: /i/, /e/, /u/, /o/, and /a/. Make a distinctive feature matrix for this system, showing the minimal number of distinctive features necessary to specify the contrasts within the system. Now compare this with the distinctive feature system for English vowels we described in Chapter 4. What is the difference between the systems in terms of their distinctive feature contrasts?

Exercise 5

The following represent some productions of English consonants by a person learning English as L₂. On the basis of the data, what distinctive feature parameters are affected? Be sure to specify when the absence of a distinctive feature specification is limited to a particular natural class of sounds (e.g. neutralization of voicing may be limited to stops).

1.	[paᴵb]	'five'	6.	[wɪs]	'wish'
2.	[sɪp]	'ship'	7.	[wɪs]	'witch'
3.	[bɪzɪn]	'vision'	8.	[θɔt]	'thought'
4.	[zʌz]	'judge'	9.	[do]	'though'
5.	[sip]	'cheap'	10.	[tiθ]	'teeth'

Differences may also be found simply in the specification of particular redundant features across systems, as we described for the different kinds of laterals which may be realized in English versus German or French. The use of differing redundant specifications for laterals did not appear to cause significant phonological interference, but differing redundant specifications can lead to some confusion across systems. Languages such as French and Spanish do not typically specify the feature of aspiration as a redundant feature of voiceless stops p, t, and k. The absence of aspiration on voiceless stops often leads the English speaker to confuse the Spanish and French voiceless stops with their voiced counterparts. In other words, without aspiration, the French and Spanish [p], [t], and [k] may be misinterpreted as *b, d,* and *g* respectively. English speakers obviously use aspiration on voiceless stops as an important cue, even if it does not qualify as a "distinctive" feature. We cannot simply assume that differences in redundant feature specifications will have no serious consequences in language learning.

There are obviously a number of variables which have to be considered when assessing what phonological differences will cause difficulty in the acquisition of another language. It is clear, however, that the appeal to distinctive features allows us to capture some of the regular patterns of phonological systems as they systematically interact with each other. From an analytical perspective, this gives us insight into the regularities of patterned interference; from a practical standpoint, this understanding may serve as an organizational principle for teaching the phonology of L_2 in a systematic way.

Phonotactic Differences

There are several ways in which phonotactic differences may lead to problems for the L_2 learner. In some cases, the distribution patterns of segments may be different across language systems. Both English and Tagalog distinguish three nasals, /m/, /n/, and /ŋ/, but English does not use /ŋ/ in syllable-initial position whereas Tagalog does. An English speaker confronted with items such as Tagalog /ŋaʔ/ 'really' and /ŋakŋaːk/ 'cry aloud' may therefore encounter difficulty producing the /ŋ/ in these positions. This is not a result of a contrastive difference but a difference in the distributional privileges within the syllable. Another difference in distribution between Tagalog and English is the occurrence of /h/. In Tagalog, /h/ may occur syllable-finally, whereas in English it may not. Thus, Tagalog items such as /amah/ 'father' and /tuːboh/ 'tube' reveal a pattern not found in English. The native English speaker will tend to eliminate the final /h/.

Another major difference in phonotactics concerns CV sequences. Syllable types and segment cluster types differ across phonological systems, and these differences are often revealed in the kinds of problems found among L_2 learners. For example, Spanish does not permit syllable-initial sibilant + stop sequences, as in English *sp, st,* or *sk*. Thus, Spanish speakers impose the Spanish phonotactic system and produce these English clusters with an epenthetic vowel ([ɛstʌdi] for *study* or [ɛskul] for *school*). In a parallel way, an English speaker learning German may be confronted with certain syllable-initial sequences not permissible in English. These include velar stops + nasals (German [knabə] 'boy' and [gnadə] 'mercy') and stops + fricatives ([psalm̩] 'psalm', [pfʊnt] 'pound'). Two possibilities exist here for imposing the English phonotactic structure. Speakers might use an epenthetic vowel to separate the nonpermissible English sequence ([kənabə]), or reduce the cluster by deleting one of the members ([nabə] or [fʊnt]). In both cases, the modification would result in a permissible English syllable type, but an unusual German pronunciation. Notice that reduction may involve more than simple interaction of the two languages involved. We would expect the unmarked member of the cluster to be deleted in the reduction rather than the marked one: thus [fʊnt], not [pʊnt], for [pfʊnt].

A final type of phonotactic difference relates to the phonological status of particular phonetic sequences. In our discussion in Chapter 5, we demonstrated that English [tš] should be considered as one phonological unit /č/, even though phonetically it consisted of a stop + sibilant sequence. In another language, this sequence might be treated as two phonological units /t/ and /š/. By the same token, another language may treat a different set of phonetic sequences as a single phonological unit. A language might treat the phonetic sequence of [ts] or [dz] as one unit in a way comparable to how English treats the [tš] sequence. Mandarin Chinese, for example, does not use phonemic consonant clusters initially, but does have a single phonemic unit which is rendered phonetically as [ts]. An English speaker learning Mandarin is likely to reduce the [ts] to [s] , treating it according to English phonotactic conditions rather than as a single contrastive unit. Similarly, initial prenasalized stop sequences ([mb], [nd], [ŋg]) might be treated as one phonological unit (/ᵐb/, /ⁿd/, /ᵑg/), as they are in a number of Bantu languages in central and southern Africa. For the language learner, these sequences present difficulties comparable to those found when other types of phonotactic sequences differ in L_1 and L_2. The sequence might be modified by deleting one of the phonetic segments (using, for example, [b] for [mb]), or by inserting a vowel to accommodate the L_1 phonotactic pattern ([məb] or [əmb] for [mb]). In effect, these units are treated as phonotactic differences by L_1 speakers, despite the fact that they are considered as a single contrastive unit in L_2.

Exercise 6

Consider how the following English items are produced by a person learning English as an L_2. Based on these productions, what kinds of syllable-initial and syllable-final clusters would you expect in this person's L_1 system?

a. *Syllable-initial*

1.	[pat]	'spot'	9.	[plid]	'plead'
2.	[tap]	'stop'	10.	[slɪp]	'slip'
3.	[kɪn]	'skin'	11.	[dwɛl]	'dwell'
4.	[pwaɪs]	'price'	12.	[swit]	'sweet'
5.	[bwɔd]	'broad'	13.	[dwaɪ]	'dry'
6.	[kwaɪ]	'cry'	14.	[twaɪ]	'try'
7.	[gwɪp]	'grip'	15.	[klɪp]	'clip'
8.	[blid]	'bleed'	16.	[glæd]	'glad'

b. *Syllable-final*

1.	[wɛs]	'west'	9.	[was]	'wasp'
2.	[waɪl]	'wild'	10.	[kaᵘnt]	'count'
3.	[læps]	'lapse'	11.	[ræŋk]	'rank'
4.	[baks]	'box'	12.	[bʌmp]	'bump'
5.	[rɪts]	'Ritz'	13.	[lɛŋks]	'length'
6.	[dɛs]	'desk'	14.	[wɪts]	'width'
7.	[kɔl]	'colt'	15.	[θæŋks]	'thanks'
8.	[tæps]	'taps'	16.	[wɪl]	'wilt'

Phonological Processes

We have repeatedly observed that language systems are susceptible to a number of different phonological processes which alter the shape of units. Because of the natural basis for various processes, it is not surprising to see similar processes in two different language systems. There is, for example, a class of nasal prefixes in Swahili which is conditioned by the place of articulation of the following segment (*m-bari* 'clan', *n-devu* 'beard', *ŋ-guzo* 'post'). This assimilation is similar to the form changes found in English (*impossible, indefinite, inconclusive*). But while recognizing certain similarities in the types of phonological processes found in different systems on the basis of some universal principles, we must also observe significant differences in detail as we compare phonological systems.

Many language systems may employ neutralization of one type or another, but the particular details of neutralization will vary greatly. Thus, the English speaker shows extensive neutralization of vowels in unstressed syllables, so most English vowels can reduce to a [ə]. Spanish, on the other hand, reveals little vowel neutralization of this type, maintaining contrasts in unstressed syllables as well as stressed ones. By the same token, standard English does not have the broadly applied German rule of final obstruent devoicing. Neutralization of contrasts in unstressed syllables, or devoicing in word-final position, may qualify as natural processes, but the particular details of these processes and the extent of their operation show considerable variation between systems. Such diversity is an important aspect of comparing systems in a contrastive analysis.

Exercise 7

In French, many word-final consonants are deleted when the following word begins with a consonant ([pəti gars] 'little boy' but [pətit ami] 'little friend'). How might the application of this process in French affect the final consonants of English items for a French native speaker? Give some examples in English of items in which you might expect consonants to be retained, and those in which you expect consonants to be deleted.

Exercise 8

There are certain similarities between the Spanish and English plural forms. Spanish has two basic forms: /s/, which occurs following items which end in a vowel ([dɛðo]/[dɛðos] 'finger/fingers'; [kasa]/[kasas] 'house/houses'), and /ɛs/, which occurs following items which end in a consonant ([señor]/[señores] 'man/men', [siuðad]/[siuðaðes] 'city/cities'). Compare these forms with the English plural forms we discussed at various points in the previous chapters, describing the precise differences and similarities. How might an English speaker produce the plural of [siuðad] and [kasa] if the English rule were applied to these Spanish items?

It is also possible for L₂ to have processes not typically found in L₁. Thus vowel harmony, not found in current English, is of considerable importance in learning Turkish. Vowels in certain suffixes must agree in terms of backing, height, and rounding with the vowel of the base word. Thus, items with a front unrounded vowel in the base would take a first person possessive with a high front unrounded vowel (/diš/ 'tooth', /dišim/ 'my tooth'). Those with a rounded front vowel in the base take a rounded front vowel in the suffix (/gil/ 'rose', /gilim/ 'my rose'). A nonfront rounded vowel leads to a rounded back vowel (/kol/ 'arm', /kolum/ 'my arm'), and an unrounded nonfront vowel to an unrounded nonfront vowel in the suffix (/ɨr/ 'song', /ɨrɨm/ 'my song'). The form of the vowel in the suffix is quite regular as governed by the morphophonemic process of vowel harmony, but this process is quite different from anything found in English.

Ultimately, of course, the comparison of different processes is reflected in the format of the phonological rules. This includes specifying the particular change that takes place, and the environment in which the rule operates. Both aspects are an important part of capturing the regularities of change in the shape of forms, and they must therefore be considered an essential part of comparing different phonological systems. Learning the application of particular processes is just as essential in foreign language learning as learning the different contrastive phonological units.

Hierarchies of Difficulty

One of the practical applications of contrastive analysis in foreign language pedagogy is establishing a hierarchy of difficulty for speakers of a specific L_1 learning a specific L_2 phonology. Levels of difficulty are predicted based on a comparison of phonological units in the two systems. Differences between systems are not all of equal magnitude. Based on our understanding of phonological organization, we anticipate that some differences impose greater obstacles than others. Generally speaking, we may say that the higher the degree of similarity between the phonological categories in L_1 and L_2, the easier it will be to learn the L_2 categories. Conversely, the more different they are, the more difficult L_2 will be to learn.

Stockwell and Bowen (1965) have proposed a general framework for establishing hierarchies of difficulty. As a basis for comparing systems, three categories of phonological units are set up:

(1) **Optional** categories are phonemes which may or may not occur in a particular phonological context.

Difficulty		Comparison		Example for the English Speaker Learning Spanish
Magnitude	*Order*	L_1	L_2	
I	1	null	Ob	allophone [ƀ] of /b/; does not occur in English
	2	null	Op	alveolar trill /r̃/ as a phoneme in Spanish; does not occur in English
	3	Op	Ob	[d] and [đ] as allophones of one phoneme in Spanish; separate phonemes in English
II	4	Ob	Op	[ɪ] and [ɛ] may be neutralized before *n* in some Southern dialects of English; contrast between high and mid vowels before *n* in Spanish
	5	Ob	null	English flap [ɾ] is an allophone of /t/ and /d/ intervocalically; Spanish does not show this variation
	6	Op	null	English has vowel phoneme /æ/; Spanish does not
III	7	Op	Op	Both languages use phonemes such as /m/, /n/, etc. in word-initial position
	8	Ob	Ob	Both Spanish and English require that a vowel follow the cluster [sw]

(2) Obligatory categories are allophones which must be used in a given phonological context.

(3) **Zero or null** categories are cases of the complete absence of a sound. Based on comparing these categories across languages, eight different types of learning structures (orders) are proposed, with three magnitudes of difficulty.

The table on page 195 summarizes the Stockwell and Bowen hierarchy of difficulty, as exemplified by a native English speaker learning Spanish. Magnitude I, Order 1 involves the most difficult learning strategy. Additional considerations in setting up a hierarchy of difficulty include the distribution of phonological classes in the respective systems, potential perceptual problems, and functional load. Functional load refers to the extent to which a given sound is used to distinguish one word from another: "the quantity of distinctive information it carries" (Stockwell and Bowen, 1965:16).

Exercise 9

Using the hierarchy of difficulty specified above, give the order of difficulty for the following relationships between categories. Assume that the L_1 is English. Example: if the thing to learn is that L_2 uses front vowels $/\underset{w}{\overset{\centerdot}{\imath}}/$ and $/\underset{w}{e}/$ in phonemic contrast, we would say that the learning problem involves the second order of difficulty, since i and e are "null" (absence of the sound) in English and "optional" in L_2 (phonemes that may or may not occur in a given position).

1. The use of the vowels [i] and [ɪ] as allophonic variations of one unit $/i/$
2. Stop + lateral clusters (*bl, pl, kl*) always followed by a vowel
3. The use of $/x/$ as a phonemically contrasting unit
4. The use of [t] as an allophone for $/d/$
5. The absence of a vowel ʊ as a phonemic or allophonic unit
6. The use of [ɣ] as an allophone of $/g/$
7. The use of $/p^h/$ and $/p/$ as different phonemic units
8. The use of nasalized vowels as phonemically contrasting units

---

Several experimental studies have shown that difficulties in learning L_2 phonology cannot always be predicted simply on the basis of comparing phonological categories in this way. One study shows that items grouped together by phonological categories may show levels of learning difficulty quite different from that predicted on the basis of a structural comparison. For example, both [ž] and [ŋ] should represent the same kind of learning problem for a native English speaker, since neither of these occurs in syllable-initial position, yet [ž] is much easier to learn in this position than [ŋ]. Similarly, both [x] and [ɣ] represent items not found in English, yet [x] proves easier to learn than [ɣ].

On the basis of such findings, we may conclude that a different perspective is necessary to determine a hierarchy of difficulty rather than comparisons made solely on the basis of distinctive features or allophonic membership in a phoneme class. Considerations of the overall organization of the phonological system and naturalness seem essential in understanding why some units are more readily learned than others. Phonological categories may have a bearing on the ease of learning, but this is only one variable in the array of linguistic considerations.

Exercise 10

How would you explain the fact that [ž] in syllable-initial or word-initial position is considerably easier for English speakers to learn than [ŋ] in this position? Consider in your response the discussion of the underlying status of //ŋ// in Chapter 7, and the discussion of naturalness in Chapter 9.

SUGGESTED READING

Weinreich's *Languages in Contact*, originally published in 1953, still remains a worthwhile introduction to the notion of phonological interference, although it must now be viewed in the light of more recent developments in phonological theory. Ritchie (1968) has also provided a reasonable approach to phonological interference in "On the Explanation of Phonic Interference." DiPietro's *Language Structures in Contrast* (1971) includes a chapter on contrastive analysis of phonology from the standpoint of generative phonology. For an actual example of the type of contrastive analysis in vogue during the 1960's, the interested reader is referred to Stockwell and Bowen, *The Sounds of English and Spanish* (1965). The journal *Language Learning* contains articles on phonological analysis and second language learning, although these occurred more frequently during the late 1960's and early 1970's than currently.

CHAPTER 13
Phonology and English Orthography

The majority of the world's written languages use writing systems that are directly related to their phonology. That is, the primary orthographic symbols are used to represent phonological units of the language in some way. English is one of these systems; the letters of the alphabet each represent some aspect of the English phonological system. The way in which phonology is represented in the English spelling system, however, is a matter of considerable dispute among linguists and educators. The popular opinion is that the English system is highly irregular and inconsistent, imposing many unnecessary burdens on its learners. For centuries now, the system has been under attack as antiquated, inconsistent, and illogical.

In the following sections, we examine aspects of English spelling with reference to the phonological system. Although the system certainly reveals complexities in its organization, English is hardly the haphazard, ill-conceived system that it has been made out to be. Understanding the basis for the different patterns of symbol-sound correspondence can give us a new appreciation for the intricacies of the system. Such information can subsequently serve to guide the English instructor who is confronted with explaining the nature of English orthography. In fact, an understanding of some of the patterns may help in improving instruction in basic educational tasks such as reading and spelling.

Levels of Representation

An alphabet might be designed to represent the units of the sound system at any of several different levels. It might seek to **represent the surface phonetic units** directly. In such a system, phonetic detail would be shown regardless of how the detail was used contrastively within the language. This system would follow the principles of phonetic transcription discussed in Chapter 2. Thus, for English, several different kinds of p might be represented in the orthography, included an aspirated $[p^h]$, unaspirated $[p]$, and unreleased $[p^\daleth]$, since all three phonetic items occur. Although some language systems have been described as having "phonetic spelling" (Finnish, for example), there are no alphabetic systems that are strictly phonetic in the sense that we discussed this notion. Most systems described as phonetic, including the Initial Teaching Alphabet for English, are really more like the phonemic spelling system we describe below. A strict phonetic alphabet might be easier for a foreigner learning a language, but orthographies are not designed for foreigners. For the most part, they are designed for native speakers, and thus take advantage of the kinds of knowledge native speakers have about their phonology.

One kind of alphabet making use of such knowledge **represents the classical phonemic units** of a language. Just as a different phonemic symbol is used for each class of sounds defined as a phoneme, a different alphabetic symbol—usually labeled a **grapheme**—is used to represent each distinct phoneme in the sound system. Spelling systems such as Finnish and Spanish have been described as phonemic, although they have some discrepancies from the ideal phonemic orthography, in which there is a one-to-one correspondence between symbols and phonemes. Strict adherence to a phonemic orthography would capture the fact that the three phonetic variations of /p/ function as one unit, and only one grapheme p would be used for /p/. This represents a clear advantage over a phonetic system, since a native speaker will automatically produce the correct phonetic forms of phonemic orthographies. Other sounds may not be represented in the most efficient way, however. For example, /s/ and /z/ are separate phonemes in English, so a phonemic system would use separate symbols for the various allomorphs of the plural. Thus, *bats*, *buds*, and *buses* should be 'bæts', 'bʌdz', and 'bʌsɪz' if the system is truly phonemic.

Another system of orthography attempts to recognize these aspects of a speaker's knowledge at the level we described in Chapter 7 as the **systematic phonemic level of representation**. In this approach, underlying units of contrast rather than classical phonemic or phonetic contrasts are the basis for different orthographic representations. Such spelling systems represent each systematic phoneme in the lexical representation with a different orthographic symbol. The changes that the form undergoes in its derivation from the underlying form to the surface phonetic form need not be overtly represented. Presumably regular phonological rules that alter the underlying shape of items can be ignored because these can be applied automatically by native speakers of a language. In other words, the orthography does not represent the changes that are predictable on the basis of the phonological rules of the language. Thus, the system takes advantage of what native speakers know about the rules of the language, as well as the systematic units within the phonology.

Consider how such an approach might treat the three different forms of the regular English plural /z/, /s/, and /ɪz/. One representation would be adequate, since the forms are quite predictable from the phonological shape of the preceding item. A native speaker automatically interprets the s of *buds* as /z/, the s of *butts* as /s/, and the s of *roses* as /ɪz/, so it appears to be adequate to use one symbol for all realizations of the regular plural suffix. Similarly, it would not be necessary to note the difference in the predictable change from final //t// to /š/ when the *-ion* suffix is added to the base, as in *demonstrate/demonstration*, or *locate/location*. Native speakers of English will automatically apply the appropriate phonological rules of the language to the underlying //t// represented in the orthography. From this perspective, the systematic phonemic representation of *sing* with an n and g might also justify the final n and g spelling even though it is produced as [ŋ] on a surface level. Recall here our discussion in Chapter 7, in which the surface /ŋ/ production was derived through a series of phonological rules that operated on underlying //n// + //g// sequences.

The viewpoint that spelling systems most appropriately represent abstract underlying units rather than surface phonemic units is often associated with the interpretation of generative phonology presented by Chomsky and Halle (1968). Certainly, they have been the most outspoken advocates for this position. It should be noted, however, that the options are not simply a representation of quite abstract systematic phonemes or classical phonemes. Between these two extremes, there exist positions which other linguists maintain are the most appropriate levels for orthographic representation. There is, for example, what might be called a **morphophonemic level of representation**. Here each phoneme is represented by a different written symbol unless the difference is the result of a productive phonological rule that changes the shape of the morpheme. When these regular phonological processes apply, one established orthographic representation is maintained regardless of the phonemic and phonetic changes. On this level of representation, a single orthographic form would suffice for the three regular alternants of the plural, and the final t before *-ion* would be represented as t. However, more abstract underlying forms (such as *kn* for *knee*) would not be justified. No cases of absolute neutralization would be represented. This level of orthographic representation fits somewhere between the more abstract level representing underlying systematic phonemes and the simple representation of classical phonemic contrasts. It corresponds to the traditional morphophonemic level in allowing different forms to be represented by the same symbol.

To a certain extent, the evaluation of how well the English orthographic system matches English phonology is dependent upon the analysis of English phonology with which it is being compared. For example, Chomsky and Halle (1968:50) conclude that English orthography "comes close to being an optimal orthographic system for English." However, this claim must be seen in light of their analysis of English phonology, in which some of the underlying systematic phonemes are never realized in the surface phonetics of English. An item such as *right* is given an underlying representation like //rixt//, *courage* //koræge// , and *giraffe* //giræffe// , despite the fact that their actual productions as [raɪt], [kɛrɪǰ], and [ǰəræf] are quite distant from this underlying form. We saw in Chapter 7 that Chomsky and Halle's claim seems somewhat exaggerated, since many of the underlying forms they posit are difficult to justify in terms of native speakers' demonstrated knowledge of English phonology. For example, there is no basis for maintaining that native speakers of English have any knowledge of a form such as //x// corresponding to graphemic *gh*. Nonetheless, we can see how their analysis of English phonology has led to their claim concerning the efficiency of English orthography.

A number of legitimate criticisms have been raised to counter Chomsky and Halle's claims about the efficiency of English orthography. However, they must still be credited with providing the impetus for discovering deeper regularities in English spelling. Consider the case of the so-called "silent *g* and *b*" in English. Our initial reaction to the *b* and *g* in items such as *bomb*, *crumb*, *sign*, and *malign* is to consider them an irrational and confusing use of an unnecessary letter. However, in related words such as *bombard*, *crumble*, *signal*, and *malignant*, [b] and [g] actually appear on the surface. This pattern has led some phonologists to posit an underlying *b* and *g* in *bomb* or *sign*, even though it is not realized phonetically in the simple base word. Whether one agrees with this analysis for current-day productive English phonology, it does provide a reasonable basis for seeing that at least some "silent letters" indicate patterned relationships between items.

Exercise 1

For the "silent letters" underlined in the following items, try to determine if a related word exists in which the segment actually occurs (for example, *doubt/dubitable*). What are the implications for the orthographic representation of the various items?

1.	column	5.	comb	9.	succumb
2.	phlegm	6.	debt	10.	damn
3.	sovereign	7.	solemn	11.	thumb
4.	hymn	8.	reign	12.	design

Exercise 1 shows that a number of the "silent letters" can be explained on the basis of their relationship with associated items. Nonetheless, some phonologists still would argue against the inclusion of these silent letters in an efficient spelling of English, because these do not appear to be particularly productive patterns. It is questionable whether native speakers of English actually associate the silent *b* of *bomb* or *thumb* with the *b* in *bombard* and *thimble* in any productive way. It is more probable that they are treated as unrelated lexical forms.

Such theoretical ideals aside, in practice we have to deal with the English orthographic system as it has become established over the centuries. At certain points in the English system, it appears that the orthographic representation is largely phonemic, while at other points it seems to represent units on an underlying, systematic phonemic level. The intervocalic consonant of *writer* and *rider* are represented differently in the orthography despite the fact that many varieties of American English produce intervocalic *t* and *d* similarly with a flap. This orthographic representation obviously refers to a more abstract level of differentiation in which the *t* of *write* is clearly different from the *d* of *ride*. Many regular phonological changes in the shape of morphemes are also indicated by a single orthographic representation, such as the regular *-ed* spelling that represents /t/, /d/, or /ɪd/, or the change from *t* to /š/ with the addition of the *-ion* affix. On the other hand, certain symbols represent the phonemic level despite morphophonemic alternation. Thus, we have *wife/wives* for /waɪf/-/waɪvz/ and *wolf/wolves* for /wʊlf/-/wʊlvz/.

Exercise 2

What level or levels of representation are indicated in the regular negative prefix in items such as *impossible* /ɪmpásɪbl̩/, *indefinite* /ɪndɛ́fɪnɪt/, and *incontestable* /ɪŋkə̀ntɛ́stɪbl̩/. How does this representation compare with the level of representation indicated in the regular past tense suffix we just discussed (*started* /startɪd/, *tipped* /tɪpt/, *bugged* /bʌgd/)? Is a pattern for representing prefixes and suffixes on different levels of representation indicated here? Compare other prefixes and suffixes to support your conclusion.

Symbol-Sound Correspondence

Some analyses identify more than 40 phonemes for English. Given the 26 letters of the alphabet available for use in the English writing system, it seems obvious that orthographic representation must go considerably beyond the simple correspondence of one letter for each significant phonological unit. Even for those analyses that posit fewer units, a single letter for each significant phonological unit is not sufficient, so the system utilizes the available symbols in some rather ingenious ways. Although we think of only 26 letters as basic to the system, there are also a number of digraphs (pairs of letters representing a single sound unit). Units such as *th*, *ch*, *sh*, or *oo* are just as basic to the English orthographic system as *a* and *b*.

Furthermore, the significance of the alphabetic symbols is not limited to combinations that are immediately adjacent to each other. The well-known use of a vowel + consonant + *e* indicates a pattern different from a vowel + consonant, as in *mate* and *fate* compared with *mat* and *fat*. Letters may even show patterns of alternation based solely on their distribution within words. We get the familiar pattern of *y* replaced by *i* when certain kinds of suffixes are added to the form, as in *mercy/merciful* and *icy/iciest*. Quite clearly, the patterning of correspondences between graphic symbols and sound units involves more than single graphic symbols. Surrounding graphic symbols, phonological context, and information from the syntactic/semantic levels of language must all be considered in determining the regular patterns of English orthography.

We have just mentioned how separated combinations of graphic symbols are used in representing different phonological values. Surrounding graphic symbols are also important in the well-known pattern of *c* representing /s/ ("soft *c*") before *e*, *i*, and *y* (*cease, city, cyot*), but corresponding to /k/ ("hard *c*") in other contexts (*cut, cream, collar*). This pattern may seem arbitrary in certain cases, but it is used to capture the regular phonological alternation *electric/electricity, plastic/plasticity*. Simple position within a word may also serve to condition a particular correspondence. For example, *gh* at the beginning of a word represents /g/ as in *ghost, ghetto*, or *ghoul*, but elsewhere it has a different phonological value (compare, for example, *tough* and *thought*). It is apparent, then, that patterns of graphemic distribution— including combinations of graphemes, sequencing, and positioning within larger units—are necessary considerations in determining the regular correspondence of English orthographic symbols. We may think of this as a type of **grapho-tactics** that parallels patterns of phonotactics. Symbols must be viewed in terms of other graphic symbols in order to capture regularity in the symbol-sound relationships.

Phonological context must also be considered apart from graphemic context as an important variable in determining regular symbol-sound relationships. This is well illustrated in the values of vowel symbols with different degrees of stress. The phonetic value of orthographic *e* in the initial syllable of *télegraph* is different from that in *telégraphy*, as is the initial *o* in *phótograph* and *photógraphy*. But each phonetic form can be predicted by looking at the distribution of stress in the words. The difference in the correspondences results from applying the regular English rule reducing vowels in unstressed syllables. Similarly, *h* in a stressed syllable may correspond to the phonological unit /h/, but may not have a surface sound correspondence in an unstressed syllable, as indicated in the difference between *prohibit* [prəhíbɪt] and *prohibition* [pròɪbíšɪn]. Surrounding segments must also be considered in accounting for certain regular symbol-sound relationships. This has already been demonstrated in how English orthography handles various morphophonemic changes without altering the basic graphic symbols. The phonological correspondence of plural forms written as -*s* or past tense forms written as -*ed* depends on the specification of the preceding segment. Other morphophonemic processes may be more complex in their conditioning effect on symbol-sound correspondences, such as the palatalization process affecting *t, d, s*, and *z* when followed by a palatal /y/ or /i/ and an unstressed vowel. For instance, *t* and *s* correspond to /š/ preceding a suffix such as -*ion* or -*ial*, as in *relate/relation, confess/confession*, or *face/facial*. Here, a regularity in the correspondence exists, but it necessarily takes into account phonological context in the derivation of phonological processes.

Certain other correspondences result from phonological context but do not reflect morphophonemic processes. For example, *a* will correspond to /a/ when

---

Exercise 3

Among the correspondences for *ch* in English are /č/ and /k/. While the /k/ correspondence cannot always be predicted for *ch*, there are some phonological contexts in which /k/ is predictable. Based on the following items, what is the relevant phonological context for predicting the /k/ correspondence with written *ch*?

1. chrome	6. chicken	11. chloride
2. choke	7. chip	12. check
3. chlorine	8. chrysanthemum	13. chronic
4. chore	9. chlorophyll	14. christen
5. christian	10. choose	

preceded by /w/ and followed by a nonvelar segment: *swamp, swan, quality*. However, when preceded by /w/ and followed by a velar, it will typically correspond to /æ/: *quack, twang, wax* (Venezky, 1970).

The basis of patterning between symbols and sound units cannot be limited to knowledge about phonology. Knowledge of the grammatical system may also be used to constrain correspondence patterns. The identification of separate morphemic units may determine particular correspondence patterns, with or without the consideration of morphophonemic processes. Knowledge about morpheme boundaries tells us that the *s* of *pies* or *dues* is part of a plural morpheme, and predictably leads to its realization as /z/. But the nonplural *s* of *pious* or *bus* corresponds to /s/ because no morpheme boundary precedes it. Similarly, *ph* sequences across morpheme boundaries such as *up-hill* or *topheavy* correspond to two different units, /p/ and /h/. When part of a single morpheme, they may function as a digraph representing /f/ as in *morpheme (morph+eme)* or *graphics (graph+ic+s)*. Such regularity can only be determined by applying knowledge about the combinations of morphemes within words.

Regularity and Variance

Although the previous discussion has pointed to the regular basis of many symbol-sound relationships, the majority of these relationships are not in-variant correspondences (Venezky, 1970:39). That is, they are not cases in which one symbol **always** corresponds to a particular sound unit. The symbol *v* in English comes close to being invariant in its correspondence to the pho-nemic unit /v/. Similarly, *j* for /ǰ/, *q* for /k/, and *ck* for /k/ have been described as invariant in their symbol-to-sound correspondence. The vast majority of correspondences in English, however, are **variant**. That is, the symbol-sound relationships are regular in the sense that they are predictable, but the phonological value of the symbols changes as a result of graphic, phonological, or grammatical conditioning.

A correspondence of initial *k* before *n* as Ø (*knight, know*) and as /k/ elsewhere (*keep, king*) is a regular but variant correspondence for *k*. Both invariant and variant correspondences may be regular in the sense that the phonological values can be predicted. The notion of regularity in symbol-sound relationships cannot be limited to those infrequent cases of invariant correspondences. Regularity refers to any case that can be predicted on a nonarbitrary basis by a learner of the system. This means that cues from the system can be used to predict the correspondence, without appealing to rote memorization of particular items.

Given our previous discussion, we must admit that there are far fewer cases of symbol-sound irregularity in English than are usually attributed to the system. But there are some. The correspondence of *o* to /ɪ/ in *women* is an uncommon and unpredictable correspondence for *o*. The correspondence of *ea* to /i/ in *bead* and *teach*, and to /ɛ/ in *dead* and *treachery*, is irregular, since there is no consistent basis for predicting different phonological corre-spondences for the symbol. This irregularity is exemplified in an item such as *read*, which corresponds to both /rid/ (*They will read a lot of books*) or /rɛd/ (*They have read a lot of books*).

Even with genuine irregular patterns of correspondence, there are differ-ent degrees of irregularity to be recognized. The case of *o* corresponding to /ɪ/ represents a very infrequent kind of correspondence relationship, whereas *ea* for /i/ and /ɛ/ is the pattern for a relatively large subgroup of words. The former case is an "exception," whereas the latter represents a difference between what Venezky labels as "major" (*ea* for /i/) and "minor" (*ea* for /ɛ/) correspondence patterns. Such a distinction in the kinds of irregularity may not be particularly significant for linguistic organization, but it seems useful in terms of systematically teaching the symbol-sound correspondences of English. Minor correspondences may be taught as sets of items, whereas exceptions are most effectively treated as true exceptions in terms of learning.

From Sound to Symbol

Our discussion thus far has implicitly focused on the symbol to sound correspondence relationship. We have been concerned with the "decoding" of symbols into sounds in a skill such as reading. For spelling, which is an "encoding" skill, different kinds of patterns may exist. Correspondences such as *j* to /ǰ/ and *q* to /k/ are invariant when going from symbol to sound unit, but we can hardly say that the converse is true. The unit /ǰ/ may be spelled *g*, *j*, or *dg* as in *gem*, *jam*, and *ridge*. /k/ may be spelled as *q*, *k*, *c*, and *ck*: *quack*, *keep*, *cup*, *back*. Some of the same types of considerations for regularity in symbol to sound relationships are found in determining sound to symbol relationships. Initial /k/ before high front vowels corresponds to *k* (*keep*, *kiss*), a pattern showing sensitivity to surrounding phonological context. Final /ks/ within a single morpheme corresponds to *x* (*box*, *tax*), but when the *k* and *s* are in different morphemes, it is spelled with a (*c*)*k* and *s* (*rack/racks*, *stake/stakes*). This pattern is sensitive to information about grammatical boundaries. Such patterns show that there is considerably more predictability in encoding English than is usually recognized, just as we showed for the decoding process. Overall, however, there are more predictable patterns in going from symbols to sounds than from sounds to symbols.

Exercise 4

a. At various points, we have mentioned how *c* preceding *i*, *e*, or *y* corresponds to /s/, whereas elsewhere it corresponds to /k/. How is this pattern manifested in the sets of items given below? What role does the inserted *k* in *politicking* or *picnicking* play in the retention of a consistent correspondence pattern? How can this knowledge assist in achieving correct spelling for these items?

> *politic, politicize, political, politicking*
> *panic, panicky, panicked, panicking*
> *plastic, plastics, plasticity, plasticize*
> *magic, magical, magicky, magicked*
> *electric, electricity, electrical*

b. In the following items, how does the apparent correspondence with /š/ relate to the pattern of *c* before *i*? Is it an irregular pattern that violates the *c* to /s/ pattern before *i*? If not, why not?

> *politician, magician, electrician*

Why Such Spelling?

Although the preceding section emphasized many regular correspondences between English sounds and symbols, the fact remains that English is still not an easy language to spell. Spelling ability can be enhanced by taking advantage of certain systematic cues about sound-symbol relationships, but the highest levels of proficiency remain something of an art. Correct spelling in English necessarily goes beyond the knowledge which a person possesses simply by virtue of being a native speaker of the language. The speller is confronted with items ranging from *psychology* and *island*, with their seemingly extraneous letters, to alternant spellings of homophonous items such as *to*, *two*, and *too*.

There are a number of reasons why the English spelling system has developed some of these apparent "inconsistencies." It is instructive to look at several of these. If nothing else, understanding of the complexities of the system is enhanced by seeing how different influences have contributed to its development. Some of the different patterns of representation within the system may defy justification in terms of the current phonological system, from which spelling might ideally take its major cues, but we must appreciate the different dimensions of natural language dynamics that are revealed in the system.

One major reason for apparent inconsistency between the phonological and orthographic systems is change within the English language. Phonological systems, like other aspects of language, are constantly undergoing change. On the other hand, orthographic conventions, once established by tradition, are generally conservative and slower to change than spoken language. Once English orthography was stabilized through the development of the printing press and dictionaries, the orthographic traditions became quite conservative. Changes in the spoken language were simply not matched by corresponding changes in the orthographic representation of forms. At one time, spelling representations matched the phonological system more directly than they do at this stage in the English language. However, English phonology has changed considerably over the centuries. New phonemic contrasts have been established, older ones lost, and the phonotactic structure of English has also changed. These changes were not always registered in the orthography. Our present *gh* in items such as *right* and *brought* represents an older /x/ phoneme once present in English. Similarly, the final *e* of items such as *name* and *smoke* at one stage represented a final vowel sound (/namə/) that has been lost. The *e* symbol has retained considerable significance as a marker in English spelling, but its phonological value has shifted from its intended correspondence centuries ago. In items such as *knight* and *knife*, we find a spelling vestige of an older phonotactic pattern in English, in which initial sequences /kn/ were permissible. Change in the phonotactic patterns of English have eliminated this sequence, but the spelling convention has remained faithful to the original.

The most dramatic change in the phonological system affecting spelling is the "Great Vowel Shift," which occurred between the Middle English and Early Modern English period (1300-1500). A series of changes in the vowels brought about a significant reorganization of the system. Roughly speaking, the earlier lengthened or "long" vowels came to be produced at a higher tongue position, and vowels already produced at the highest position became diphthongs. Thus, an item such as *sweet* changed from /swe:t/ to /swit/, *ride* changed from /ri:d/ to /raɪd/, *spoon* from /spo:n/ to /spun/, *down* from /dun/ to /daʊn/, and so forth. This shift in the pronunciation of the vowels was made without a corresponding shift in spelling. Thus symbol-sound correspondences changed in significant ways. The double vowel letter, once used to represent a long vowel (*sweet*, *spoon*) now represents a high vowel. The correspondence is still regular in many respects, but the vowel phonemes have changed while the graphemes have remained the same.

Another factor producing different spelling correspondences comes from foreign language influence. English has borrowed rather freely from other languages in extending its vocabulary, and spelling reflects this borrowing in several different ways. In some cases, items retain their foreign spellings, and thus introduce a different correspondence relationship between sound and symbol. Items such as *bouquet* and *ballet* from French have a final *t* that has

no phonetic correspondence. The *j* in *junta* (Spanish) has an /h/ correspondence rather than the typical /ǰ/. Cases such as French *ge* representing
/ž/ (*rouge, beige*), or German *sch* representing /š/ (*schnauzer, schnapps*)
are other well-known examples of a symbol-sound correspondence different
from items derived from Anglo-Saxon. Borrowed items, then, may simply
bring along with them a different spelling pattern.

Not all borrowed correspondence relationships are introduced so directly.
In some cases, a spelling pattern may be introduced through the process of
transliteration, as is the case with items taken from Greek. Greek, of course,
uses a different alphabet, but items derived from Greek were respelled into
the English system by setting up equivalent English letters (English *ch* for
Greek χ, *ph* for φ, etc.). While this is efficient for some items, it introduces
different correspondences for the transliterated items at points where English
and Greek differ in their phonological systems. For example, the *ch* and *ph*
transliterations introduce different correspondences for English (*ch* as /k/ in
chasm, chorus; *ph* as /f/ in *philosophy* and *phonology*), since they represent
Greek distinctions that are not present in English. Similarly, the transliteration of *ps* and *pn* (*psychology, pneumatic*) represent sequences in Greek
phonotactics not permissible in English. The production has been accommo-
dated to the English phonological system, while the direct spelling transliteration is retained. The end result of such a process is similar to cases of direct borrowing of foreign spellings: a subsystem of correspondence conventions different from English items of Anglo-Saxon origin.

Exercise 5

It has been suggested that the investigation of word etymologies is a good
source for learning the finer details of spelling patterns in English. Do you
think this proposal might provide a systematic basis for teaching some of the
patterns operative within English symbol-sound correspondences? Before giving an answer, consider that some items in English are spelled on the basis of
"analogy." In these cases, spelling takes its cue from a predominant pattern
regardless of the historical development of an item. An item such as *delight*
was spelled with the *gh* of *right, light*, and *fight* even though it did not
come from an item with an historical /x/. Similarly, *schooner* is based on the
model of *school*, following the Greek derived *ch* as /k/, even though it is not
an item derived from Greek.

Given the changes that have taken place in English and the various subsystems of conventions adopted within the spelling system, alternative spellings have sometimes emerged for **homophonous items** (two or more morphemes
that are pronounced the same). We get spellings such as *right, write, rite*,
and *wright* all representing /raɪt/, or /so/ spelled as *so, sow*, and *sew*.

In some cases, different spellings of homophonous items represent
earlier pronunciation differences. The spelling of *knight* and *night*, or *see*
and *sea*, represents an historical phonological difference that has been
eliminated. This does not handle all cases, however. Some spelling reform-
ers have introduced different spellings simply to ensure that different meanings or grammatical functions of items are distinguished in writing (for example *to, too, two*). Whatever the reason, the selective use of different spellings for homophonous items is a practice that sets our written language apart
from our spoken language. And, it is a tradition that creates considerable
difficulty for the beginning speller, who is taught to maximize phonological
cues in learning how to spell. In these cases only syntactic and semantic
information can be used to determine which spelling is appropriate.

Exercise 6

Using a dictionary that gives etymological information about words (such as the *Oxford English Dictionary*), consider why the following homophonous items have different spellings. Were the items which are spelled differently once also pronounced differently?

doe, dough   *their, there, they're*
pain, pane   *to, too, two*
pair, pare, pear

It might seem ideal for the orthographical conventions of English to be regularized exclusively in line with the current phonological system, but attempts to do this have met with widespread resistance. It is probably more realistic for educators to concentrate on understanding the extensive patterning that does exist in the current system and the various subsystems that have been incorporated into it. In a sense, the present system is a tribute to the dynamic nature of a phonological system. It reflects changes from within the system and changes from contact with other systems. Important social and historical factors have also influenced the spelling system through the centuries. Its study offers insight into the developing phonology of the language, as well as the intricate patterning of the current system. English spelling is not a linguistic and educational conspiracy against the lives of students of English. It is a reflection of the many dimensions which have made our phonology what it is today.

SUGGESTED READING

General orientations to the nature of orthography, representing different approaches to phonology, are found in Carol Chomsky, "Reading, Writing, and Phonology" (1973), Venezky's "English Orthography: Its Graphical Structure and its Relation to Sound" (1967), and Steinberg's "Phonology, Reading and Chomsky and Halle's Optimal Orthography" (1973). Steinberg's article is a reaction to Chomsky and Halle's claim that English orthography represents a near-optimal system for English phonology in terms of its underlying representations.

The various contributing sources to the current orthographic system are surveyed in Barnitz, "Interrelationship of Orthography and Phonological Structure in Learning to Read" (1978). Venezky's volume on *The Structure of English Orthography* gives a detailed inventory of correspondences between graphemic and phonological units, and can be very helpful as a reference work. Charles Read's research on children's early spelling patterns (1975, 1980) has provided new insight into the way children use their phonology creatively in the initial stages of learning how to write.

BIBLIOGRAPHY

Abercrombie, David. 1967. *Elements of General Phonetics*. Chicago: Aldine.

Anderson, Stephen R. 1974. *The Organization of Phonology*. New York: Academic Press.

Barnitz, John G. 1978. "Interrelationship of Orthography and Phonological Structure in Learning to Read." Technical Report No. 57. Center for Study of Reading. Urbana-Champaign: University of Illinois.

Bell, Alan and Joan B. Hooper, eds. 1978. *Syllables and Segments*. Amsterdam: North-Holland Publishing Co.

Berko, Jean. 1958. "The Child's Learning of English Morphology," *Word* 14: 150-177.

Bernthal, John E. and Nicholas W. Bankson. 1981. *Articulation Disorders*. Englewood Cliffs, N.J.: Prentice-Hall.

Bloch, Bernard. 1941. "Phonemic Overlapping," *American Speech* 16:278-284 (reprinted in Makkai, 1972).

_____ and George L. Trager. 1942. *Outline of Linguistic Analysis*. Baltimore, Md.: Linguistic Society of America.

Bloomfield, Leonard. 1933. *Language*. New York: Holt, Rinehart and Winston.

Bronstein, Arthur J. 1960. *The Pronunciation of American English*. New York: Appleton-Century-Crofts.

Brosnahan, L. F. and Bertil Malmberg. 1970. *Introduction to Phonetics*. Cambridge: Cambridge University Press.

Chomsky, Carol. 1973. "Reading, Writing, and Phonology," in Frank Smith, ed., *Psycholinguistics and Reading*. New York: Holt, Rinehart and Winston.

Chomsky, Noam. 1964. "Current Issues in Linguistic Theory," in Jerry A. Fodor and Jerrold J. Katz, eds., *The Structure of Language: Readings in the Philosophy of Language*. Englewood Cliffs, N.J.: Prentice-Hall.

_____ and Morris Halle. 1965. "Some Controversial Questions in Phonological Theory," *Journal of Linguistics* 1:97-138 (reprinted in Makkai, 1972).

_____. 1968. *The Sound Pattern of English*. New York: Harper and Row.

Dinnsen, Daniel A., ed. 1979. *Current Approaches to Phonological Theory*. Bloomington: Indiana University Press.

DiPietro, Robert J. 1971. *Language Structures in Contrast*. Rowley, Mass.: Newbury House.

Francis, W. Nelson. 1958. *The Structure of American English*. New York: The Ronald Press.

Fromkin, Victoria A. 1971. "The Nonanomalous Nature of Anomalous Utterances," *Language* 47:27-52.

_____, ed. 1973. *Speech Errors as Linguistic Evidence*. The Hague: Mouton.

Gleason, H. A. 1955. *Workbook in Descriptive Linguistics*. New York: Holt, Rinehart and Winston.

_____. 1961. *An Introduction to Descriptive Linguistics*. Revised edition. New York: Holt, Rinehart and Winston.

Greenberg, Joseph H., ed. 1978. *Universals of Human Language, Volume 2: Phonology*. Stanford, Calif.: Stanford University Press.

Halle, Morris. 1959. *The Sound Pattern of Russian*. The Hague: Mouton.
_____. 1962. "Phonology in Generative Grammar," *Word* 18:54-74 (reprinted in Makkai, 1972).
_____. 1964. "On the Bases of Phonology," in Jerry A. Fodor and Jerrold J. Katz, eds., *The Structure of Language: Readings in the Philosophy of Language*. Englewood Cliffs, N.J.: Prentice-Hall (reprinted in Makkai, 1972).
Harms, Robert A. 1968. *Introduction to Phonological Theory*. Englewood Cliffs, N.J.: Prentice-Hall.
Harris, Zellig S. 1944. "Simultaneous Components in Phonology," *Language* 20:181-205 (reprinted in Makkai, 1972).
_____. 1951. *Structural Linguistics*. Chicago, Ill.: University of Chicago Press.
Heffner, Roe-Merrill S. 1949. *General Phonetics*. Madison: University of Wisconsin Press.
Hockett, Charles F. 1958. *A Course in Modern Linguistics*. New York: Macmillan.
Hodson, Barbara W. 1980. *The Assessment of Phonological Processes*. Danville, Ill.: The Interstate.
Hooper, Joan B. 1972. "The Syllable in Phonological Theory," *Language* 28:525-540.
Householder, Fred W. 1965. "On Some Recent Claims in Phonological Theory," *Journal of Linguistics* 1:13-34 (reprinted in Makkai, 1972).
Hyman, Larry M. 1970. "How Concrete Is Phonology?" *Language* 46:58-76.
_____. 1975. *Phonology: Theory and Analysis*. New York: Holt, Rinehart and Winston.
Ingram, David. 1976. *Phonological Disability in Children*. London: Edward Arnold.
_____. 1981. *Procedures for the Phonological Analysis of Children's Language*. Baltimore, Md.: University Park Press.
International Phonetic Association. 1949. *The Principles of the International Phonetic Association*. London: University College.
Joos, Martin, ed. 1957. *Readings in Linguistics: The Development of Descriptive Linguistics in America Since 1925*. New York: American Council of Learned Societies.
Kenstowicz, Michael and Charles Kisseberth. 1977. *Topics in Phonological Theory*. New York: Academic Press.
King, Robert D. 1969. *Historical Linguistics and Generative Grammar*. Englewood Cliffs, N.J.: Prentice-Hall.
Kiparsky, Paul. 1968. "How Abstract Is Phonology?" Bloomington: Indiana University Linguistics Club.
Labov, William. 1972a. *Language in the Inner City*. Philadelphia: University of Pennsylvania Press.
_____. 1972b. *Sociolinguistic Patterns*. Philadelphia: University of Pennsylvania Press.
_____ and Teresa Labov. 1978. "The Phonetics of *Cat* and *Mama*," *Language* 54:816-852.
Ladefoged, Peter. 1971. *Preliminaries to Linguistic Phonetics*. Chicago: University of Chicago Press.
_____. 1975. *A Course in Phonetics*. New York: Harcourt Brace Jovanovich.
Lehmann, Winfred P. 1976. *Descriptive Linguistics: An Introduction*. Second edition. New York: Random House.
Makkai, Valerie B., ed. 1972. *Phonological Theory: Evolution and Current Practice*. New York: Holt, Rinehart and Winston.
Pike, Kenneth L. 1947a. "Grammatical Prerequisites to Phonemic Analysis," *Word* 3:155-172 (reprinted in Makkai, 1972).

Pike, Kenneth L. 1947b. *Phonemics: A Technique for Reducing Languages to Writing.* Ann Arbor: University of Michigan Press.

Pulgram, Ernst. 1970. *Syllable, Word, Nexus, Cursus.* The Hague: Mouton.

Read, Charles. 1975. *Children's Categorization of Speech Sounds.* (NCTE Research Report, No. 17.) Urbana, Ill.: National Council of Teachers of English.

_____. 1980. "Creative Spelling by Young Children," in Timothy Shopen and Joseph M. Williams, eds., *Standards and Dialects in English.* Cambridge, Mass.: Winthrop.

Ritchie, William C. 1968. "On the Explanation of Phonic Interference," *Language Learning* 28:183-197.

Robins, R. H. 1967. *General Linguistics: An Introductory Survey.* London: Longmans.

Robinson, Dow F. 1975. *Workbook for Phonological Analysis.* Huntington Beach, Calif.: Summer Institute of Linguistics.

Rockey, Denyse. 1973. *Phonetic Lexicon of Monosyllabic and Some Disyllabic Words, with Homophones, Arranged According to Their Phonetic Structure.* London: Heyden & Son.

Sapir, Edward. 1925. "Sound Patterns in Language," *Language* 1:37-51 (reprinted in Makkai, 1972).

_____. 1933. "The Psychological Reality of Phonemes." Originally published in French: "La Réalité Psychologique des Phonèmes," *Journal de Psychologie Normale et Pathologique* 30:247-265 (reprinted in Makkai, 1972).

Schane, Sanford A. 1971. "The Phoneme Revisited," *Language* 47:503-521.

_____. 1973. *Generative Phonology.* Englewood Cliffs, N.J.: Prentice-Hall.

Sloat, Clarence, Sharon Henderson Taylor, and James E. Hoard. 1978. *Introduction to Phonology.* Englewood Cliffs, N.J.: Prentice-Hall.

Smalley, William A. 1961. *Manual of Articulatory Phonetics.* Tarrytown, N.Y.: Practical Anthropology.

Smith, Neilson V. 1973. *The Acquisition of Phonology: A Case Study.* Cambridge: Cambridge University Press.

Sommerstein, Alan H. 1977. *Modern Phonology.* Baltimore, Md.: University Park Press.

Stampe, David. 1973. *A Dissertation on Natural Phonology.* Unpublished PhD dissertation. Chicago: University of Chicago.

Stanley, Richard. 1967. "Redundancy Rules in Phonology," *Language* 43:393-436.

Steinberg, David D. 1973. "Phonology, Reading, and Chomsky and Halle's Optimal Orthography," *Journal of Psycholinguistic Research* 2:239-258.

Stetson, Raymond H. 1951. *Motor Phonetics: A Study of Speech Movements in Action.* Amsterdam: North Holland.

Stockwell, Robert P. and J. Donald Bowen. 1965. *The Sounds of English and Spanish.* Chicago: University of Chicago Press.

_____ and Ronald K. S. Macaulay, eds. 1972. *Linguistic Change and Generative Theory.* Bloomington: Indiana University Press.

Swadesh, Morris. 1934. "The Phonemic Principle," *Language* 10:117-129 (reprinted in Makkai, 1972).

Trager, George L. and Henry Lee Smith. 1951. *An Outline of English Structure.* (Studies in Linguistics, Occasional Papers 3.) Washington, D.C.: American Council of Learned Societies.

Trnka, Bohumil. 1966. *A Phonological Analysis of Present-Day Standard English.* University, Ala.: University of Alabama Press.

Twaddell, W. Freeman. 1935. "On Defining the Phoneme," *Language* Monograph No. 16 (reprinted in Joos, 1957).

Venezky, Richard L. 1967. "English Orthography: Its Graphical Structure and Its Relation to Sound," *Reading Research Quarterly* 2:75-105.

Venezky, Richard L. 1970. *The Structure of English Orthography.* The Hague: Mouton.

Vennemann, Theo. 1972. "On the Theory of Syllabic Phonology," *Linguistische Berichte* 18:1-18.

Walsh, Harry H., ed. 1979. *Phonology and Speech Remediation: A Book of Readings.* Houston, Texas: College-Hill Press.

Weiner, Frederick. 1979. *Phonological Process Analysis.* Baltimore: University Park Press.

Weinrich, Uriel. 1953. *Languages in Contact.* New York: Linguistic Circle of New York.

Wolfram, Walt and Donna Christian. 1976. *Appalachian Speech.* Arlington, Va.: Center for Applied Linguistics.

_____ and Ralph W. Fasold. 1974. *The Study of Social Dialects in American English.* Englewood Cliffs, N.J.: Prentice-Hall.

Yeni-Komshian, Grace H., James F. Kavanagh, and Charles A. Ferguson, eds. 1980. *Child Phonology, Volume 1: Production.* New York: Academic Press.

_____, eds. 1981. *Child Phonology, Volume 2: Perception.* New York: Academic Press.

INDEX